Zaragoza Bound

Zaragoza Bound

A Chronicle of the Durruti Column

Roberto Martínez Catalán

Translated by Paul Sharkey

Zaragoza Bound: A Chronicle of the Durruti Column
Roberto Martínez Catalán © 2025
Translation © 2025 Paul Sharkey
This edition © 2025 AK Press

ISBN 9781849355827
E-ISBN 9781849355834
Library of Congress Number: 2025936922

AK Press
370 Ryan Avenue #100
Chico, CA 95973
www.akpress.org
akpress@akpress.org
510.208.1700

AK Press
33 Tower St.
Edinburgh EH6 7BN
Scotland
www.akuk.com
akuk@akpress.org

First published as *Rumbo a Zaragoza: Crónica de la Columna Durruti* (Rasmia Ediciones, 2019)
Chapter 1 is a revised version of "Armed Anarchist Organization: Debates and Proposals during the II Spanish Republic," in *Germinal. Revista de Estudios Libertarios* no 12, July–December 2014.

Cover image from CNT. 1936–1939. Archivo Cinematográfico de la Revolución española, used by permission
Cover design by John Yates, www.stealworks.com
Printed in the USA on acid-free paper

Dedicated to Cándido Otín Barreu, a former Durruti Column fighter, whose acquaintance I had the pleasure of making when he was one hundred years old. He was a humble fellow with a good heart. May he rest in peace

"Freedom, Sancho, is one of the most priceless gifts that Heaven bestowed upon men; there is no treasure that lies buried under the soil nor which is covered by the sea that can match it; life can and should be gambled for the sake of freedom and of honour whereas captivity is the greatest misfortune than can befall men."

—Miguel de Cervantes, *Don Quijote de la Mancha*

The door to the street lay wide open and a bunch of militians were taking their ease in the yard, my father waiting upon them. And then one of them cried out:
—Eh? Buenaventura!
And a small group that had been retreating stopped at our door. Durruti had transferred command and was heading back to the front and to his column. We invited then in for a drink. How well I remember it! My father with a bottle of El Mono *anis* in his hand, yes, I remember it perfectly, the wonders of recall, and he was pouring the liquor and the militians were sipping at it, before washing it down with a mouthful of cold water from the bodega's earthenware pitcher.

Durruti was in a hurry, declining the *anis* but welcoming the cold water. I went to fetch him a glass. While he was drinking from it my father said something.... When he was done, he wiped his mouth with the back of his hand and, looking at my father, he laid his hand on my head and said:
"We are making this revolution for their sake, for them."
And that was how I first met Durruti.

—from Agustín Camón's memories of his childhood, in *Crónicas del 36*

Contents

List of Abbreviations xi

Introduction. 1

I. Armed Agencies and Debates Around Defense of the
   Revolution During the Second Republic 5

II. Zaragoza Bound: The Revolution Awaits. 33

III. Durruti and his Column: Between the Ideal and
   the Reality of War 73

IV. Militarization of the Column and the Eclipse of
   the Libertarian Movement: The End of the Dream. 85

Epilogue: A Hard Lesson to Swallow 113

Notes. 119

Index 181

Abbreviations

Organizations

AIT/IWA	Workers' International Association
CAMC	Central Antifascist Militias Committee of Catalonia
CNT	National Confederation of Labor
ERC	Republican Left of Catalonia
FAI	Iberian Anarchist Federation
PSUC	Unified Socialist Party of Catalonia
POUM	Workers' Party of Marxist Unification
UGT	Workers' General Union

Archival Collections

AEP	Ateneu Enciclopèdic Popular
AGGC	General Civil War Archive (Historical Memory Documentation Center, Salamanca)
AHCB	Barcelona City Historical Archives
AHN	National History Archive
ANC	National Archive of Catalonia, in San Cugat del Vallés
AS	Salamanca Archives (Salamanca Historical Memory Documentation Center)
BNE	National Library of Spain
BPA	Arús Public Library
CDMHS	Salamanca Documentation Center for Historical Memory
CEDALL	Anti-authoritarian and Libertarian Documentation Center
CIRAM	International Center for Research into Anarchism (Marseilles)
HMV	Valencia Municipal Newspaper Library
IISH	International Institute of Social History

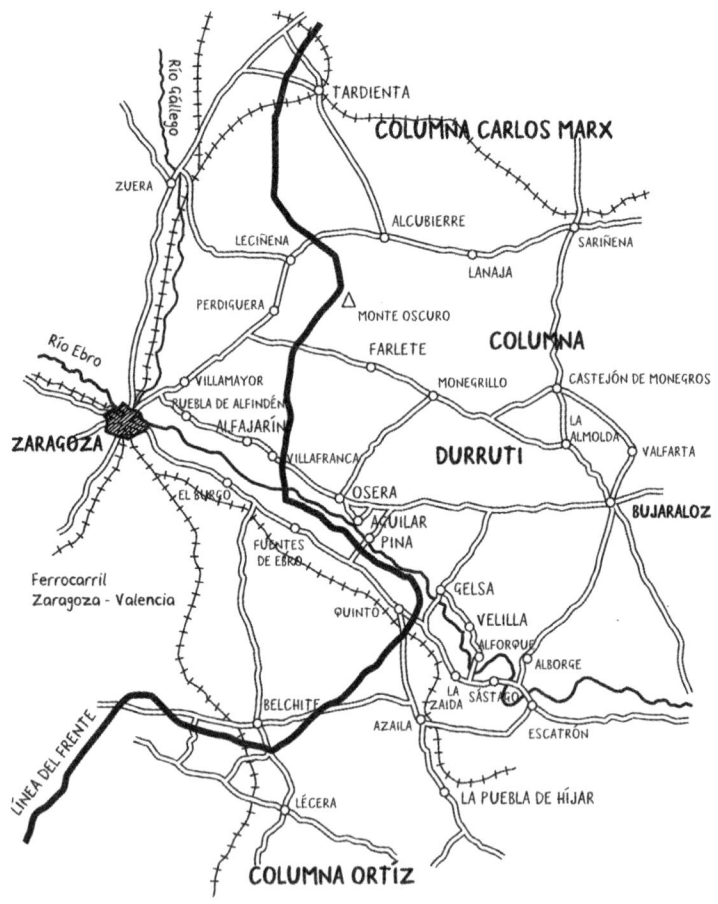

Map of the central sector of the Aragon front around November 1936. Inspired by a map from Los Gimenólogos as found in *En busca de los Hijos de la Noche. Notas sobre los Recuerdos de la Guerra de España de Antoine Gimenez* (2009), p. 390.

Introduction

"The revolution is a war and to speak of war is to speak of the destruction of people and things. That we have yet to devise a more peaceable means of moving forward is of course a disgrace for humanity, but so far everything new in history has only been accomplished after a baptism in blood."
—**M. A. Bakunin**, *The Bears of Berne and the Bear of St Petersburg*

Not all anarchists have seen violence used to end the existing society and replace it with one that is guided by the precepts of free federation, self-management, and nonviolence as an inescapable, inevitable fact. But most anarchists have considered the necessity of it in mounting the final revolutionary uprising.[1] Seeing as no ruling class or classes have ever surrendered power without a fight.[2]

During the Second Spanish Republic, Spanish anarchists spearheaded many uprisings with the intent of establishing their earthly paradise. Whether spontaneous or organized and mounted on a specific date—like the ones on January 8 and December 8, 1933—each instance resulted in resounding failures, weakening the libertarian movement's organizations, particularly its trade union and mass organization, the National Confederation of Labor (CNT).[3]

Eventually, the yearned-for opportunity and historical occasion to put their ideological principles into practice arrived thanks to a failed army coup that would evolve into a civil war. The collapse of the republican state's machinery of coercion created a power vacuum; as Hannah

Arendt points out: "In the context of violence competing with violence, the Government's superiority has always been absolute, but such superiority lasts only as long as the government power structure survives intact—meaning as long as its orders are followed and the Army or police forces are ready to use their weaponry. If this is not the case, the situation is abruptly altered. Not only is rebellion not snuffed out, but the weapons themselves change hands."[4]

Spanish anarchism's brief but intense golden age—the age of "revolutionary gains"—was beginning. In terms of armed organization, these gains took the form of the raising of militias that set off for the front to face down the mutinous soldiery and spread the revolution, and in the creation of the rearguard with a genuine array of control patrols, border patrols, investigation groups, and other units that functioned like a revolutionary police.[5] The libertarian movement equipped itself with this motley armed wing to defend its plans for an alternative society.

Delving into this multifaceted aspect of Spanish Civil War–time anarchism, this study is an attempt to shed a little more light on the organization, operation, and evolution of the Durruti Column (as well as the libertarian militias generally) from its inception up until its absorption into the Republic's People's Army. Set in the context of the overall political, military, economic, and social trends in the republican rearguard, we'll explore how it evolved right up until the utter defeat of the revolutionary process that began in the wake of the army's mutiny. There are various reasons for the focus on the Durruti Column: It was the first column of note raised in Barcelona, the power base of the CNT and the headquarters of Catalonia's Central Antifascist Militias Committee (CAMC), and it served as a model for subsequent columns that set off from Catalonia or operated in Aragon.[6] Second, it was commanded by José Buenaventura Durruti, one of the libertarian movement's strongest and best-known personalities. And finally, and most importantly, its objective was the city of Zaragoza, the liberation of which, it was thought, would represent a crucial step forward for the war and the revolution.

Before getting into details about the Durruti Column, however, we need to analyze the practical basics and theoretical baggage from which the anarchist movement began on the outbreak of the war, as these inevitably shaped its initial characteristics and those of the rest of the libertarian columns. We shall concentrate on examination of the debate surrounding the insurrections, "defense of the revolution," and the discipline imposed during the preceding five years of the Republic, as well as on the bodies that acted as the CNT's armed shield and prepared for the final clash that would bring down the capitalist order. In the course of this task, we will pay special attention to the Los Solidarios group, relaunched during the Republic as the Nosotros group, as it was the ultimate embodiment of the so-called "men of action."[7] Many of its members were prime movers in the 1933 uprisings but they also held important positions at the head of armed units and a variety of military bodies during the Civil War: Buenaventura Durruti, Domingo Ascaso, Antonio Ortiz, Gregorio Jover, and Miguel García Vivancos were militia and/or divisional commanders, as was Ricardo Sanz, who was initially in charge of the organizing of the militias in Catalonia and later Inspector-General of the Aragon and Catalonian fronts.[8] Moreover, Aurelio Fernández occupied a position of leadership within the CAMC's Investigation Committee and later on the Generalitat's Homeland Security Council, bodies that oversaw the Control Patrols. García Oliver was the CAMC's Councillor for War, Secretary of Defense within the Generalitat cabinet, a member of the Supreme War Council, and organizer of the People's War Schools, as well as serving briefly as commander of the "Los Aguiluchos" Column.

Unbeknownst to its members, the Durruti Column was an out-and-out reservoir of future military leaders. In a way this was inevitable since "action men" and "intellectuals" had always been given special consideration within the CNT and wielded a sort of charismatic leadership that was not included in any of its statutes or regulations.[9] So it was only natural that, once the war and the revolution were under way, men who had distinguished themselves through their recourse to violence and arms would have held down the main positions in the armed units and agencies set up to direct operations and oversee public order. The force of circumstance would quite simply drive them that way. But let's not jump the gun, and instead begin at the beginning.

I
Armed Agencies and Debates Regarding Defense of the Revolution During the Second Republic

"The Spanish Republic, as presently constituted, poses a great threat to libertarian ideas, unless we anarchists act vigorously, we will of necessity descend into social democracy. There is a revolution to be made and it must be made as soon as possible. . . . We cannot wait for the Republic to consolidate itself in its current form. Even now, General Sanjurjo is calling for an additional 8,000 Civil Guards."
—**Durruti in *La Tierra*, September 2, 1931**

At the beginning of the Second Republic, Spanish anarchism, as an armed movement, took as its starting point the traditional anarchist critique of militarism and all coercive authority in general.[1] As far as anarchists were concerned, the army had always been one of the worst blemishes upon the State; it was not only the State's defender but it also schooled individuals in immorality, in that within it they forfeited their freedom and turned into a obedient machine.[2] Their view of the police was even dimmer, as police personnel enforced their repressive assignments voluntarily, as their stock in trade, rather than out of compulsion as most of the soldiery did.

Concerned to match means with ends, anarchists never thought to create disciplined, hierarchical armed corps designed to make or defend the revolution. So the chosen formula for defending revolutionary society was the "people in arms"—the armed working people—who would mobilize as required. Positing no transitional period, like the Marxists argued for, on the day after the revolution, anarchists were to seek the destruction of all authoritarian power and thwart the emergence of new ones: both the police and the army were numbered among those authoritarian powers. From time to time there was talk of "people's armies" or "revolutionary armies," though such talk was almost always synonymous for the traditional "people in arms," rather than a reference to any regular army with a hierarchy, a unified or centralized command, and a strict discipline.[3] On the other hand, until a revolutionary society could be actualized, there had to be some means of self-defense and of combating the State and the various enemies extant, and to that end the only legitimate means entertained, in terms of armed organizations (in addition to individual actions, although the latter is not an organization in any sense), were guerrilla units and, above all, small clandestine groups welded together by affinity.

There is a long tradition, in anarchist history, of small, clandestine armed groups devoted to a wide range of illegal activities. These date back to anarchism's very beginnings and Bakunin, whose view was that a sort of vanguard of conspirators needed to be formed to offer guidance to the masses of the people.[4] In Spain, "the comarcal gatherings in '76 led to the setting up of action groups," "warfare" units answerable to the sections of the FRE (Spanish Regional Federation) and, until such time as an opening for revolution arose, these were to "look into the best means of waging war, while equipping themselves with resources, weapons, and munition and mounting reprisals." Such groups explored this style of organization and survived until 1880.[5] During the years of *pistolerismo* (1919–1923), action groups were resurrected, their purpose this time being to put pressure on the bosses to initiate improvements in working conditions, and to respond to State- and employer-sponsored terrorism. Finally, come the Republic, action groups lingered on as different armed units operating as pickets, defending demonstrations, and promoting local uprisings.[6]

Fueled by various events during the Republic, a series of new theoretical debates and practical approaches regarding armed organization and defense of the revolution were explored. A precipitating event was the spontaneous uprising triggered by a labor dispute in the Upper

Llobregat in January 1932. It was not the first uprising, as we can give that award to the so-called "Bloody Week in Seville" in July 1931, but it did have a lot of impact.[7] The ease with which the revolutionaries initially gained the upper hand and the short-lived proclamation of libertarian communism constituted, for many, hints that the revolution was imminent; they had only to broaden the revolt next time and ensure that it was not isolated in a location readily open to recapture by State forces. And that failed uprising had another significant collateral consequence: it helped oust from the CNT's higher committees the moderates or "*treintistas*" who were in favor of a strategy of carefully laying the groundwork for revolution through the strengthening of the unions, which necessitated a measure of peaceful coexistence and give-and-take with the republican authorities.[8] The CNT then fell into the hands of those who proclaimed that the revolution was not a matter of preparedness but a matter of determination, that no further economic or social preparations were needed, and who advocated for open, ongoing confrontation with the Republic.[9]

So, with an eye to coordinating any further insurrections across the country, the CNT determined, at a National Plenary in May 1932, to set up confederal defense cadres. According to Abel Paz,

> With the motion regarding "confederal defense cadres" the CNT was outfitted with a defensive [and, let it be said, offensive] should: The idea ... was nothing new because they had always pretty much existed within the CNT alongside anarchist groups. In the notorious years of [employer-funded] terrorism, they had been described as "trade unionist revolutionary action groups" and they acted as the CNT's armor plating. After the proclamation of the Republic, the suggestion that they should proceed with setting up confederal defense cadres inside the unions had been raised [and endorsed] at a national plenum, but due to the confusion that prevailed inside the CNT due to the [factional] strife, that idea was never actually implemented.[10] At the May plenary there was some movement toward their creation since the motion had talked about not just setting them up but also

of their federating at the national level [through the Defense Committees] with an eye to the all-out prosecution of the revolutionary struggle.[11]

Or, to borrow García Oliver's words "equipping anarcho-syndicalism with a paramilitary apparatus so that, when the day came, it might take on and beat the armed forces."[12] A more detailed description of their functions can be found in Alexander Shapiro's report regarding his stay in Spain, which coincided with the January 1933 uprising: "The National Defense Committee, as well as the Regional and Local Defense Committees, are bipartisan bodies made up of an equal number of representatives from agencies affiliated to the Confederation and representatives from FAI [Iberian Anarchist Federation]-affiliated organizations. The sole responsibility of these defense committees ... was to stockpile the weaponry required in the event of an uprising, organizing assault teams in the various working-class *barrios*, orchestrating resistance by troops in their barracks, etc. The Defense Committees commanded no executive authority. They merely had to remain at the CNT's disposal once their preparatory efforts had concluded."[13]

On the other hand, writings started to emerge dealing with the thorny issue of the defense of the revolution and whether or not a hypothetical revolutionary army might be needed and what its features might be. It is important that we make clear that none of the advocates of the revolutionary army advocated from the perspective of a standing institution but rather laid it out as a necessary evil in successfully addressing a period of strife and fighting that would pave the way toward the proclamation of the revolution. Once libertarian communism had succeeded worldwide, the army, like any other repressive force, such as the police, would be done away with once and for all, as would any arms plants, in accordance with the classical teachings of anarchism—and of Marxism, it should be said.[14]

The first such text to appear was a pamphlet from Horacio M. Prieto, who subsequently went on to serve as the CNT's general secretary: its title was "Anarcosindicalismo: cómo afianzaremos la revolución." Dated January 22, 1932, in the very throes of the uprising, it is hard to tell whether the events underway may have influenced the contents or whether it was merely the product of earlier thinking, but the fact is that it raised a lot of controversial ideas that most anarchists found hard to swallow.[15] As to the understanding of defense of the revolution, starting off from the libertarian tradition, it suggested that military leaders be elected in a democratic assembly of their own soldiers. But, lo and behold, here comes the first novelty: for as long as such commanders held that position, they were to be obeyed without question "especially with the fighting in progress"; in any event, an assembly of soldiers could sit in judgment of them later. Secondly, even though the soldiers' assemblies might discuss the plans put forward by the higher committees and offer their own suggestions, they could "never" query their "watchwords" or orders. In other words, in the context of warfare, obedience to commanders and the central command was de rigueur. Finally, there was another very telling detail: workers in arms and munitions plants were subject to "military discipline." All of this was explained away with the remark: "Our comrades' profoundly libertarian sensibilities, this unjustified fanaticism about the free will of the individual, which is so deeply imprinted in the character of our finest militants, has always run up against hard facts, the demands of history and the present society, which, now more than ever, necessitate strict adaptation to the difficulties inherent in the ever more cumbersome and complicated growth of the human family."[16]

In September that year, the weekly *Tierra y Libertad* carried a couple of articles originating from France and surrounding the issue of "defense of the revolution." The first of these, by Jean Marestan, was a reply to an article by Sébastien Faure titled "Regarding Defense of the Revolution," published in *Solidaridad Obrera*, amounting to a challenge to the resolutions passed by the Languedoc Anarchist Federation, which he deemed authoritarian. For a start, Jean Marestan quite correctly pointed out the climate of violent opposition wherein the revolution would inevitably have to operate:

> There is every likelihood—not to say certainty—that should the social revolution break out right now or sometime soon,

somewhere in the world, it would take place against the backdrop of the conditions regularly observed in any of the revolutionary upheavals that have occurred thus far. Revolt is triggered by poverty or by wars. Bloody battles reminiscent of the horrors of international warfare are joined on the streets. Hordes of people, unsure of what the future holds in store for them, seize all that they can for their own personal benefit, whilst, on the other hand, the famished masses swoop on the food warehouses, not pausing for a thought about whether they will then run short, nor how they will be replaced somewhat later. If the uprising is beaten, it is drowned in blood. If victorious, it will be obliged to look to its defenses for months and even years on end, in the face of enemies within and attacks from outside, whilst the exacting task of reorganizing is carried out.[17]

And then Marestan went further: "Your response [addressing Sébastien Faure] is: 'My reckoning is that, should a popular uprising occur . . . there is no possibility of anarchists' being mere onlookers.' And, quoting Malatesta, he added: 'Their role, therefore, is to push revolutionary action as far as it will go, in accordance with their unshakable determination to bring about a situation where it is impossible for anyone to force themselves on others.' But in order to bring that situation about, you reject, as a matter of principle: all military power, even that under collective command and any police force, even should it be proletarian." And he reached the emphatic conclusion: "Let me state that, with the best will in the world, no other approach seems better suited to guaranteeing that the incipient uprising will be defeated and extinguished."[18] Sébastien Faure's retort to this letter abided by the orthodox anarchist line:

> The army and the police—even should the former be established and controlled by the collective and the latter be proletarian—are going to remain two despicable armed institutions prompted by the spirit of discipline, regimentation, and obedience, brutish morality, coercion and authority, a spirit and a morality

diametrically opposed to the anarchist spirit and morality.... I am neither a Gandhian or a Tolstoyan ... and I have a great interest in the issue of defending the Revolution.... But my contention is that those methods of defense must not be at odds with how anarchists have come to think in terms of a libertarian society and that we must avoid inflicting a lie on it.[19]

This controversy clearly echoed the polemic triggered within French anarchist circles during the latter half of the 1920s by the "Organizational Platform of the General Union of Anarchists," (also referred to as the "Organizational Platform of the Libertarian Communists" or the "Arshinov Platform"). It might be of some interest to dwell briefly upon it since the drafting of it and propositions it articulated were not so much based on any theoretical considerations as upon its sponsors' experiences in the Russian Revolution (1917–1921). Over the course of that event, anarchists had played a telling and sometimes premier role, as in the battles against the reaction and the White armies in Ukraine, but that had not saved them from being swept aside completely by the Bolsheviks. As far as the Platform's authors—a bunch of Russians in exile in Paris—were concerned, the reason for their defeat was traceable to the ineffectuality of the anarchist movement itself, what with its disorganization and the vagueness of its political principles. Nevertheless, those shortcomings were not confined to the Russian anarchist movement but afflicted the entirety of the anarchist movement worldwide and derived from an underlying flaw that was a "misinterpretation of the principle of individualism within anarchism," it being "all too often [mistaken for] the absence of responsibility."[20]

As a solution, they proposed a new type of political organization similar to a party, the aforementioned Platform. The Platform was based on the principle of collective responsibility, with its executive committee, though still clinging to federalism, and with a tactical and theoretic unity for which a clear and concise revolutionary program was needed to be accepted by all of its members.[21] Regarding the defense of the revolution, in accordance with what had happened in Russia, they pointed out that the civil war was ushered in by the revolution,

It will take several years not several months.... In order to preserve the revolution's gains ... [the workers] must create agencies to defend the revolution, to counter the onslaught of the reaction with a fighting force equal to the task. During the early days of the revolution, that militant force will be made up of all the armed workers and peasants. But this spontaneous armed force will only be valid in the early days, when the civil war has yet to peak and the two warring sides have not yet established regularly constituted military organizations.... Like any other war, the civil war could not be conducted successfully by the workers without the application of the two basic principles of any military action: a shared plan of operations and a unifying shared command.[22]

The revolutionary army was to be built upon four basic principles: 1. Its class character. 2. Volunteer service (no conscription). 3. Free revolutionary discipline or self-discipline, which did not mean the absence of rules of conduct or that everyone was free to follow the discipline of his own choosing but rather the code of discipline laid down by the fighters themselves.[23] 4. Complete deference to the masses of workers and peasants represented by their organizations.[24] And, to end this section, they concluded: "Rather than its being founded in accordance with specific libertarian communist principles, the army *per se* is not to be deemed a fundamental factor. It is merely the outworking of the revolution's military strategy, to which the workers will inescapably be drawn by the very processes of the civil war. But this step should draw attention right from the outset. It must be painstakingly examined to avert, in its efforts to protect and defend the revolution, any irretrievable delay, as delays in times of civil war may prove damaging to the denouement of any social revolution."[25] Nevertheless, the Platform's polemic and proposals had very little impact or influence on the Spanish anarchism of the day, whether the movement in exile or at home.[26]

Getting back to 1930s Spain, a couple of months after publication of Jean Marestan's letter and Sébastien Faure's retort, *Tierra y Libertad* in its "Suplemento" published a survey on various organizational aspects of the revolution and included a question regarding defense: "In terms of defense of the revolution, what force will it be able to call upon and how should it be organized?"[27] The first response came from "GEOFILO A.N.T." who saw an important role falling to the defense cadres, which was tantamount to acknowledging those bodies' rather specializing in matters of defense but at the same time added: "We shall of course have to take the utmost care not to fall into the great snare of setting up a standing army; it is for the producers themselves to exchange their work tools for the weapons of defense when necessity demands it."[28] Actually, it would not be long before the recently launched defense cadres entered into action, not to defend the revolution but rather to topple or at least destabilize republican rule.[29]

Toward the end of 1932, through the National Defense Committee, the body coordinating the various Regional Defense Committees, the CNT's National Committee was hatching its first nationwide uprising.

Initially, the plan was to unleash the uprising in tandem with a general strike in the rail sector. When the National Railway Industry Federation (affiliated to the CNT but a minority presence in the industry) proved reluctant to call a general strike that would likely fail, and the CNT National Committee's refusal to proceed with the uprising in the absence of assistance from the strike, the Regional Defense Committee of Catalonia, fronted by Durruti, Francisco Ascaso, and García Oliver, made up its mind to trigger the uprising and drag the Confederation along in its wake. One reason for the haste was that an explosion at a building in Barcelona had provided the police with a lead on the weapons stockpile for the uprising, as well as how its organizers were taking a risk that the whole plan for Barcelona might come to nothing without prompt action. Even so, Shapiro also points out how "they [the members of the Catalonian Regional Defense Committee] were keen to try their hand at a coup d'etat and were out to 'make the social revolution' without paying the slightest heed to whether the circumstances were or were not suitable and, above all, paying no heed at all to the interests of the National Confederation of Labor."[30] In this regard, according to the notion of a "revolutionary gymnastics" peddled by García Oliver, what mattered was taking on the forces of law and order in order to implant in anarcho-syndicalist militants "the habit of revolutionary action, avoiding individual outrages and sabotage attacks and staking everything on targeted action against the structures of the capitalist system until they could overcome the complex of fear of repressive forces."[31] Even if the confrontation ended in defeat—with the resultant aftermath of militants imprisoned, wounded, or killed, and the enemy's capture of their weapons—such action could still prove positive.[32] As García Oliver explained in an article, "La baraja sin fin" (The Never-ending Shuffle), anarcho-syndicalism never played its last card (as the bourgeois reporters wrote) with its uprisings.[33] Therefore, none of its defeats were final, and one revolutionary uprising followed the last in a never-ending sequence. Even though, if taken literally, the idea was thought to be correct, it patently spoke of a dangerous, overblown optimism and it was dismissive in its appreciation of the waste implicit in any defeat.

The Regional Defense Committee of Catalonia chose to trigger the uprising at 8:00 p.m. on January 8, 1933. Not only did the revolution fail to "take," but improvisation and a load of questionable circumstances surrounding its proclamation caused enormous confusion and a tide of recriminations.[34] The uprising found itself restricted to isolated pockets strewn across Catalonia and Levante and Andalusia, where the tragic Casas Viejas incident occurred. There was a lot of the traditional Bakuninist vanguardist approach in this insurrectionist strategy, whereby a minority of particularly tuned-in and prepared militants might, by some display of daring, act as the detonator and trigger a mass uprising.[35] Even so, it was no easy task. To begin with, and no matter how brutally the forces of order might act on occasions, a struggle mounted through demonstrations, strikes, or sit-ins designed to extract hard and fast improvements and those that took those same forces on at gunpoint or with explosives was an entirely different beast, especially for anyone with family responsibilities.[36] The risks were clearly higher and a majority would see no grounds for taking them. Besides, the fact that the CNT was anarcho-syndicalist "absolutely did not mean that its members were thoughtful anarchists conversant with the thinking and principles of anarchist thinkers . . . there is every chance that its worker membership simply thought that it represented the best vehicle for pursuing their demands."[37] In sum, the bulk of the CNT's membership were primarily in pursuit of tangible economic and work-related improvements. As José Bonet pointed out: "while it is true that we could call upon the people's sympathy, it is no less true that the workers stood aside from the struggle or played a very indifferent and passive role in events. . . . The working class is more responsive to issues of a material and economic order than any other sort . . . which is why the uprising boiled down to a bunch of dyed-in-the-wool militants who counted on very little from the bulk of the Confederation's workers. The same cannot be said of the tangibility of economic-style demands that the CNT was tasked with wresting from the bourgeoisie."[38] Secondly, to complicate things even further, there was the CNT's meager presence in rural areas "with its scattered local trade unions subject to orders and propaganda emanating from the cities."[39]

Outstanding among the criticisms directed at this style of "revolution decreed from above" was the report drawn up by Alexander Shapiro, secretary of the International Workers' Association (IWA/AIT) with help from Eusebio Carbó.[40] The chief complaint raised there concerned the deference that had crept into the practice of the entire Confederation vis-a-vis what should have been an agency in its service: the Regional Defense Committee of Catalonia. The CNT National Committee and in particular its general secretary, Manuel Rivas (who was simultaneously secretary of the National Defense Committee), appears, on the basis of friendship among other things, to have caved in to the Catalans' ultimatum and sent out a telegram to the various regional committees stating that Catalonia had risen in revolt. As a result of which, in accordance with a resolution passed on December 29, 1932, the uprising by the Catalan regional (or any other) had to be followed by the remaining regionals, which would similarly rise in revolt.[41] Shapiro's view was that the National Committee should have asserted itself and championed the Confederation's interests. It should have used all of its moral influence to preempt the hasty uprising at all costs, even if it had entailed losing the equipment stockpiled by the Defense Committees.[42] Henceforth, the CNT was not to allow any agency beyond its direct and constant control to embark again upon a large-scale revolutionary action, no matter how high the moral standing of its members."[43]

Even as the arguments around the January 1933 uprising raged in the columns of the *Suplemento de Tierra y Libertad*, responses to its survey about the defense of the revolution were continuing to pour in. Juanel (the nickname of Juan Manuel Molina, secretary of the FAI's Peninsular Committee) immediately pointed out that the topic itself was "rather a thorny one," going on to say that until such time as the novel circumstances had been consolidated and all resistance coming from capitalism and the State had been overcome, they would have to look to "every means of ensuring it." Which seemed to suggest that he was well-disposed toward the raising of an army or something like one. But once he got into the details, he clung to a cautious ambiguity, avoiding the use of terms such as army, discipline, or unified command. Thus he wrote: "at the outset, defense of the revolution . . . will entail the need to fight in large collective units; ones organized to perfection and well-articulated."[44] In spite of everything, it was not long before a response came and in the very next edition Antonio Conejos Vicente replied very candidly: "There is no implanting our ideals in the soil of a 'certain blockade' and 'organized force' for the defense of the revolution. If it comes to thinking about organizing armies and manufacturing arms, we would do better not to start. We must seek to shape an informed and happy people; everything else will resolve itself, because a people obsessed with advancing its never-ending well-being ought to be invincible."[45]

In the same vein, that September *La Revista Blanca* published an article sent in from Buenos Aires. Essentially it was a critique of repression or terror as a means of defending the revolution but it also addressed the organizing of revolutionary armed forces. The author pointed out: "in the event of it being necessary to defend the revolution's gains by force of arms, that will always be done better and in more timely fashion by the people themselves, if they have an interest, rather than by some government or central direction. The Russian revolution of 1917–1918 is the best illustration of that. *Since the masses of the Russian people had faith in the revolution, it took place almost without bloodshed;*

and, when the need arose, it was [sic] *readily defended by the masses, willingly and with an effectiveness that could never have been matched by any disciplined, well-trained, and centralized army*. . . . Allowing the establishment of specialist police and military forces would signify that the revolution has stopped mid-way and that, inevitably, the popular masses and the anarchists will have to start the struggle all over again."[46] To demonstrate the interest and conflicts that this debate stirred up we might highlight the article "Sheer Fascism" published in *Tierra y Libertad*, in which the author sought to dismiss the idea of organizing militias or a revolutionary army as authoritarian (or, to cite the article's title, fascist): "The talk in our circles hereabouts . . . has spoken slickly about discipline and the virtues thereof. . . . The excellence of 'well-disciplined armies' has been assessed and there has even been some who dream of nothing less than 'libertarian armies.' Where is this taking us? . . . 'militant' gents, I know a good comrade who used to describe them as soldiery 'depending on what sort of militants they are.' By a strange coincidence, supporters of libertarian militias. . . . Poor liberty that you should require an army before you can shine your light on earth! Poor libertarians, if liberty needs to be 'imposed' upon us by an army of 'well-disciplined' Thebans."[47]

The second and last anarchist uprising at the national level came in December 1933 and the immediate trigger was the victory of right-wing candidates in the legislative elections in November–December that year. During that election campaign, the CNT and FAI had mounted an aggressive propaganda campaign in favor of abstention, advocating social revolution in the event of the right's success; so, when that eventually came to pass, they felt impelled to set an example and demonstrate that they were not playing ball with the right by attempting to carry out their own program.[48] A revolutionary committee was set up in Zaragoza on November 26 and tasked with orchestrating the uprising, scheduled for December 8. Prominent within the committee were Durruti, Cipriano Mera, Isaac Puente, and Joaquín Ascaso.[49] As on the previous occasion, doubts were raised and there were complaints about haste; many took the view that they were not ready. Outstanding among the latter was García Oliver, no less, who was undergoing an ideological about-face that would lead to his putting a proposal in front of the Zaragoza Congress for a revolutionary army; according to FAI militant Alejandro Gilabert, "García Oliver, drawing the lessons of the January uprising, took the line that they simply had to move toward a paramilitary organization, which might use the FAI's anarchist groups and the Confederal Defense groups as its springboard."[50]

The revolutionary committee disregarded the objections and once again launched the CNT into an uprising guided not so much on strategic grounds as by undiluted voluntarism and optical considerations such as preserving "the credibility of the CNT" or honoring "the pledge made."[51] Furthermore, Durruti, and perhaps the rest of the uprising's promoters, were still influenced by the notion of "revolutionary gymnastics" which, as we have seen, prized action above any consideration of whether the outcomes would or would not be favorable.[52] This uprising was particularly forceful in the Aragon and La Rioja regions, spilling over across the rest of Spain, mainly into Extremadura, Andalusia, Catalonia, and the lowlands of León; but, as on previous occasions, the hoped for general uprising failed to materialize. The insurgents were reduced to isolated, easily mopped up flare-ups that were not able to pose enough of a serious threat to shake the discipline of the forces of order, especially the army, which, being made up of conscripts, was regarded as more inclined to mutiny.[53] The defeat and ensuing repression left thousands of militants dead or in prison and it left the CNT broken and in disarray. It was clear that it could not carry on this way: the strategy of unrelenting uprisings regardless of the objective circumstances[54] weakened the CNT a lot more that it did the State and gave wings to reaction.[55] Besides, a change of strategy was called for simply because the CNT, now a shadow of what it had been at the beginning of the Republic, did not have the capability to carry on operating on the basis of revolutionary outbreaks.

The wrong-headedness of insurgent voluntarism would be exposed even more when, in October 1934, the socialists launched their own revolutionary uprising. As on previous occasions, the rebellion was unable to arrange a general uprising and in the end was confined to scattered flare-ups doomed to failure. This time, though, unlike on other occasions, the Asturian revolutionaries managed to defeat the forces of order in the region and establish a revolutionary regime for two weeks, with the army of Africa needing to step in to bring it to heel. This was the first time that the revolutionary forces managed to gain control of a sizable region, albeit only for a time, and this represented an important qualitative escalation. While it was under way, the anarchists found themselves unarmed and powerless to lend a hand in the uprising, other than in Asturias itself where they had remained on the sidelines in the preceding attempts and were less depleted. The fact is that the socialists never sought assistance for their revolutionary uprising and were out to go it alone, but there is no denying that the anarchists could have capitalized upon the disorder to fish in troubled waters.

The October 1934 Revolution reaffirmed the need to redefine the insurrectionist strategy. In its "Motion on the Establishment of Defense Committees," dated October 11, 1934, and drafted in the heat of developments in Asturias, the National Committee of Defense Committees lamented: "And [in future] let us have no more of what we have witnessed in the past, whereby, due to a general awareness that we were unprepared for a struggle with even the merest assurances of success, we had to let events pass, immersed in the grief of powerlessness and having to endure the adverse comments."[56] That motion first repudiated "insurrectionist gymnastics" once and for all.[57] "There is no revolution in the absence of preparation; and the more intense and intelligent the latter, the more likely the former will be to carry the day. We must put an end to the penchant for improvisation and hot-headed inspiration as the only viable approaches in times of difficulty. That mistake, of trusting to the creative instincts of the masses, has cost us very dearly. The weapons of war crucial to the fight with a State that has experience, mighty resources [in terms of arms], and superior offensive-defensive standards cannot be come by through spontaneous generation."[58] And it went on to offer a detailed description of the new organizational format and functions of the Defense Committees and, picking up on Shapiro's criticism, looked upon these as "an organic approach ancillary to the CNT," one based upon the latter's "volunteer militants."[59] The equal partnership with the FAI was done away with and its status as an organization answerable to and subject to the CNT's orders was underpinned.

The "Motion" took the view that "the basic group or defense cadre should be small, in order to facilitate its clandestinity and suppleness, as well as a profound familiarity with the character, expertise, and skills of each militant."[60] They were to be made up of six militants "albeit that on occasion the odd additional member can be brought in in order to handle 'higher profile' tasks."[61] And those six members were to share the responsibilities as follows: "A secretary, handling the basic task of liaison with other groups from the same barrio and the fostering of new groups. A second militant was to make it his business to identify ... [and record the personal particulars of] enemies existing within the area allotted to the group. A third militant was to study and assess the vulnerability and importance of buildings and sites inimical to the workers' movement. Their mission was to draw up plans and statistics regarding personnel, items, and arms existing in "barracks, police stations, prisons, churches and monasteries, political and employer centers, strongholds, etc." A fourth member of the group was to investigate strategic and tactical locations, namely, "bridges, underpasses, sewers, basements, house rooftops or escape doors, and access to other streets or a yard affording an escape route and shelter." A fifth militant was to look into public services: "lighting, water, garage facilities, tram depots, metro, transport routes and their vulnerability to sabotage or seizure." A sixth militant was to see to it that locations where arms, money, and supplies for the revolution—"armories, armed private dwellings, banks, credit institutions, clothing depots, foodstuffs, etc."—were identified and their raid-ability investigated.[62]

> Thus, after October 1934, the defense groups would be characterized by their restricted numbers at around six militants each, charged with very specific tasks. They were intelligence-gathering and combat teams who were to "act as the very vanguard of the revolution" and would "directly inspire the people." Meaning that come the moment of the insurrection they had to prove capable of mobilizing a larger number of secondary groups and then later

the entire populace.... Its theatre of operations was a very specific precinct within each barrio. A ward Defense Committee was set up in every barrio to coordinate all these defense cadres and would receive a monthly update report from each group secretary. The barrio secretary-delegate forwarded a summary to the District Committee; and the latter in turn would forward this to the Local Defense Committee "and the latter to the Regional and then to the National Committee." This organizational arrangement, suited to the larger cities, was simplified for the villages where the different groups coordinated directly with the local committee.[63]

Ultimately, the defense cadres, which had hitherto been essentially a fighting vanguard, came to look upon themselves primarily as intelligence-gathering and revolutionary preparedness groups[64]; although they abided by the federal structure in the form of the pyramid of committees so beloved of the CNT and so had to coordinate and control.[65]

Lastly, Agustín Guillamón points out that "the defense cadres were for the most part made up of trade union cadres." And once the would-be coup-makers had been seen off "some of those trade union cadres came to set themselves up as *centurias* of the People's Militias, which promptly marched off to fight the fascists on Aragonese soil. Thus, within the various CNT columns, there might be talk of the metalworkers' *centuria*, or the woodworkers' *centuria*, or construction workers' *centuria*, made up of militants from the same trade union."[66] Also, during the early weeks following "the people's victory" they tackled (among other things) the tasks of "recruiting militians and supplying provisions to the columns leaving for the front."[67]

In Catalonia, the practicalities of implementation of this new agreement on Defense Committees was the subject of a motion tabled by the anarchist groups Indomables, Nosotros, Tierra Libre, and Germen at the Plenum of the Barcelona Federation of Anarchist Groups in January 1935.[68] It moved that a Local Revolutionary Preparedness Committee be formed, made up by two members of the Local CNT Federation and another two from the Local Federation of Anarchist Groups, which would itself set up an auxiliary commission. The task of the Committee and its Commission was "to look into means and methods of struggle, the tactics to be followed and the articulation of organized insurgent forces."[69] That motion looks like a clear ploy by the FAI to recapture some of its lost protagonism and status, since the functions of the new committee had, logically, to belong to the Local Defense Committee. But the interesting thing is the interpretation of revolution laid out in the preamble to the motion and that served to justify it. First of all, it reiterated the jettisoning of the earlier insurrectionist strategy: "The social revolution is not to be construed as a stroke of daring after the fashion of Jacobinist coups d'état."[70] And then came criticism also of spontaneity and voluntarism in respect of defense of the revolution: "[The social revolution] will be the consequence and outcome of the denouement of an inevitable civil war, the duration of which there is no predicting.... If a coup d'état in these modern times requires enormous technical and insurrectionist preparations, with resources and personnel trained to perfection for the appointed purpose, a civil war is going to be that much more demanding in terms of a fighting machine that cannot be cobbled together by enthusiasm alone but that has to be structured and articulated with the greatest possible amount of forward planning and personnel numbers."[71] This motion, incorporating the same preamble plus a few tweaks made by Andalusia and Extremadura, was carried at the FAI's National Plenum of Regionals in January–February 1936.[72] Its endorsement meant that there was acknowledgment of the need to equip oneself with an armed organization suited to getting to grips with the period of warfare that would usher in the revolution but at the same time the idea of a revolutionary army was dismissed, as was evident from one of the items passed in a different motion: "Defense of the new regime is not to be entrusted to professional armies or police forces but should be handled by all workers, without the latter's losing touch with their workplaces."[73] Instead, the revolution's success was being entrusted to a wide-ranging network of Defense and Revolutionary Preparedness Committees, an arrangement entirely compatible with traditional anti-militarist principles, albeit a lot less effective. It was hard to see any other stance being espoused by the FAI, a specifically anarchist organization that was always characterized by and stood apart from the CNT because of its greater "purism."

It is noteworthy that, under the Republic, the libertarian movement made no attempt to raise rural guerrilla detachments to embark upon a guerrilla war, that being something of a popular tradition in Spanish history. It could be argued that whereas, under Francoism, and in a much harsher context, there was a maquis, then something of the sort could have been even more to be expected at that time. Nevertheless, and setting to one side a few eulogies to guerrilla wars and guerrillas, the possibility was never considered.[74] The closest thing to it to be found was a proposal put forward by the FAI regarding the groundwork being laid for the very first nationwide uprising.[75] At the Zaragoza Congress in May 1936, a FAI representative who had served on the National Defense Committee when the uprising occurred explained: "We came out in favor of an uprising prepared by the CNT.... We were denied two things vital to its success. First: the creation of five or six major guerrilla campaigns across the country for the purpose of supporting the revolution at village level by investing it with substance and rolling it out."[76]

There are a number of reasons why such lack of interest might be credited: first of all, anarchism in Spain was primarily an urban movement, with scant foothold in the countryside.[77] Though it is true that where anarchism had its greatest rural support was in the south of the Peninsula, specifically the region that, due to the climate of social strife (robberies, arson attacks on farmsteads, occupations) and the more recent record of banditry, looked better suited to a guerrilla-type movement.[78] Secondly, the planners behind the 1933 uprisings—prominent among them the most charismatic members of the Los Solidarios-Nosotros group—brought an eminently urban approach to the uprisings: guerrilla units were to have emerged once the rising had succeeded in part of Spanish territory and if the revolution needed defending and spreading. But there was no pre-planning done, aside from the odd generic appeal, so the raising of them was left to the initiative of local activists and the wider population.[79] Besides, even though they reckoned that the revolution had to start in the countryside and close in on the cities, the "agrarians," because of their pronounced individualist ideology and thus hostile toward organization, also never pressed the need to allow guerrilla groups to emerge and be supported; in any case, they were supposed to emerge spontaneously.[80] But as José Peirats later pointed out: "a guerrilla war cannot be improvised. There must be pre-planning of support, bases, and communications networks. What did the CNT-FAI do in that respect in its attempted revolutions in 1933? Taking to the streets in the urban areas, proclaiming libertarian communism from the town halls, laying siege to the Civil Guard barracks or affording them the option, should they so choose, to evacuate the area in order to muster in some strategic position elsewhere in the comarca and, having reached some critical mass there, to launch their counterattack. When the latter occurred, the revolutionaries used to give up their revolution, surrendering, or dispersing. Such dispersion might have borne fruit, had the aforementioned support bases or mountain hideaways for their arms, munitions, and explosives—there is no shortage of mountains in Spain—been arranged beforehand." And that writer also cited the flimsiness of the foothold in the countryside: "And had they in, say, Catalonia, won the peasantry by dint of less rabble-rousing and skewed propaganda, posing fewer threats to its petty interests."[81] It should also be pointed out that the much more repressive context of Francoism contributed mightily to the emergence of a maquis, since the Franco regime's revanchist and vindictive nature prevented a huge number of left-leaning people from reintegrating into society, forcing them to go into hiding, take to the hills or go into exile unless they wanted to finish up behind bars or dead.[82] The Communist Party's outreach from France, smuggling in hand-picked guerrilla teams, was crucial to the organizing of most of the guerrilla *agrupaciones*: but we should not overlook the fact that that would not have been feasible had there not been a huge pool of runaways available for recruitment.

On the other hand, the October 1934 revolution did revive the debate on alliance with the UGT and other labor forces, the understanding being that one of the crucial factors in the victory in Asturias had been that that region boasted the only alliance encompassing socialists, anarchists, and communists and including the communist

Armed Agencies and Debates Around Defense of the Revolution

left unaffiliated to Moscow.[83] While this argument raged, *La Revista Blanca* carried a number of comments regarding defense of the revolution; these showed once again how controversial this theme was and how varied opinions were. M. Ramos, a radical individualist who was not even a member of the CNT, "not regarding it as an anarchist association," kicked off with this criticism: "Some years back, Charles Malato suggested anarchist regiments (?) to defend... the anarchist ideal, and Isaac Puente, who was not unaware of that, pointed to the necessity for libertarian militias (!) to establish and uphold what he calls libertarian communism. To my mind, no matter how you dress it up, that amounts to socialism, pure socialism: government, out-and-out government, just as government and government of the worst sort was the 'inspired' Paul Boncour's 'inspired' idea when he proposed mobilizing... the elderly, women, and children whenever the 'sacred' French homeland seemed in jeopardy."[84] To which a highly outraged Isaac Puente tellingly replied: "Could you let me know in which of my writings, or where in any conversation I may have had with anyone, I POINTED TO THE NEED FOR LIBERTARIAN MILITIAS? I have no memory of ever having advocated such nonsense."[85] Two editions later, Ramón Fuster, a communist, had this to say on the matter: "In terms of defense of the revolution, among some anarchists there are still some lingering and very deplorable misconceptions. Pointedly, in these very pages just a few days ago, comrade Isaac Puente spoke out indignantly against disciplined worker militias defending the new order. Let us answer comrade Puente with a few words from another anarchist, Luigi Fabbri: 'The territory of the revolution must be defended, and that includes militarily; that much is evident. For as long as the need persists, an army will have to be maintained and there will have to be such ancillary and like-minded bodies with which every anarchist principle is in open contradiction. For as long as the need persists, an anarchist organization may well not be a possibility, in the early stages at any rate.'"[86]

Before the army mutiny ushered in a completely different picture, the most telling debate would come with the Zaragoza Congress. There, the CNT was about to resolve several pending issues such as unification with the Opposition Unions, laying down its future policy line, and, for the very first time, laying out a detailed program of its notion of libertarian communism, its speculative libertarian society of the future. It was at one of the meetings in the run-up to the Congress that the Barcelona Manufacturing and Textile Union—to which nearly every member of the Nosotros group was affiliated—that, as stated earlier, García Oliver set out his proposal for a revolutionary army.[87] The intention was "to build up a paramilitary organization as an effective means of opposing the coup d'état that he felt was imminent."[88] Although he was backed by some of his comrades from the Nosotros group, there was notable opposition from Buenaventura Durruti who, espousing a more purist approach, warned of the dangers of sliding into authoritarianism: "It is true," he declared,

> that García Oliver's theory is more effective from the point of view of military organization, than the guerrilla warfare that I champion. But I am sure that that paramilitary organization will lead to defeat of the revolution because that body will start out having its way in the name of efficiency and will exercise authority and wind up foisting its power upon the revolution. It was in the name of effectiveness that the Bolsheviks killed off the Russian revolution, which they assuredly had not intended to do, but it was inevitable that that should happen. Let us allow our revolution to plow its own furrow.[89]

But over Durruti's objections, Oliver's motion was passed, and Juan Montserrat, Francisco Ascaso, and García Oliver were appointed delegates to the Congress.[90]

The official motion, published in *Solidaridad Obrera*, opened with the requisite justification:

> If we could count for the defense of the revolution upon the resistance of the world proletariat against intervention and its prevention of its governments' intervening . . . it could be claimed that we might abide by a strictly libertarian interpretation of defense of the Revolution. It needs saying that, in those

circumstances, there would be no defense-of-the-revolution problem, and as a result there would be no need to resort to violent defense of it. Trying that is a duty as enormous as preparing the world proletariat for insurrection. But just in case preparations for defending the Revolution might not be feasible, or in case, their having not gone as far as necessary, they fail, it would also be appropriate for us also to be ready to defend our Revolution by force of arms. But this defense cannot be made on the basis of the theoretical assumptions of our humanitarian and anti-militarist ideas.... That outward defense is going to have to be prepared in accordance with the most advanced methods of military expertise, but with that in mind, should this become impossible or fail, people will turn to the national guerrillas as the ultimate expression of their resistance. Between across-the-board arming of the people and the creation of a revolutionary army, the latter is preferable because it would be more effective and less costly in lives ... the theory of arming people across-the-board ought to be construed and applied in the sense that, in the event of the Revolution's coming under attack from outside, the people ought to step in en masse, each standing by his post, and wherever best serves the overall interests of the defense of the revolution.

In conclusion, what was being proposed was the "creation of a revolutionary army in whichever circumstances defense of the Revolution itself demands." And that army would be answerable "to a Confederal Defense Council, made up of one delegate from each National Federation of Industry or Sector plus a delegate from the Confederal Production, Distribution, and Rights Council."[91] Albeit that no doubt out of discretion the motion before congress offered no further detail, that revolutionary army was to be followed up—García Oliver argued—by the organization and extension to all of Spain a network of defense cadres and their committees, in some regions still in their infancy and—now this was a great novelty—by the raising of a hundred-men units as a complement to the guerrilla network. Such centurias would make up the main units of the Proletarian Army.[92] In contrast to the Defense cadres, which were attached to a barrio or township, or some specific territory, these centurias, genuinely presaging the ones that would later make up the anarchist militias, appeared to represent flying columns standing by to mount operations that required a certain pooling of resources, such as marching off to the front lines to seek out the enemy or to recapture a village or city once the war as under way.

According to Ricardo Sanz's testimony, once the congress convened, the debate that had raged throughout the country in the run-up had turned the matter into somewhat less of a controversy: "The proposition which would at a different time have triggered unanimous objections from the Congress given the character and above all the anti-militaristic education of anarcho-syndicalism, and the reservation displayed by most of them [the delegates] showed that the ground had been prepared. A lively discussion broke out for and against the proposition."[93] But "in the end, the motion put forward by the Barcelona Textile Union was rejected by a majority vote. Of course, it could hardly have gone otherwise."[94] In the end tradition carried the day, despite the motion being very moderate (in that it was respectful of anarchist principles): there was no suggestion that large units be raised, although the centuries could presumably come together to create larger units if need be, nor was there any firm discipline nor unified command established—so the Confederal Defense Council does not seem to have amounted to a General Staff as such—these things being fundamental in any army, as the Platformists had pointed out. Ultimately, the notion of an army came closer to a cluster of militias or guerrilla bands than an army per se; this was suited to a short war of movement, a guerrilla war, but it would prove seriously deficient if the war dragged on and if the emergence of lengthy front lines and large-scale military operations imposed the need for greater coordination. Nevertheless, acceptance of the need for an army, even of that sort, might have been the first step in the direction of shrugging off the ideological taboos that existed regarding armed organizing and defense of the revolution and could have saved some time once the war was underway. It is very likely that the rejection had more to do with squabbling over word choice and the fear and distaste that the word "army"—and everything associated with it—triggered in broad swathes of the anarchists, than the actual contents of it.[95] Here, it is striking that the only counter argument that has survived from the Congress was Cipriano Mera's sardonic crack: "Could comrade García Oliver perhaps let us know his preferred color of 'insignia' and braid?"[96]

When it came to the "Defense of the Revolution" part of the resolution that was passed on "The Confederal Conception of Libertarian Communism," which espoused a traditional line, stated: "A standing army represents the greatest danger to the revolution, because the dictatorship that is called upon to deliver the *coup de grâce* would be molded under its direction. . . . The armed People will be the greatest guarantee against any attempt, from within or without, at restoration of the destroyed regime."[97] And then, in a vague way that actually did not amount to much that was concrete, it added: "If that time comes [invasion from abroad], the People will mobilize swiftly to stand up to the enemy, with the producers returning to their workplaces once they have completed their defensive assignment. That general mobilization will apply to all individuals of either sex who are fit to serve and who do so by carrying out the many assignments needed in the fight. The confederal defense cadres, spreading into the centers of production, will be the most precious auxiliaries in the consolidation of the revolution's gains and equipping the workforce there for whatever large-scale battles we may be called upon to fight in its defense."[98] All the big questions such as the organizing of units, a unified command, or discipline were left hanging, none of them resolved.[99]

Likewise, within the resolution on the "Confederal Conception of Libertarian Communism," we might do well to underline the section "Obligations of the Individual to the Collective and the Notion of Distributive Justice":

> Libertarian Communism is incompatible with any system of correction, which implies the eradication of the current corrective justice arrangements and therefore of the arsenal of punishment (prisons, jails, etc.) . . . social determinism is the chief cause of so-called offending in the current set-up and, as a result, with the

> root causes of offending gone in most cases, the latter will cease to be. So, it is our considered view.... That man is not by nature evil and that crime is the logical consequence of the state of social injustice in which we live.... In order to meet his needs as well as affording him some scope for rational, humane education, those causes have to go. Therefore, our understanding is that when an individual fails to meet his obligations, morally as well as in his role as a producer, it will be up to popular assemblies to devise some fair solution, in a harmonious sense. Libertarian Communism will, therefore, build its "corrective action" upon Medicine and Pedagogy, those being the only preventives that modern science deems so entitled. Whenever some individual, prey to pathological phenomena, trespasses against the harmony that we ought to obtain between man, pedagogical therapy will see to it that the imbalance in him is remedied and that his ethical sense of social responsibility, naturally denied to him by an unhealthy inheritance, is stimulated.[100]

Not only was the offender to face no punishment per se, but there was also no thought of there being some armed corps charged with overseeing the maintenance of order and civic safety, not even a short-lived one prior to the attainment of that stage of social perfection. All in all, the resolution was nothing more than a reiteration of the classical outline of libertarian communism, in theory—a society free of coercion or government and made up of a range of freely federated communes—but did not delve into further detail regarding which measures and issues might need to be taken and grappled with prior to arriving at this idyllic situation. In accordance with its traditional principles, there was no contemplation of any sort of an intervening stage between the existing status quo and libertarian communism.

Throughout the years of the Republic, debates about armed organization had been prolific and remarkable and they involved important personalities from the libertarian movement. As a result of these debates and the different experiences gained, insurrectionist voluntarism was abandoned in favor of a more pragmatic strategy that placed greater emphasis on the preparation for, and circumstances in which, the uprising would be unleashed, as well as on the Defense and Revolutionary Preparedness Committees that would play an important part in defeating the army mutiny in a number of cities, such as Barcelona. However, as far as the defense of the revolution, though some had warned about the difficult circumstances that would surround the early days of the revolution and sought and proposed formulas for attempting to meet the needs that civil war would impose—while respecting as much as possible libertarian principles—in the end the preferred option was to keep those principles untainted and look no further than the Defense Committees. Besides, it's quite possible, as César M. Lorenzo pointed out, that the majority of CNT members would continue to believe that "the Revolution would explode one afternoon as if by some magic spell and, the very next day, in the blink of an eye, everything would fall into place in the best of all possible worlds."[101] Then, since the struggle was going to be a short one, there was no need to organize the various armed forces of the revolution along military lines, or to set up repressive agencies in order to oversee, say, the rearguard.

Once the war was began, and setting aside the initial role the aforementioned committees might be play—and that could only be a modest one, given their characteristics—everything was being left to improvisation, spontaneity, and the people in arms.[102] In this regard, it looked as if the wheel had turned and returned to its starting point. Less than two months later, in the wake of the army revolt of July 17–18, that program and the whole conception of the revolution would have to undergo the test of events.

II
Zaragoza Bound: The Revolution Awaits

"Come out of your houses. Pounce on the enemy. Don't wait another minute longer. You need to put your shoulders to the wheel this very instant. In which task the militants of the CNT and FAI should be to the fore. Our comrades should be in the van of the fighters. If death be necessary, then die they must. . . . We can tell you that Durruti and the speaker will be setting off at the head of the expeditionary columns. We have sent a squadron of planes to drop bombs on the barracks. The militants of the CNT and FAI must live up to the duty that the present moment asks of them. Do not hold back. Do not wait for me to finish this speech of mine. Come out from your houses and burn and destroy. Thrash fascism."
—García Oliver's address over the airwaves as reported in *Solidaridad Obrera*, July 23, 1936

Paradoxically, the army mutiny and the rebellion of the armed corps against the government, a rebellion mounted with the intention of preserving the social order, opened the door to a revolutionary process. "Fascism or social revolution," the slogan oft-repeated in libertarian circles, had finally come true but in a rather different sense than had previously been imagined. The success of one had not banished or defeated the other; instead, they had divided up Spanish territory between them: fascism where the army revolt had succeeded, and revolution where it had been defeated.[1] This was possible because initially the clashes had undermined the potential, unity, and discipline of the forces loyal to the Republic and, secondly, had led to the arming of the masses through a number of transfers of arms carried out by the republican authorities and, especially, the raiding of barracks. A couple of decrees announcing that all the units taking part in the rebellion were being disbanded and all the troops whose officers had defied republican legality demobbed, added further to the disarray in the army. The aims of those decrees was to encourage desertion from the rebel ranks, but they backfired on the government, as they were effective only in the areas where the revolt had been defeated and troops that the government might have been able to try to redeploy under trusted officers been sent packing.[2] The republican state per se was still around, though it has lost status in the eyes of the workers and, now bereft of its means of repression, found itself powerless to hold back the popular tide as power passed into the hands of a host of armed groups and revolutionary barrio and local committees that functioned like out-and-out miniature governments (or, as Grandizo Munis dubbed them, governing committees.[3]) On the economic side of things, the Republic had forfeited its monopoly on violence and political authority, and a wave of expropriations and collective forming was under way.

In Catalonia the defeat of the coup forces after some fierce fighting on the streets of Barcelona, was crucial in turning the entire region against the uprising.[4] In addition to leaving the Generalitat teetering and whittled down to little more than a symbol, it turned the CNT into the master of the streets and the unchallengeable arbiter of events.[5] It was against this backdrop that the mythic Regional Plenum of Local and Comarcal Trade Union committees was held on July 21 to debate the next step. Would the CNT send the Generalitat packing and proclaim libertarian communism? Or would they "go for broke," as García Oliver was calling for—"a pretty euphemism" to which he resorted in order to avoid having to say "taking power"?[6]

Or instead, would they postpone the revolution and first collaborate with all the other antifascist forces in defeating the common foe?[7] This latter proposition won out by a huge majority: partly because of ideological scruples, and partly out of fear of foreign intervention and

Catalonia's being cut off from the remainder of Republican Spain.[8] That decision initiated a problematic alliance that was merely circumstantial, between an array of political factions with entirely contradictory programs, the relations between which had up until that point been marked by frictions. Elsewhere in Spain, wherever the revolt had failed, the upshot was more or less the same: collaboration between all antifascist forces won. As Julián Casanova explains, the territorial, political, and military fractures surprisingly introduced a modicum of stability: "Nobody was strong enough to steer the ship to the port of his choosing."[9] The existence of a deeply fragmented but strong workers' movement was an important barrier to anyone deciding to try and finish off the moribund republican State.[10]

This gamble on collaboration, however, did not mean that the Catalan anarchist leaders once more surrendered political power completely to their adversaries. They stayed on at the Liaison Committee, which the Generalitat established for the organization and coordination of the militias that were due to set off for the front, but they disagreed that it was a mere appendage of the Generalitat and imposed their own view of what it should be, endowing it with a brand new name and an authority and independence that it had not originally had.[11] And so the CAMC was born, a body halfway to a government as such, in which the CNT and FAI reserved the main departments for themselves, those that, given the wartime context, were related to the oversight and organization of the militias and public order.[12]

Add to this difficult coexistence between a limited Generalitat and a CAMC that did not govern at all, in itself potentially damaging to the unification of the war effort, there was what very quickly proved to be a major error: the authorization by the CAMC to its constituent organizations in its founding decree—signed by José Asens, Durruti, García Oliver, Aurelio Fernández, and Diego Abad de Santillán on behalf of the CNT and the FAI—to open up centers for the recruitment and training of militias.[13] That measure was to be followed by the allocation of the various barracks around Barcelona (which had until then been under CNT control) to all the political forces.[14] After having opposed the Liaison Committee's scheme for Civilian Militias, geared to the formation of armed forces under Generalitat control, now renounced CAMC oversight of the organization of its Antifascist Militias. The result, as is all too familiar, was that the armed columns were formed by the various political organizations, making it very hard for the CAMC to coordinate them and thus hampering the direction of military operations, the very thing that should have been its chief concern. This would undermine the CAMC's position and that of the libertarians themselves, who occupied a preeminent position within it.

The existence of unified militias did not guarantee, of course, that the rivalries the antifascist camp was affected by would not be reproduced within it, as would later happen with the Republic's People's Army but it might still have been better than the sort of federation of party and trade union militias that was created. Likewise, the switch to an army as such might have proved easier and quicker. Only in Asturias, where the experience of the 1934 Revolution had helped bring all the left-wing workers' forces together, was that mistake averted and "the centurias and columns were not strictly segregated along the lines of ideological differences; the anarchists and the socialists, the communists (of which there were few) and certain republicans rubbed shoulders in the same units."[15] In the rebel camp, the Carlists and Falangists also raised their own militias and the coup d'etat led to a certain atomization of power and political cantonalism, but there, by contrast, right from the very beginning of the war, unity of action in military matters was achieved. First of all, because the army took decisive charge of military operations and civil authority, enforcing its rigid discipline and clamping down on factional squabbles. Secondly, because all of the conservative elements supportive of the rebellion, though they also covered a broad spectrum, were essentially united around the shared aim of maintaining the economic and social order.[16]

Nevertheless, there was a small chance of things turning out differently: the libertarian movement simply did not have the requisite theoretical baggage to act as the driving force and chief organizer of these hypothetical unified militias. The creation of militias, no matter how informally organized initially, was a novelty in itself and was largely inevitable, as is demonstrated by the Plenum of Catalonia's

Local and Comarcal FAI Group, meeting on August 2, 1936, where there was acceptance of "the fait accompli of popular militias as an unavoidable necessity in the civil war under way."[17] Similarly, the survival of the Generalitat alongside the CAMC was a point of conflict and resistance when it came to the organization of those unified militias, so that at any time it might have felt necessary to win out by sending the Generalitat on its way and cranking up the CAMC as the only regional authority in Catalonia—meaning a proper government. This suggested an additional difficulty for libertarians as their long tradition of anti-politicism—repudiation of government in any guise—left them unequipped to take that step, in the short term anyway. What was required first was a period for reflecting upon and revisiting their principles. For the time being, what they had their sights on—especially the leaders of the CNT-FAI—was a "freezing" of the existing revolutionary situation, retaining a duplication of powers at the top until such time as suitable circumstances might arise for moving on through the implementation of libertarian communism.[18] But that could not go on forever. The situation characterized by the atomization of power was, perforce, transitory and, rather sooner than later, as in every previous revolution, the reconstruction of the crumbling political superstructure would have to begin. If they did not try to seize the reins in this process, others would not hesitate to do it in their place. Moreover, the solution of everyone forming their own militias did not look like an overly significant concession on the part of the CNT which, due to its numerical superiority in Catalonia, was assured of oversight over the greater number of militians and columns.

At this point, we should ultimately ask why García Oliver, being the strongest voice on the CAMC, agreed to this arrangement (assuming that he had not put it forward) and did not try to put his revolutionary army into practice.[19] From the outset it's worth remembering that his proposal bore a closer resemblance to a cluster of guerrilla bands than to an army proper, but the most important point was that he thought of that revolutionary army in terms of a confederal army, wholly and exclusively under the control of the CNT and not as an army in which a range of revolutionary forces might partake and work together. This can also be deduced from the way he envisioned the revolution as a whole: as "the seizure of power" and administration of society by the anarchist trade unions.[20] (Although García Oliver side-stepped the expression "the seizure of power" due to the repudiation it attracted.)[21] Thus, he writes in his memoirs that, at the Plenum on July 21, 1936, he proposed that what started on July 18 should be concluded "with the Militias Committee standing down and events being forced in such a way that, for the first time in history, the anarcho-syndicalist unions should 'go for broke,' meaning organize libertarian communist life throughout Spain."[22] Given that the CNT did not account for the majority of the working class, never mind the overall population, some rightly labeled this proposal as an "anarchist dictatorship."[23] The most striking thing about the matter is that it seems that all of the participants there were pondering a hypothetical proclamation of libertarian communism and furthering the revolution along those or very similar lines, and the understanding was that the CNT as an organization should "prevail after the revolution."[24] Neither at that point nor, more significantly, in any subsequent debate surrounding this topic, was there any discussion of turning the main committees that had mushroomed right across the country—once they had been democratized and coordinated until they constituted a central authority—into the governing agencies of a future revolutionary regime. A formula a lot more coherent than the establishment of some sort of a trade union dictatorship or collaboration with other antifascist factions regardless of ideology, something that might have attracted the support of other revolutionary factions, as well as of workers of no particular political persuasions.[25] Instead, they thought of those revolutionary committees as just temporary bodies doomed sooner or later to fade away, and there was no doubt about this because they were extraneous to their organizational models.[26] In short, and harking back to the subject that opened this paragraph, and García Oliver's conception of the revolution and the organization of a revolutionary army: having declined to institute an "anarchist dictatorship," it was going to be hard to sell an "anarchist army." Leaving each organization free to set up its own armed militia was the only alternative left.

Meanwhile, Aragon had fallen to the rebels—the conspirators had succeeded in the three provincial capitals there and every town of significance, except for Barbastro. According to García Oliver, at the very first meeting of the CAMC, following approval of the order establishing and assigning the portfolios around the representatives, reference was made to the "threat of a fascist military march from Aragon and the appropriateness of getting columns of volunteer militias ready to contain them," with the idea being expressed "and promptly agreed upon, that the best containment would be a swift march that might make it possible to capture, first, Zaragoza, and then Huesca. Once that had been agreed, Durruti offered—and no one refused—to take command of the first militia column," whereupon he "asked that Major Pérez Farrás accompany him as the column's expert military commander."[27] This account, which explains the source of the decision to set up what would be the Durruti Column, differs from Ricardo Sanz's account. Sanz places the discussion in the Generalitat and credits Companys with a leading role in it:

> After the Militias Committee had gathered, thoughts turn immediately to paying a visit to the President of the Generalitat of Catalonia, Don Luis Companys, and a broad exchange of views followed.... Companys set out his view—which was shared by all present—that the capture of Zaragoza and most of the villages in Aragon by the rebels posed a serious threat to Catalonia. It was conceivable, he stated, that the rebels might mobilize their forces immediately in order to pit them against Catalonia and so the latter wasting no time, should raise a mighty column made up of volunteers and to head it, two people should be appointed whose military and labor credentials offered enough of a guarantee for those who might enroll in it ... In the end, there was agreement that the Column ... should be under the command of some very well-known individuals of proven antifascist credentials: Major Pérez Farrás, a member of the Esquerra party, as military expert and as its civilian delegate, the renowned libertarian fighter from the CNT, Buenaventura Durruti.[28]

It is plausible that Companys's intention in seconding his trusted Pérez Farrás to Durruti's side was an attempt to counterbalance Durruti's authority lest that first column fall under the sway of the CNT.[29] Whatever the facts of the matter, both testimonials, along with a couple more quotations drawn from García Oliver's autobiography and the fact that two months after the outbreak of the war a series of second line fortifications more or less following the boundary between Aragon and Catalonia were under construction, prompted José María Maldonado Moya to come to the mistaken conclusion that the "intention of the Catalan leaders, from the Generalidad president to those who actually wielded command of the militia forces that set off from Catalonia—the anarchists—was never the capture of Aragonese cities. Their sole intention was defense of Catalan soil."[30] At least insofar as it relates to the anarchists this is a roundly reductionist statement. Even though those columns were also setting off in defense of Catalan soil, there is no denying that their main aim was to achieve an advance that they believed could prove decisive for the defeat of the rebels and in the expansion and deepening of the revolution.

In actual fact, Zaragoza, a city second only to Barcelona in terms of the CNT's foothold there, was afforded an especially important status, as is indicated by the recurrent headlines and articles carried by the libertarian press about it and the imminence of its capture during the early months of the war.[31] There was a general clamor of "On to Zaragoza!"[32] Strategically, the city represented a very important communications hub linking the Catalan region to the Central Meseta and offering access to La Rioja and Navarra, the capture of which would have allowed a connection with the isolated republican strip to the north. A lot of people saw its liberation, indeed, as paving the way to venturing to introduce libertarian communism. Here, José María Maldonado glosses over a very telling scene outlined by García Oliver, who in his autobiography, writes that on June 23, 1936, he gathered the Nosotros group together and, after criticizing the fact that "going for broke" had been rejected, he suggested that they cash in on the mustering of men expected the following day for the departure of the first column and launch a revolutionary rising that might drag the Confederation along in its wake (just as they had tried to do earlier in January 1933). In 1933, Durruti had opposed the move on the grounds that the timing did not seem right to him and that the rising should be postponed until after the capture of Zaragoza, something that he thought could not take any more than ten days, since with just Catalonia as their support base they would be reduced to a tiny foothold, geographically speaking.[33] The fact is that we have serious grounds for asking whether García Oliver ever made the suggestion: for a start, several testimonies raise doubts as to the conviction and/or commitment with which he had championed the chances of "going for broke" back on July 21, 1936.[34] Secondly, Ricardo Sanz points out that the last time the group gathered together was on July 20, 1936, during the storming of the Atarazanas barracks.[35] For his part, Antonio Ortiz, acknowledges this meeting took place, but makes no mention of the suggestion.[36] But the point of the account is that—just as there is a grain of truth in most lies—it shows Durruti espousing a stance that subsequent details show that he definitely embraced and that was also the majority view within the Catalan libertarian movement.

So, on July 29, 1936, at a meeting of the CNT National Committee, the delegate for Catalonia, in a statement that is also indicative of how the top echelons of the Catalan CNT had been (and still was) applying the brakes to its rank-and-file, declared that "the bulk of the membership seems disposed, as a result of the Organization's ascendancy [to] proceed with the establishment of Libertarian Communism throughout Catalonia ... If the columns of comrades that have set off for Zaragoza take that city, there will be no chance of a minority's upholding [holding back] the bulk of the Organization the way it has up until now. They will ... proceed with the implementation of our ideals, regardless of the conditions with which the rest of the Regionals may be having to contend." That possibility was also not to the liking of those in attendance who reckoned that there was no way that libertarian communism should be proclaimed for the time being, as they were outnumbered in many other regions.[37]

The organization of the Column was completely haphazard, which was inevitable given that they were starting from nothing. After the announcement that columns were being raised to march on Aragon, the workers began to flood into their respective unions and into the former Defense Committees, which had resurrected themselves as Revolutionary Ward Committees, to enlist and be issued with weapons, blankets, and other gear.[38] Those Ward Committees also offered a very rudimentary military training, instruction in "the most elementary rules of combat, as well as in the throwing of hand grenades and the handling of rifles."[39] Naturally, these volunteers grouped together on the basis of affinities, searching out acquaintances and friends and forming groups of militias drawn from the same trades, defense cadres, barrios, Libertarian Youth. . . . Durruti and Pérez Farrás, for their part, sought reinforcements from among the army and police units that had kept their oath to the Republic and that had not disbanded once the fighting ended.[40]

At 9:30 a.m. on July 24, Durruti delivered a wireless address on behalf of the CAMC, urging those willing to accompany him to muster on the Paseo de Gracia at ten o'clock that morning, and warning the workers of Barcelona, especially those in the CNT, not to surrender the posts they had captured and to remain alert and watchful and respond to potential incidents.[41] That was a somewhat ambiguous warning that was directed more at some effort by the Generalitat to reassert its authority than to a resurgence on the part of the fascist rebellion.[42] Abad de Santillán, in charge at the CAMC of the organizing of the militias, acknowledges that, just hours before the Column moved out, he could not have said where the militias would be coming from, let alone their weapons or transport.[43] In the end, shortly after midday, the volunteers set off for Zaragoza "with indescribable delight, pride, and spirit," cheered on by the public.[44]

The July 24, 1936, edition of the *Crónica diaria de la Generalitat de Catalunya* (Generalitat of Catalonia Daily Gazette) offers us a detailed description of the assets making up the Column: "it comprised ninety-six vehicles, including around thirty buses and sixty trucks loaded with militias; various trucks carrying rations, four CAMPSA tanker-trucks, an army tank carrying drinking water and some fifteen trucks carrying twelve modern artillery pieces and munitions. Part of the expedition was made up of fifteen Red Cross military ambulances and several nurses ... a number of armored trucks that had been cobbled together ... [recently] in the Hispano-Suiza workshops, plus one truck carrying a team of telegraphers to establish communications."[45] As to the numbers and where they came from, the non-existence of registers makes it impossible to provide precise figures, so we have no choice but to go for an estimate. In view of the vehicles making up the expedition, and even if higher figures have been suggested, the Column on its departure could not have been made up of the two-thousand-odd men suggested by Vicente Guarner or Abel Paz.[46] The vast bulk of them were drawn from the CNT but there were some groups of soldiers, Civil Guards, and Assault Guards, a handful of Esquerra Republicana de Catalunya (ERC) members who had signed on to follow Pérez Farrás, plus a tiny minority of members of the Workers' General Union (UGT).[47] As far as officers, though it was initially unclear who was in charge, Durruti—abetted by the fact that most of his companions were CNT personnel—emerged as the sole, undisputed "Column Commander."[48] This was symbolically acknowledged through a change of column name, from the Durruti-Farrás Column to what simply became known as, from August 1936 onwards, the Durruti Column.[49]

Pérez Farrás, by contrast, was relegated to the status of advisor with no power, and was basically without any influence at all. He disapproved of how things were being handled and was utterly sidelined from any sort of effective leadership or oversight, and would eventually quit the Column, returning to Barcelona sometime during the latter part of September.[50] Durruti's personal military advisor, basically from the column's departure, was artillery sergeant José Manzana.

Back on the afternoon of July 24, a second, mostly anarcho-syndicalist column, headed by Antonio Ortiz and made up of some eight hundred personnel who had not been able to leave with Durruti, set off by train determined to help capture Zaragoza.[51] According to Martín Terrer, an artillery sergeant who served with this second column, those personnel represented the left-overs, as the CNT's elite had left with Durruti.[52] Together, the two columns raised some three thousand militias for a mission on the scale of Zaragoza, which as the base of

43

the Fifth Organic Division, held huge arsenals and was the base of sizable armed forces and public order personnel.[53] Here, Abad de Santillán points out that "it was estimated that some twelve thousand men would be needed to enter Zaragoza," but "it was believed that the initial expeditionary column had too many fighters and that it would encounter no obstacles in its mission."[54] This reckless optimism added to the frictions that existed between all the antifascist organizations, prompting them to withhold manpower, arms, and munitions in the rearguard with an eye to self-protection and efforts to have their own way once the rebels had been defeated.[55] Abad de Santillán even talks about sixty thousand rifles held in the rearguard when there were only thirty thousand in service on the Aragon front. And there was more ammunition in the rearguard than at the front;[56] even though that estimate may seem exaggerated—even granted that there was large scale retention of gear held in the rearguard—it is questionable whether, prior to July 1936, that number of rifles had ever existed in Catalonia. The shortage of combatants on the expedition to Zaragoza would be eased in part by new arrivals joining it along the way and also later on, but it was undoubtedly a major obstacle to its success.

Over the ensuing days and weeks, the trickle of columns bound for the various sectors in Aragon would continue.[57] For all their origins and partisan nature, they were largely reflective of the revolutionary process that had started off in the republic's rearguard and they shared—with variations depending on each instance—a range of features: 1. They were made up of "diluted militians," remnants of the army and police, plus volunteers drawn from the left-wing parties and trade unions, the ones drawn from the workers were the majority.[58] 2. There was little to distinguish those in charge from the ordinary ranks. 3. All decisions were discussed democratically. 4. Discipline was rooted more in the collective will than any hierarchical imposition.

Another striking detail was the presence of female militians who were subsequently gradually pulled back into the rearguard or consigned within their units to non-combatant roles as, say, cooks, nurses, secretaries. The libertarian militias, in addition to all of the above, stood out especially for the absence of military saluting, stripes, marching in formation, or any other outward display one might expect of any traditional army.[59] As a rule, as Pelai Pagès i Blanch concludes, they represented an organizational model that reflected the anti-militarism that the popular classes had evinced ever since the eighteenth century and the dream of egalitarianism, the model of the classless society for which anarchists, socialists, and communists had been striving for decades.[60]

These columns, regardless of the high levels of courage and morality they displayed, were to reveal serious shortcomings, especially in the early stages, especially where discipline, coordination, or internal cohesion were concerned.[61] Most of the militants displayed almost utter ignorance of warfare. At best their experience of arms usually went no further than their participation in uprisings, riots, and raids over the previous years, but those struggles had nothing in common with the clashes that were about to begin in the open countryside. Here, García Oliver's testimony proves illuminating: "From the confederal Defense Committee we had successfully conjured up a type of revolutionary fighter, which the passage of time showed was highly effective. The Defense Cadres were suitably equipped for street fighting in the larger cities. They were trained in a value system that might lead to success in urban fighting; they were extremely secretive, punctual in their rendezvous, abiding strictly by watchwords, maintaining the esprit de corps inside the cadre, were flexible in their movements, fought shy of the stationary tactics, such as digging in behind a barricade or on some balcony or some window, because, sticking to any of those positions meant defeat and death. In relation to cities, those and other tactics were best suited."[62] In the open countryside, however, they were soon to discover that knowing how to dig in in some position, design a system of trenches, shelters, and casemates, and proper deployment of one's firepower was vital. Some of the officers who had not mutinied marched off with the columns in the capacity of military experts to counter this lack of expertise; however, their effectiveness was rather limited by the distrust they generally inspired—a distrust partly justified by frequent desertions and acts of treachery.[63] It took some time and material and personnel losses before the militants from the workers' organizations absorbed the basic lessons of modern warfare.

Zaragoza Bound

On July 25, 1936, on the way through Lérida, the Durruti Column crossed paths with another column raised by the Workers' Party of Marxist Unification (POUM) and commanded by Manuel Grossi and Jordi Arquer. Grossi, who requested the meeting, recalls the conversation between the commanders of both columns. He began, "In view of the success achieved in Barcelona and in the rest of Catalonia in the fight against fascism and once it has been defeated by the workers' concerted action, the workers will be marshaled with the various CNT-FAI-POUM workers' organizations, etc., it is my belief that in order to press home our success against our class enemies and achieve victory, before leaving Lérida for the battlefield . . . we must come to some arrangement regarding unity in combat. That would inspire our militians in the fray by injecting into them a mutual trust that must of course also have an impact on ourselves as commanders. Moreover, decisions subject to joint examination might offer greater assurances of victory. To which Durruti replied: 'The CNT on its own is up to winning the war and consolidating the revolution, relying upon no forces beyond its own' . . . Arquer piped up: 'That view may well be very much comrade Durruti's own and that of some of the other leaders of the CNT, but it is not too widely held, since we can rest assured that all the CNT's combatants, like those from the other workers' organizations want to see unity in every aspect of the struggle against their class enemies.' Durruti then stated: 'Ultimately, we will see that later once we can talk about victory. Take it from me, we will show tolerance.'"[64] This evidence is rather revealing as to Durruti's initial stance on the war and the revolution; indicating that he had great confidence that the war was going to be brief—which, by the way, is what nearly everybody thought at the time—and that its outcome would be favorable to the anarchists.[65] He saw no need for collaboration with columns of different political persuasions.

On the morning of July 25, and subsequently, Durruti reached Caspe with part of his column. That town, lying a few kilometers south of the Ebro River, had been captured by the rebels thanks to back-up from a mutiny by Civil Guard Captain Negrete. On July 24, a team of militians from Barcelona had attempted to claw back the town and were partly forced back following a ferocious firefight. Against this backdrop, the arrival of Durruti tilted the balance once and for all in the militians' favor as the rebel forces retreated once he showed up.[66] Within hours, all of the forces that had had a hand in the recapture of the town gathered at the town hall and, after a rather heated discussion, it was agreed that the Durruti Column would cross the Ebro and proceed along its left bank in the direction of Bujaraloz to establish the central front.[67] The right bank would fall under the remit of the Ortiz Column, which would absorb the remaining small columns operating in the area. This decision represented a serious strategic miscalculation, as the city of Zaragoza, apart from its El Arrabal barrio, is located in the south of the Ebro on its right bank (also known as the South Ebro or Jubert Column). The right thing to do at that point was for the stronger column to head swiftly south to where it would no longer have the river as a barrier in front of it, the aim being to try to reach the capital city of Aragon before the resistance could be crushed and the defenses well organized. There was no risk involved in crossing the Ebro but the closer they got to Zaragoza, where the enemy had concentrated his forces, the more problems they were likely to run into.

And so the Durruti Column carried on its way along the left bank of the Ebro, reaching Bujaraloz, Valfarta, and La Almolda on July 26, leaving Candasnos and Penalba behind it.[68] Its progress was proceeding like some triumphal march, running into no opposition. From Bujaraloz, the column set off for Osera and Pina de Ebro and it was halfway there when the column had its first encounter with the reality of modern warfare: the enemy air force attacked them (not that there was anything spectacular in that—between one and three planes were involved, depending on one's source), leaving a number of them dead or wounded and primarily triggering a tremendous rout. According to what was later told to Jesús Arnal, the priest who, in one of the quirks of history, wound up as Durruti's secretary, only the medics and the officers stood their ground.[69] In light of this situation, Durruti opted to head back to Bujaraloz to marshal his forces again, to be briefed on the enemy positions lest he fall into an ambush, and to improve the organization of his column, installing its headquarters in the town and setting up the column's first administration.[70] The unfortunate thing is that these tasks, positive enough in themselves, would delay them there for over a week.

Inside Zaragoza, the general strike called by the trade union organizations lingered on but for want of the arms with which to defend itself, it could not hold out for much longer. All of it despite the fact that Durruti, in a heartfelt address to his militians after their shameful rout, stressed that they needed to strike swiftly: "The sooner we attack, the greater the chances of our success. So far, victory has been on our side, but it is not going to be consolidated unless we take Zaragoza immediately.... We must not have tomorrow a repetition of what we have seen today."[71] As Javier Ortega Pérez explained, "the anarcho-syndicalist columns' closing on Zaragoza did not quite mean [or rather, not just mean] the capture of a military objective; the overarching aim was to tilt the map of the conflict in the direction of a situation where there was no war" ... in the direction of circumstances—to be more blunt—where, with the mutineers defeated, the revolutionaries might push things as far as they would go, not excluding the breaking up of the republican State and the proclamation of libertarian communism (in Catalonia and Aragon anyway).[72] Had this come to pass, this would have been a step toward a new and deeper phase of the Spanish Revolution—though there was no telling what political form this might take.

On August 4, *Solidaridad Obrera* reported that, as of August 2, "the organizing of groups of militians into centurias under the command of a centurion [elected by the fighters], and the sub-division of these into ten-man groups [each with its respective delegate] is now complete."[73] So the centuria had been embraced as the basic unit, in accordance with what García Oliver had suggested. The article, "Fighting ability and war tactics" by José Blanco, a member of the Column, appears to suggest that the organization into centurias began in Bujaraloz.[74] However, Abel Paz mentions a number of centurias up and running by the time of the departure from Barcelona.[75] Similarly, José Mira writes that "the infantry was organized into centurias and by the first few days they were already up to the 10th."[76] As a result, the most likely thing is that, by the time that the Column stopped over in that town, there were militians already organized into decurias and centurias and the assignment of the rest was underway. That organization into centurias and decurias was not by any means complete by August 2 was demonstrated by the fact that, as Alejandro Soteras Marín recounts, the 12th and 13th centurias were set up after the capture of Pina.[77] As for the decurias, during that same month they were to be replaced by twenty-five-man groups, a sub-division that was not so small but was more practical.[78] When the Column set off it was little more than a shapeless mass of combatants that would, thanks to a "process of trial and error," progressively adopt an organizational structure.[79]

Five centurias were to make up one *agrupacion*, which would represent the larger unit, headed by an elected commander who, together with the delegates from the centurias, made up the Agrupación Committee. Right at the top there was the War Committee, made up of Durruti, Ricardo Rionda, Miguel Yoldi, Francisco Carreño, and Lucio Ruano, plus the various agrupacion delegates.[80] This organizational format would be copied by the rest of the libertarian columns.[81] This continued, to a greater or lesser extent, by the other political formations and would prevail up until the militarization in early 1937.[82] It should, finally, be pointed out that to this basic structure were added a number of groups distinguished by their origin or activity on the front and that had their own particular organizational format. In the case of the Durruti Column, we might single out the International Group, the Investigation Group made up of metalworkers and under the command of Justo Bueno Pérez, with its monitoring-and-repression mission in the rearguard.[83] Plus the various guerrilla groups like La Banda Negra, Los Dinamiteros, and the "Sons of Night."[84]

The Column's progress resumed on August 8 with the capture of Gelsa, Osera, and Pina de Ebro after negligible or no resistance; the enemy dug in on the far side of the river.[85] On August 12, Monegrillo was overrun without any problems.[86] On the 14th, it was the turn of Farlete before moving on to the Calabazos Altos from which position Zaragoza could be sighted at some twenty kilometers distance.[87] In the liberated area, the small villages of Castejón de Monegros, Alborge, Alforque, Velilla, and El Aguilar de Ebro had been bypassed. South of the Ebro, however, the situation was not so encouraging: the advance was encountering serious resistance and slowing down, added to which the fact that it was actually the weakest column operating in that sector. The upshot was that the Ortiz Column had been held up.

Durruti was eager to press on with his advance, but orders came from the CAMC that he was to halt and wait until Ortiz had control of Belchite and Quinto.[88] Durruti's military advisors agreed.[89] Durruti was resistant to the idea of temporarily placing Zaragoza on the back burner but eventually caved in and ordered the Column to mark time.[90] It could be argued that this decision lost them a golden opportunity to capture Zaragoza, but the fact is that the opportune moment had long since passed. Although it had increased its manpower to some 4,500 fighters, the Durruti Column only had access to 3,000 rifles and was consequently a minor force compared with the army and police units dug in inside Zaragoza.[91] The army and police units were bolstered over July 23 and 24 by some 3,000 *requetés* coming from Pamplona.[92] But what mattered most was that the rebellion had had more than enough time to embed itself, drown the general strike in blood, and make its defensive arrangements by blowing up the bridges across the Ebro leading to the city.[93] In a sense, Durruti was trapped in a dead end: "the position he had taken up," Abad de Santillán recounts, "was the one least suited to the capture of Zaragoza ... the bridges across the Ebro had been blown up and Durruti was unable to cross the river and reach the gates of Zaragoza before the South Ebro columns or the ones we had dispatched in the direction of Huesca."[94] In these circumstances, an attack on Zaragoza was risky and might easily have resulted in a disastrous defeat that would have left the column decimated, if not destroyed. Durruti's exceedingly cautious approach, his sluggishness, combined with the wrong-headed decision to cross back over the Ebro at Caspe, thwarted any chance of capturing Zaragoza in a lightning attack.[95]

In the rest of the Aragonese front, the rapid initial advance of the antifascist forces, made almost in a vacuum, was also slowing down and a regular front was beginning to emerge. At that very time, the expedition against Majorca was being launched, even though any reinforcements to breathe fresh life into the offensive might have been of great assistance.

The expedition was an operation orchestrated behind the back of the CAMC by the Generalitat, with support from the Unified Socialist Party of Catalonia (PSUC), the central government, and even the CNT's own Marine Transport Union.[96] The aim was to challenge the authority of the CAMC and secure a victory that might have been claimed by the Generalitat. However, in the end, the discredit to the CAMC, which was powerless to direct or even to keep track of all the military operations hatched inside Catalonia, would be added to the expedition's failure and its shambolic evacuation over September 2 and 3, in the course of which a good part of its war materials were lost.[97]

Concern at the sluggishness of operations and a sneaking suspicion of failure were palpable at the Plenum of Locals and Comarcals described by García Oliver.[98] At the Plenum, Durruti, in the face of criticisms coming from his comrades, actually surrendered the leadership of his column into the hands of the meeting, thought in the end everything was left as it had been.[99] Politically speaking, the military setback represented by the halt to the push against Zaragoza and the slowing down of progress along the rest of the front was seen by libertarians as the outworking of the collaborationist approach. On August 17, at a Plenum of Locals and Comarcals, the CNT made the decision to wind up the CAMC, though the CNT's membership were not told, and in any case, it would be some time before it took effect. "The view was taken that in order to avoid a duplication of powers as represented by the CAMC and the Generalidad government, the former had to leave the stage and the Council of the Generalitat of Catalonia be constituted, to pursue more positive activities without the friction of a conflict of powers and in order to fend off the democracies' pretext that they would not assist us 'because the anarchists were giving the orders.'"[100] Instead, it was proposed that battery of Commissions and Councils (of Supplies, Economy, Culture, Defense) be set up. The intention was, as Agustín Guillamón correctly points out, "to control the government without serving in it."[101] Fat chance.

Important political developments were also taking place at the national level. On September 4, after the Giral government—made up exclusively of republicans—had wallowed in powerlessness for more than a month, Francisco Largo Caballero formed a new cabinet with a majority of rather moderate socialists plus a minority of republicans, one representative from the Basque Nationalist Party (PNV), and two communist ministers. The CNT, having been offered only one minister without portfolio, decided to stand aside. However, appreciating that the incoming government was making a fresh start, was a lot more representative, and had enough of a working-class foothold to set about reshaping the central government, the CNT embarked upon a series of internal discussions in an effort to devise some way of avoiding being sidelined. The aim was "that the machinery of the state's oversight mechanisms not be left in the hands of the other political organizations";[102] and to oversee that authority, insofar as was possible, in order to use it to its own advantage and avert the anarchists' and the revolution's being gobbled up the way they had been in Russia.[103]

In line with what had been agreed in Catalonia, on September 5, a CNT delegation proposed to Largo Caballero that within each ministry there be established an auxiliary commission made up of representatives from the CNT, the UGT, the Popular Front, plus a government delegate.[104] That proposal was unrealistic and poorly thought out and was of course rejected. In the wake of that rejection, the CNT decided at a National Plenum on September 15 to discuss the creation of a National Defense Council made up of five CNT delegates, five from the UGT, and four republicans. It too would be headed by Largo Caballero, while Azaña would remain as president of the Republic. It was a proposal for a government lineup (because, when all is said and done, that was precisely what it was, though with a label that was more palatable to the CNT) with a correlation of forces that was a lot more in the CNT's favor, but it came too late even to be worth considering.[105] It was obvious that if any UGT leader had entertained the chances of coming to some arrangement with the CNT, it would have come to nothing when compared to the political forces upon which Caballero had relied in the formation of his government. Besides, acceptance of any such proposal would have risked the image of republican legitimacy and respectability that Caballero was then attempting to "sell" internationally.[106] With the proposed National Defense Council rejected, the CNT's then general secretary Horacio Martínez Prieto would start the "horse trading" with Largo Caballero over direct and unashamed partnership in the government of the Republic.[107]

The reality is that the libertarian movement, full of scruples and ideologically incapable to face the scenario that had opened up, and improvising and revising its principles as it went along, after having let the first few weeks pass without trying to roll out some kind of counter-power or revolutionary government, began to realize that it was being overtaken by other political forces. The only region where they took the initiative and managed, for a few months, to "institutionalize the revolution" (in the words of Julián Casanova)—meaning "conjure up a brand-new political order as the expression of these revolutionary changes"—was Aragon.[108] There, on October 6, at an Extraordinary Plenum of trade unions held in Bujaraloz at the instigation of the CNT Regional Committee and in which the main leaders of the anarchist columns participated, it was decided to set up the Regional Defense Council of Aragon, better known by its abbreviated name, the Council of Aragon.[109]

Moreover, the dragging out of the war and the progressive establishment of a front line had significant military and economic implications; for a start, the switch from the initial war of movement to a more positional warfare highlighted the shortcomings of the militia's organization even further; secondly, it would necessitate the organization of production and supply in sustaining these armed forces over an extended period of time. Some anarchists thought that the formation of a front was a mistake and that they should have opted instead for guerrilla warfare.[110] The fact is that no matter how fond the libertarian press was of referring to the militians as guerrillas or freedom fighters, it was unrealistic and they were more or less doomed to a conventional war. By its very nature, guerrilla warfare cannot—or should not—openly engage an army rather than carrying out harrying operations, laying ambushes, and thereby avoiding frontal combat and giving ground when required, and launching an attack at one location only when it has the upper hand and could guarantee victory. It was designed, not so much to occupy territory as to grind down and undermine the enemy; sabotaging his infrastructure, gathering intelligence, attacking the supply, pinning down and stringing out his forces in the rearguard. Steering clear of establishing a defensive front and opting for a widespread guerrilla war would have meant leaving behind the population and territory just liberated at the mercy of fascist incursions. Moreover, that territory represented the columns' main source of sustenance and was the location of an alternative social arrangement that was in progress. As Durruti stated in one interview: "A defeat for my column would be fearsome, as our retreat would resemble that of no other army; we would have to take with us all the inhabitants of the villages through which we have passed. From the line of fire, the whole way to Barcelona, along the route we have traveled, there are combatants and nothing else. Everyone is working on behalf of the war and the revolution."[111] In short: guerrillas might be an asset to an army but were no substitute for one.[112]

Inside the Durruti Column, and other columns, guerrilla squads were formed that mounted numerous raids and incursions, even though the opportunity to organize an ongoing guerrilla war in the enemy's rear was neglected.[113] In mitigation, however, it should be said that the rebels had carried out brutal, methodical repression in the territory they occupied for the precise purpose of, among other things, thwarting any sort of opposition or resistance.[114] So many of the potential support bases for a guerrilla movement of that sort had been eradicated or could be paralyzed by fear.[115]

The Durruti Column, therefore, had no option other than to embed itself by forming a front from Velilla de Ebro and following the course of the river through Gelsa, Pina, and Osera before turning north in the direction of the foothills of the Sierra de Perdiguera, with the war effort shifting toward the outskirts of Huesca and the area immediately south of the Ebro. There was another factor that would curtail the Column's activities: the alarming dearth of arms and munitions that was starting to make itself felt right across the entire front. On August 14, in a conversation with Mikhail Koltsov, the correspondent from the soviet newspaper *Pravda*, Durruti stated that he had access "only to old rifles in numbers insufficient to arm everyone" and, as for ammunition "that was a real nightmare."[116] Durruti was bombarding the CAMC with requests for arms: on a daily basis, Abad de Santillán recounts, "he would treat us to a diatribe ... about everything he needed in order to prosecute the war and emerge the victor," but "we were in no position to give anything to him or to anybody else, because we had nothing."[117] Thus, powerless to undertake any great venture, the column was reduced to strengthening its defensive positions, to skirmishing and a few guerrilla operations and raids.[118]

In *Solidaridad Obrera* of August 15, 1936, for instance, one could read about a scouting operation in the direction of Aljafarín: on the 21st, about skirmishes between the 8th *centuria* in Osera and enemy forces dug in on the far side of the Ebro in Fuentes; on September 6 about a raid on Villafranca de Ebro, and on September 10 about the attack on the enemy headquarters in Fuentes and the ensuing withdrawal with captured war materials and prisoners. For his part, Antoine Gimenez, a member of the "Sons of Night" guerrilla group, recounts that between late August and early September, an incursion was mounted to open up one sluice-gate and close another, in order to bring water to Pina's irrigated fields, and the temporary seizure of a bridgehead on the far bank of the Ebro as a diversionary ploy.[119]

Shortages on the front led, in late August, to the first requisitioning attempts in the rearguard,[120] plus calls for arms to be moved up to the front—calls that Durruti[121] and his column's bulletin *El Frente*[122] were involved in. At the beginning of September and after the Sabadell PSUC had refused to hand over the weapons they had in storage, Durruti dispatched a centuria under the orders of Francisco Carreño to seize them. This incident did not trigger a violent clash because, in the end, the CAMC persuaded Moix, the local PSUC leader, to hand them over with good grace.[123] As a rule though, the fruits of such calls and attempts to commandeer were very poor. The existence of multiple armed bodies in the rearguard was a symptom and a result of both the absence of a government (be it described as Council, Committee, or Junta) strong enough to enforce its monopoly on violence. Within the libertarian movement, such attempts to disarm the rearguard, whether coming from the CAMC or, later, from the Generalitat, always ran into stiff resistance from the rank-and-file and especially from the network of Ward Committees in Barcelona and its Defense Sections (also known, in the jargon of the republican period, as Defense Committees), which feared, not unreasonably, that they might mean that they themselves were being disarmed even as their enemies were gaining in strength, thanks to the resuscitation of the state's security forces. Aware that the control of arms represented the only guarantee that their revolutionary gains would survive, they insisted that prior to or in tandem with the disarming of the rearguard, the old police forces—and their weaponry—should be dispatched for front line service.[124] Abad de Santillán, by contrast, naively or at best idealistically, argued that libertarians should, if need be, disarm themselves first, in order to acquire the "moral high ground" from which to compel others to follow suit. And he argued that, had they done so, the war might have been won in just a few months.

In my own opinion, there was an opportunity soon after the revolt to overwhelm the rebels right across the Aragon front, had all arms been dispatched there, since it seems that there was no shortage of volunteers.[125] Even though this might not on its own have meant that the war was won, it would unquestionably have been a huge stride forward in that direction. However, once the rebel military had secured their victory in the major population centers and established their defensive deployment, the situation had changed considerably: at the outset of the war, whilst the front lines were fluid and a war of movement prevailed, courage and daring might well have made up for the lack of discipline, training, and coordination of the militia columns, but as the front lines were being established and the conflict was switching to a positional war, the technical edge enjoyed by the military was having that much more of an impact. Similarly, any initial advantage that this might have conferred would be quickly diluted until the tables turned when military aid from Germany and Italy started to reach the rebels, because it also must be remembered that Abad de Santillán's estimate of arms held in the rearguard appears to be exaggerated. "Neither Carod nor Jordi Arquer, the political commissar of the POUM column in the Sierra de Alcubierre, thought that the arms being held in the rearguard would be enough to make any significant difference to the situation."[126] The question of munitions was especially problematic and dangerous.[127] Abad de Santillán himself, elsewhere in his book, acknowledges that, even in the event of the rearguard's having been deep-cleaned of weapons, it would not have been long before they would have run into "a cartridge shortage."[128] From which we may deduce yet again that the chances of victory because of such gear's being held in the rearguard applied during the early stages of the conflict, and, with the passage of time, were evaporating. In conclusion, by that stage in the war, the disarming or otherwise of the rearguard was a secondary issue; with arms and munitions, some sort of push against Huesca or Belchite and Quinto might have been mounted but not much else. As Jacques De Gaule aka Juan Gómez Casas points out: "any action mounted on the front . . . would have gobbled up the arms of groups in the rearguard in the blink of an eye."[129]

Once the would-be coup d'état degenerated into a protracted civil war, the huge volume of weapons and munitions needed to keep the front lines supplied could be procured from only two sources: the native war industry which, prior to the outbreak of hostilities, had been very weak; and, above all, suppliers abroad, which would swiftly prove to be a key factor in the development and denouement of the war. In Catalonia, some of the metalworking and chemical industry was successfully turned over to military production; but despite that success, this recently created war industry was still inadequate and afflicted with shortcomings, the most significant being the lack of specialist machinery and raw materials.[130] Therefore dependency on supplies from abroad—in one form or another—was inevitable; and those supplies were impossible to produce without hard currency or objects of value (particularly precious metals), to which only the central government had access in large amounts. However, the latter, headed by Largo Caballero, was refusing to supply war materials or hard currency to the regions of Catalonia and Aragon, the main fiefdoms of the libertarians. In September 1936 it even turned down a request from the Generalitat that the machinery from one of three cartridge factories in Toledo, which had been "idle for several years past, due to the model's being obsolete and its products no longer profitable" be relocated to Catalonia.[131] It and the other two plants would shortly thereafter fall into the hands of the rebels. This incident highlights the fact that the government would rather see the Aragon front stymied, no matter any military set-back that might entail (in that it allowed the rebels to focus their efforts in other fronts) than arm the militias that were outside of its control and that might pose a threat to the authority the government was busily rebuilding.[132] Military considerations took second place to the political considerations of its bolstering its authority and combatting a revolution that was threatening to overwhelm it.

The libertarians' September 26, 1936, entry into the Generalitat government—euphemistically recast as the "Generalidad Council" in order to overcome any resistance and the ensuing dissolution of the CAMC—hardly helped at all.[133] Even though the central government had repeatedly refused to hand over weapons or hard currency as long as the power of the CAMC was so "manifest."[134] In light of this situation, Abad de Santillán recalls, a plan was hatched for some of the Bank of Spain's gold reserves in Madrid to be seized and removed to Catalonia. That was an operation for which Durruti argued, as he thought it necessary.[135] The seizure of gold was to have been carried out by the Tierra y Libertad Column.[136] All the preparations were in place when "push came to shove"—as Abad de Santillán puts it—"the sponsors of the scheme proved reluctant to take responsibility for a move that would have enormous historical implications. The plans were passed on to the CNT National Committee and some of the best-known comrades. The plan sent those friends into a funk: the main argument raised in their refusal to let the plan proceed—and it was about to be implemented at any moment—was that the animosity that already existed toward Catalonia would merely be increased. What could be done? There was no way of ending up at loggerheads with our own organizations and we had to let it drop," he concludes.[137] That it was a risky scheme that might have triggered a civil war within the civil war that was already under way, there is no doubt, but when all is said and done it was the only option left open to libertarians unless they wished to be left dangerously dependent on those in charge of the resources of the central state. With the operation rejected, the bulk of the gold would be shipped first to the powder store in Cartagena and was then, on October 25, shipped off to Moscow.[138] That, plus the fact that the USSR was to become the leading and virtually the sole country supplying arms, with the somewhat token exception of Mexico, would quickly confer huge power and influence upon the communists while leaving the libertarians in a very bad position.

The war and all that revolved around it such as supply lines, control of the currency reserves and precious metals, and international support were inevitably shaping developments in the republican rearguard. Contrary to what anarchists had often imagined, the revolution was not going to be a great but brief eruption after which the construction of the new society would begin, and the war—like it or not—operated in accordance with rules of its own and these could no longer be ignored, unless one wanted to be doomed to defeat. After a few weeks of the fighting, it became obvious that some sort of cooperation needed to be agreed to between the different antifascist militias, and their internal discipline boosted.[139] With regard to the first of these, Durruti had to reconsider his initial stance and accept that there was no escaping military coordination between columns of differing political persuasions. Tellingly here, though of a later date, were the minutes of the conference of Political and Military Leaders on the Aragon front held on October 13, 1936: its overall conclusion was that every effort should be committed to the front, political squabbles set aside and a unified operational command, acceptable to all, organized.[140] The first step in that direction had come in mid-August when García Oliver, conscious that his leadership of the CAMC was "more apparent than effective, insofar as none of the column commanders was abiding by it," set up the Aragon Front War Committee.[141] García Oliver put Colonel Villalba—a professional soldier and a choice designed to defuse political rivalries—in charge of it.[142] Even so, frictions surrounding him did crop up, and for that reason, come mid-October, the unified command was reshuffled, with its High Command led by Alfonso Reyes being established in Sariñena as a replacement for the previous War Committee.[143] The change of name and leadership was accompanied also by a significant reorganization, with the establishment within the High Command of the conventional specialized sections (operations, intelligence, organization, medical) with the entire front reliant upon Catalonia being split up into three demarcations and two sectors.[144] This was a huge step forward, after which, according to Guarner "the front's High Command was organized to perfection," albeit that in practice the factional nature of the columns amounted to an original sin that would at all times afflict the direction of the war.[145] There was also the problem that the columns manning the southern half of Teruel province were left out of these efforts, mounted from Catalonia, to establish a unified command, as they themselves were drawn from Levante and as a result were answerable (theoretically as well, because in practice each of them enjoyed great autonomy) to the Popular Executive Committee in Valencia.

The military compartmentalization, a product of the politics that needed to be overcome, was otherwise going to make defeat of the rebels extremely difficult. And of necessity that would entail the construction or reconstruction of central authority and the raising of an army—be it revolutionary or traditional—answerable to it. It is hard to conceive of any other option.

Getting back to military operations, against the new backdrop of requisite military cooperation, toward the end of August 1936, the Durruti Column was called upon by Villalba to cooperate in operations around Huesca, and responded with two *agrupaciones* that took part in the capture of Siétamo, which was occupied finally on September 13 after multiple attacks and counterattacks, and the capture of Loporozano and Monte Aragon, which fell on September 30.[146] However, the rebels managed to re-establish the front line outside the very approaches to Huesca city and avoid the noose's tightening completely around them. At the time, and as part of their overall plan, the rebel military assigned their forces in Aragon the aim of holding their ground: while the vast majority of their army of maneuvers was thrown against Madrid, the capture of which was crucial if they were to secure international recognition. Aragon was supposed to be the "anvil" on which the enemy would founder.[147] In which case it was supremely important that, for the time being, control be retained over the three provincial capitals and the routes by which they were connected. To that end the defense concentrated around those three cities and a few other particularly sensitive positions, especially if communications were to be preserved, leaving large parts of the front guarded only by cavalry squadrons or supportive locals from the nearby villages.[148] Zaragoza, for instance, was protected north of the Ebro by defensive positions in Zuera, Perdiguera, Villamayor, and Puebla de Alfinden and on the southern side, positions in Fuentes, Pina station, Quinto, and Belchite.[149] And a well-equipped flying column capable of entering swiftly into action wherever needed had been held in reserve as back-up.[150] Similarly, this meant did not mean that the rebels confined themselves to remaining on the defensive, waiting for enemy attacks in order to repel them; instead, in accordance with any well-understood type of defense, they went on the attack when they saw an opportunity to improve their positions and grind down the enemy. All in all, this made for an organization of the front that proved highly effective and superior to the militia columns' front lines.[151]

During the latter half of September, activity in the central sector of the Aragon front remained restricted to shelling, shooting, and skirmishing without further consequences, with the front line not moving. At the start of October, though, the rebels seized the initiative with an offensive that would create serious difficulties for the Durruti Column. It all kicked off on October 4 when a powerful column under the orders of Lieutenant-Colonel Urrutia attempted to cut the Osera-Monegrillo highway and capture the first of the villages, only to be beaten off. On the morning of the 8th, after having bolstered his attack capabilities, Urrutia launched a pincer movement against Farlete. The rebel column, made up of plentiful infantry, machine-guns, cavalry, artillery, a few tanks, and with air support, outstripped the centurias stationed there in numerical and material terms. Even so, in a clear demonstration that the column's organization had been improved as well as the militians' having been trained and improved their discipline, they managed to hold their ground and stand firm, using their munitions sparingly until the progressive arrival of reinforcements began to turn the tide and they were able to go on the counterattack. In the end, by evening, the attackers decided to fall back "when there were only two or three bullets left in the [Durruti] column's best equipped cartridge belt and it would have been obliged to fall back to who knows where [had the enemy persisted]."[152] Three days later, on October 11, the rebels switched the direction of their attack, looking for some weak spot on the front, this time out toward Leciñena, a village defended by the POUM's Lenin Column, which would pull out of the town on the 12th after its defenders had exhausted all their ammunition.[153]

The Durruti Column's initial response was to occupy Monte Oscuro, the highest peak in the Sierra de Alcubierre and half-way between Farlete and Perdiguera. It met no resistance as no one had previously thought to secure that position and they were the first to arrive there.[154] And on the 15th, with the intention of cutting the Villamayor-Leciñena highway and free up the Lenin Column's sector—making it easier for it to mount a counterattack or at least buying some time for it to rebuild its lines of defense—it targeted Perdiguera. That position might bring them a little closer to the Zaragoza they craved and threaten its communications with Huesca. The grassroots membership of the CNT was anxiously awaiting the capture of both cities so that it might press ahead with the revolution.[155] The attack on Perdiguera started off promisingly: on October 16, part of the International Group involved in the operation stormed the outlying houses in the village. On their left, though, those centurias charged with severing the highway to Zaragoza to thwart the arrival of reinforcements failed to achieve the expected progress, leaving the Internationals in positions well ahead of the remainder of the column. The rebels swooped on this chance to surround and attack them, and a number of the Internationals were killed, including their delegate, Louis Berthomieu.

It seems that the Internationals were left to their lonely fate because the runner sent to tell them they should fall back got lost. Nevertheless, it is striking that some of those who survived the slaughter were convinced that they had been deliberately sent into a trap by Lucio Ruano, which makes one wonder why he might have wanted to be rid of them. Perhaps there had earlier been some sort of a clash between him and the Internationals.[156] This was the first incident in a long series in which Ruano, a future commander of the column, would be involved over the ensuing months. In the wake of the Perdiguera shambles, the fighting carried on with less intensity for a few days before stability was restored to the front.[157] The ultimate outcome was that the threat of a breakthrough had been thwarted and the Durruti Column was able to advance its lines by a few kilometers, albeit with losses of precious human assets like Berthomieu.

With the situation salvaged, the high command in Sariñena cast its eyes once again in the direction of Huesca which seemed to be within reach. On October 21, after some softening up by the artillery, a considerable attack was launched, only to be repelled. The operation was replicated the following day with the same outcome.[158] This setback was a perfect encapsulation of the equilibrium and stagnation that had been established, not just in the Huesca sector or the Durruti Column's sector but throughout the whole of the Aragon front. The rebel forces, slightly outnumbered but well equipped and operating out of solid defensive positions, were perfectly well able to ward of the attacks from worse organized, and essentially very poorly armed militia columns with deficient access to munitions.[159]

By contrast, the rebel advance on Madrid was moving at great speed and was by then dangerously close to its approaches. It looked like the city was nearing capture unless there was some reaction or something to turn the situation around. From early October, there began to be rumors about the chances of sending Durruti in with part of his column to stiffen the resistance. "At the very first meeting of the Generalitat Defense Department," Abad de Santillán points out, "there had been talk of the chances of sending Durruti to Madrid."[160] The first firm proposal came from Horacio Martínez Prieto, the CNT's general secretary, who is alleged to have asked Durruti on October 19, to head off immediately to Madrid "but, the latter being obsessed with Zaragoza"—to borrow the words of H. M. Prieto's son, César M Lorenzo—"had declined."[161] Obsessed or not, there is no denying that Durruti was very busy trying to secure the armaments with which to finish off the offensive against Zaragoza. In addition to the various calls for weapons to be moved up to the front, there was the Sabadell "expedition" and his taking part alongside Pierre Besnard (the IWA general secretary) in a delegation that met with Largo Caballero.[162] We should also highlight the unauthorized raising of funds carried out in France by Durruti's *compañera*, Emilienne Morin, and Ascaso's sister.[163]

Durruti was also a focus of attention because of his criticisms of the political trend in the rearguard. On September 28, the central state, even as its authority was starting to recover its machinery of coercion, passed a decree that all commanders, officers, and ranks in the militias—found after audit by the General Inspection of Militias to merit it—be added to the army's active service lists.[164] This was followed the very next day by another order declaring that the militias were being regularized and their members subject to the old Code of Military Justice, which would take effect on October 10 in the central zone, and on October 20 in the other zones. Those not in agreement with this were free to quit the militias before those dates.[165] Catalonia, which was operating separately from the central government, followed Madrid's example and passed its own militarization decree on October 24.[166] That decision, reached without consultation with the militias in the front lines, provoked widespread unease in the libertarian columns. A delegation from the Jover, Ascaso, Los Aguiluchos, and Ortiz columns attended the gathering of Committees in Barcelona on October 31 to register their objections. Things ended "a lot more friendly" than they had begun.[167] For its part, the Durruti Column on November 1—the day that the former Code of Military Justice came into effect—sent the Generalitat a message on behalf of its War Committee and signed by Durruti, spelling out its refusal to countenance this and reasserting its own freedom of organization. The grounds set out were that "hierarchical military organization" belonged to a past that had been bypassed as a result of the popular backlash against the "fascist military provocation," that the column was operating smoothly and that the new order could only lead to "suspicion, reservations, and repugnance" and would instead lead to "a genuine state of dis-organization" and, lastly, offered no solution to the problem of supplies, which was the main reason for the stymying of operations.[168]

Not that Durruti's objections would be confined to that official text! On November 4, four anarchist ministers joined the government of the Republic—all four given secondary portfolios unrelated to the war, public order, or finances.[169] That same day, Durruti delivered a radio broadcast using harsh terms to call for an end to political rancor and championing the gains of the revolution—characterizing those opposed to them as enemies—and attacked social inequality, the privileges enjoyed by councilors (including those from the CNT and FAI), the pilfering and disorganization in the rearguard and urging the establishment of a "Code" governing economic matters and the mobilization of all males between the ages of sixteen and fifty. And, of course, that militarization decree: "If this Generalidad-ordered militarization is supposed to scare us and foist a steely discipline upon us, you are mistaken. You are mistaken, councilors, with the decree militarizing the militias. Since you speak of steely discipline, I say to you, come to the front with me. That is where you will find us who accept no discipline because we are aware enough to do our duty. Then you will see our order and our organization. And then we will head back to Barcelona and question you about your discipline, your order, and your control, which are non-existent."[170] His statement gave a definite hint that he might well head back to Barcelona to impose order.

Immediately reacting to that speech, Companys convened, the very next day, November 5, an extraordinary meeting at the Generalitat Palace of all of the councilors and representatives of the political organizations to deal with resistance to the militarization order as well as the recently passed orders endorsing the disbandment of the revolutionary committees and their replacement by Popular Front town councils. "Durruti was the cause and target of the debate, although everybody avoided speaking his name."[171] It is striking that during that meeting Marianet (Mariano Rodríguez Vázquez), no less the general secretary of the Catalonian CNT, in response to complaints from Companys and Comorera (the latter from the PSUC) about what they termed "uncontrollables," went no further than to point out that this was no more than signs of "resistance needing to be overcome without triggering rebellions, and of individuals yet to be convinced." The issue, therefore, was not so much the appropriateness or otherwise of disbanding the revolutionary committees and the militarization order, but of ensuring compliance.[172] The high-ranking bigwigs from the CNT who had begun to slide down the slippery slopes of concessions found Durruti's stance inconvenient, and the Catalanists and communists, busy forcing the revolution on to the back foot, saw it as a direct threat. As is obvious from a secret report drawn up by the soviet consul in Barcelona—in which we read that the commander of the Karl Marx Division (formerly the De Barrio-Trueba Column), "inspired" by the Russians and with an eye to "deactivating" the Durruti Column, on November 5 had broached with the military advisor the chances of dispatching it to Madrid.[173] "However, Durruti roundly refused to carry out the order for all or part of his forces to be sent to Madrid . . . [and it was immediately agreed] with president Companys and the military advisor that they would see to it that a mixed Catalan column (made up of detachments from a range of parties [in this case, of organizations, since the CNT is a trade union]) was dispatched."[174]

That decision was to be forced on November 6 at a gathering of the commanders of the columns manning the Aragon front. Antonov-Ovseenko's report tells how, amid an obvious ordeal, "after a brief report on the situation in the outskirts of Madrid, the commander of the K. Marx Division declared that his division was ready to be sent to Madrid. Durruti was utterly against the sending reinforcements to Madrid: his words were scathing of the central government 'which was preparing for defeat'; he described the situation in Madrid as desperate and concluded that Madrid had a purely political rather than any strategic significance."[175] Instead, Durruti called for a decisive push against Zaragoza that might then veer south and head for Madrid.[176] An indirectly helpful operation, as set out in the report from Iosif Ratner dated October 12–14, that had been proposed earlier. Ratner noted that "the Catalans raised the following suggestion: that Madrid supply them with two million cartridges and they would take Zaragoza and from there will strike at Siguenza; that would be the best way of helping Madrid. The central government did not agree to this and asked for reinforcements to be sent to the Madrid front immediately."[177] This reluctance of Durruti (who "wields extraordinary influence over all the Catalan anarcho-syndicalists serving in the front lines") to send troops to Madrid, Antonov-Ovseenko goes on eloquently, had to be overcome at all costs. A forceful intervention was required. And Durruti gave in, saying that he could send a thousand hand-picked combatants to Madrid. Following an impassioned address by the anarchist Abad de Santillán, he agreed to send two thousand and immediately issued an order for his neighbor on the front—Ortiz—to send another two thousand, Ascaso another thousand, and the K. Marx Division a further thousand. Durruti said nothing of the Esquerra republicans even though the command of the latter's column stated that it could send a battalion. In all, six thousand eight hundred bayonets were awaiting relocation prior to November 8. Durruti then put his lieutenant [this appears to have been Miguel Yoldi[178]] in charge of the mixed column (which he agreed to consider as a "Catalan division"[179]) and he stated that "he would accompany the column in person up until the appointment [of his lieutenant as commander, that is].[180]

But things didn't stop there. Having successfully twisted Durruti's arm into surrendering some of his men, the pressures coming from libertarian circles to ensure that he and no one other than him would lead that column became persistent and proliferated. On November 9, a Plenum of CNT Locals and Comarcals affiliated to the CNT of the Center region agreed to lobby for Durruti's presence "in light of the lack of defensive readiness in which the capital found itself, and in view also of the fact that the psychological approach might make a huge contribution to resistance."[181] David Antona and Miguel Inestal were delegated to travel to Valencia, where the central government and leadership bodies of the various political organizations had relocated just a few days before to convey this resolution to the CNT National Committee. Upon their arrival these two delegates found staunch support and cooperation from Federica Montseny, who helped ensure that their appeal was supported by the National Committee, which immediately set in motion the overtures to persuade Durruti.[182] Years later, Federica explained that the aim was to counter the influence that the communists were gaining through their prominent role in the defense of Madrid, an influence that would increase further thanks to the impending arrival of the International Brigades; she points out that Marianet told Durruti: "You must make the most of your prestige and the fighting qualities of your column; otherwise we will be sidelined politically."[183] However, since Durruti's political stance had become a discomfort to some anarchist leaders, it was easy to think (as García Oliver and Antonio Ortiz did[184]) that one or more of those same leaders might have had other motives when they were so insistent upon Durruti's rushing to Madrid's rescue. I am referring to the fact that they too were out to "decommission" Durruti, to move him far away from Catalonia and Aragon as a means of undermining the more uncompromising revolutionary position within the libertarian movement. This is not to say, of course, that they wanted him dead. Personally, I believe, like Horacio Martínez Prieto, that Durruti was too widely loved and admired in libertarian circles for any anarchist to want to see him dead.[185] It seems that it was during a military conference urgently convened by Abad de Santillán (who was Secretary at the Generalitat's Department of Defense at the time) and which may well have taken place on the night of November 9, that Montseny and he overcame Durruti's lingering reluctance.[186]

Once approval had been secured for the formation of the aforementioned mixed column, or Catalan division, the political squabbling regarding its final makeup and armaments would continue. Antonov-Ovseenko's report recounts how, initially, the forces that made it up were supposed to march, armed as they were, directly from the Aragon front to Madrid. However, when word reached Durruti that there were certain fresh arms available in Barcelona—Winchester rifles, with a number of Swiss rifles among them—he seized upon this to hold up their shipment and sent his men, unarmed, into Barcelona:

> leaving their (Mauser) weapons where they had been manning the front and calling for them to be taken up by (unarmed) reserves from Barcelona.[187] His anarchist neighbors did the same. In this way, Durruti had his way, and the Aragon front was not weakened. Around five thousand unarmed front-line troops

had gathered in Barcelona and Durruti immediately raised the issue of arming them at the expense of the Assault Guards, Republican National Guards (formerly the Civil Guards[188]), and soldiers of the rearguard. To replace the Mausers what those troops carried, Durruti suggested that they be issued with the technically inferior Winchester rifles—this was the crux of the matter. In this way, Durruti was boosting the efforts of the CNT and FAI to undermine the armed backers of the current government of Catalonia.

Even so, the soviet consul continues in terms that speak for themselves "with great pains we managed to thwart that plan that would, at best, have held up the dispatch … to Madrid for several days (the Winchesters had not yet arrived)." In the end those Winchesters were allocated to Durruti's forces. And the report adds:

> Another reason for our rejection of the plan [aside from the fact that it was undermining the Catalan government's armed back-up, of course] was the anarchists' military unreliability and the planned leadership's political unreliability. We insisted upon the Stalin Regiment, the thousand hand-picked fighters from the Durruti Column and the Libertad detachment (it had fought well in the environs of Madrid and was being overhauled) from Barcelona's being sent to the front. … In addition, Durruti was sent a thousand fighters plus a battalion of left republicans. In all, some six thousand five hundred bayonets, twenty-five machine-guns, fifty light machine-guns, and twelve pieces of ordnance [artillery].[189]

This fighting strength matches the breakdown given by Abad de Santillán, who writes that they amounted to "some 6,000 men with a few batteries." And adds that "together these forces were to operate under the orders of Durruti as their political leader and of Blanco Valdés as their military advisor. But—and here is an important detail missed by the soviet consul—the column dispatched by the socialists refused to submit and acted on their own accord."[190] This characterization of "socialists" should be understood as referring more to "communists." In Catalonia at the beginning of the war the socialists and communists had amalgamated into the Unified Socialist Party of Catalonia (PSUC) but despite the title, the organization was completely under the control of the communists, as was the Catalan UGT.[191] As a result, in Catalonia, supposedly socialist organizations were in fact crypto-communist ones. The Libertad-López Tienda Column—made up mainly of UGT members and the PSUC and which had set off from Barcelona a few days earlier—refused to follow Durruti's orders.[192] The K. Marx Division contingent, which arrived later, also refused Durruti's orders.[193] After all, once Durruti was en route to Madrid, the communists were not going to help him achieve a resounding success in its defense; instead, they would do everything they could to discredit and boycott him.

So, out of the 6,000 to 6,500 fighters dispatched to Madrid, the numbers under Durruti's command appear to have been closer to between 3,000 and 4,000, 1,500–1,700 of whom were drawn from his own Column in Aragon.[194] José Mira in particular points out that the 1st and 8th agrupaciones "which had played such a sterling part in the capture of Siétamo," plus the 44th, 48th, and 52nd centurias; were joined by a few more hundreds en route, including Bonilla's Asturias Battalion, and young Jesús Salillas Artigas's centuria, bringing the number up to between 1,500 and 1,700. And Durruti called in several trusted comrades—specifically, Miguel Yoldi, Ricardo Rionda, Manzana, and Mora to join his War Committee.[195] Lucio Ruano stayed behind to take charge in Aragon alongside Campón, Bargalló, Cuba, Pablo [Paolo] Vagliasindi, Esplugas, and Busquets.[196]

In such precarious circumstances, with a much smaller force than had been agreed and armed with old Mexican Winchesters and Swiss rifles, Durruti set off to save Madrid.[197] Or so it was supposed. Very soon, he and his men would find themselves caught up in a veritable slaughterhouse. The trap had been closed. Zaragoza was left to wait once more. There is every indication that Durruti was confident that his absence would be brief and, once the situation in the Spanish capital had been saved, he would soon be back in Aragon to finish outstanding business. The November 13 edition of the Durruti Column's bulletin—the day he set off from Barcelona—carried a communique from "Headquarters," which read: "The separation will be brief. The work needing done in that sector will not take long."[198] And Enrique Líster, another protagonist of the defense of Madrid, years later wrote that "the Durruti Column showed up with the rather showboating aim of rescuing Madrid. Furthermore, they wanted to see this done quickly so that they could get back to Aragon as soon as possible."[199] The fact is that Durruti would never again gaze at the Pilar towers in the distance or the trams inside Zaragoza.[200] On November 20 he perished in Madrid after being hit by a bullet from an unknown source and the column was left bereft of its leader.[201] And the vacuum left behind would not easily be filled.

III
Durruti and his Column: Between the Idea and the Reality of War

> "The people in the rear must remain at their posts. . . . We are staying on the front. Each in his place. There is no reason to be afraid; we will not leave until we have won. Then let the people judge us and we will see. But for now I don't want to talk, understand? Now let us drop everything except the war."
> —**Durruti from a balcony in Bujaraloz's town square**

On August 2, the same day *Solidaridad Obrera* carried an article praising the spontaneity of the armed struggle, the Durruti Column completed the assignment of its militians to centurias and decurias (one hundred-man and ten-man groups respectively) with a delegate democratically elected on the front line.[1] That initial sub-division would shortly be improved upon by the replacement of decurias by twenty-five-man groups and the addition of agrupaciones for larger units. This plainly reflected that, no matter what the article said, the harsh reality of war was beginning to impose an overhaul of the traditional anarchist thinking regarding armed organization: launching a search for and shaping of an organizational arrangement that might—to the extent that this was feasible—reconcile the demands of the war and their revolutionary, anti-militarist principles.[2] This was a process with which all other libertarian columns also had to grapple, albeit with differences in terms of arrangements adopted and results obtained.[3]

The main issue needing resolution was a lack of discipline. There was little point in arranging the column into smaller units and establishing a chain of command if orders went disobeyed and everyone was at liberty to do what he wanted. With the exception of serious offenses like theft or rape, which were severely punished, normally by death—in the early phases of the war, anarchists had trusted their militians' self-discipline, their ability to do their duty without the need for any coercion or imposition.[4] Note the difference here with what the Platform had prescribed. This appeal to the consciences of individuals, which was enough in some cases, was, in other cases, sadly fostering selfishness and abuse, under the pretext of freedom. The proliferation of "maverick (*incontrolados*) groups" was, in that regard, a fair indicator of the lack of control. In the specific instance of the territories in which the Durruti Column was operating, on more than one occasion, these groups shot alleged fascists in contravention of Durruti's express opinion, as he always tried to keep the repression to a minimum.[5] Another and more widespread issue was militians' going AWOL into the rearguard or the relentless applications for leave. In this regard, Jesús Arnal recounts how some people had joined the Column "because they looked upon the war as a pastime ... and so they would serve a few days in the front lines and, whenever the notion took them, would slip back into the rearguard to brag about acts of daring that had never taken place." The ten pesetas a day pay was another factor that prompted a lot of youngsters to sign on for a time and "whenever they returned to their village on leave, they were, so to speak, masters in that they had money."[6] Plainly there were some volunteers prompted by motives that were anything but lofty. Contrary to what had sometimes imagined, the outbreak of revolution had not automatically raised levels of consciousness, not in everyone anyway.

In such circumstances, if self-discipline failed to produce the desired outcomes, if some of the militians were not prepared or simply not ready to embrace it—among other reasons, because war always attracts adventurers, risk takers, and all sorts of undesirables—then it was inevitable that they would resort to traditional coercive discipline.[7] The November 1, 1936, message sent to the Generalitat suggested that self-discipline was the Column's main guide.[8] Emma Goldman wrote romantically one year after Durruti's death that "no military stricture, no disciplinary punishment . . . was in place to uphold the Column's coherence."[9] Nevertheless, if we set aside propagandistic declarations and ideological prejudices, the fact offered perfect illustration of the fact that Durruti, in order to enforce order within its ranks, matched word of mouth and example with coercive disciplinary measures. Not as harsh as those of a conventional army, to be sure, but still coercive.

The Column's bulletin, launched once things had stabilized, was used as a loudspeaker in the promotion of a campaign against the various acts of indiscipline that posed a threat to the Column's efficacy and cohesion. On August 27, 1936, the War Committee published a text with the telling title of "ONWARDS, EVERYONE: NOT ONE STEP BACKWARDS." "Day in and day out, this Committee receives countless applications for leave with entitlement to leave the column for one or more days. That represents a constant traffic in militians and a coming and going of personnel that upsets any possible oversight of the centurias, rendering any orderly assignment of services impossible. We came here from Barcelona. The roads in our wake are clear and unobstructed. Let anyone unprepared to forge ahead without a backward glance turn his back on us once and for all."[10] Two days after that, it insisted that the "hour of sacrifice" was upon them and that all "family considerations" had to be set aside.[11] The bulletin included a piece addressed to the uncontrollable groups without naming them:

> Let us stem our urge to act individually and forward our proposals to the delegates and committees in charge [it opened slickly]. There have been some instances of house searches, arrests, and the odd execution carried out without the intervention or prior knowledge of the Committees. Anyone acting like that is operating outside of the ethos of the Column, trespassing against its cohesion and the level-headed principles that inform its leaders. . . . [There was a clear warning that this had to stop.] Remember that militians must act at all times in a level-headed, deliberate fashion, like men of ideas. In an unjust society, anything can be forgiven, but when we are laying the foundations of a nobler, more equitable social organization, actions like

these cannot be countenanced. There is no excuse for banditry in these circumstances and anyone indulging in it will get what he deserves.[12]

More telling regarding the shift in mentality that had to be brought about is the article "We are Freedom's Army and Should Obey Those Watching Over Our Lives," which appeared on September 2, 1936:

> There is a rather infantile and simplistic notion of discipline that needs amending. The alternative is suicide.... We are an army of Freedom and should obey our delegates who have taken on the responsibility of watching out for our lives.... So no weapon should be discharged unless the enemy is within range.... Our militians' spirit of sacrifice, their enthusiasm, occasionally induces them to carry out acts of genuine heroism but that are suicidal and that the war committees are disposed to avert. No one should move from his station for scouting or outrider operations without an order from the delegate from his group or his centuria.... We are in the throes of a social war and as guerrillas we should behave ourselves. All militians should be aware that any act of indiscipline, which might compromise the lives of his comrades and the success of our fight, will be punished by his being disarmed and compulsorily return, to his own disgrace and as an example to others.[13]

We know from José Mira and from Durruti himself that that homeward journey had to be made on foot (without any facilitation, reasonably enough) and that also applied to those engaging in defeatism or who, after invoking certain pretexts, insisted upon heading for home because they were there in a voluntary capacity.[14] This was primarily a symbolic punishment intended to expose them to disgrace and social reprobation. Nevertheless, some individuals cared very little about the social sanctions returned to the rearguard, honorably or dishonorably, whatever they felt. On one occasion, Durruti came upon several militians who had abandoned their lookout posts and were blithely drinking wine in a nearby village. He reprimanded them, demanding their CNT membership cards and eventually threw them out of the column, but "far from being cowed, they seemed rather pleased with themselves."[15] This attitude infuriated Durruti who decided that they would be dispatched back into the rearguard without trousers and in their underwear "so that all may see that they are not anarchists but mere trash!"[16] Another regular punishment was hard labor: "Anyone who had shown cowardice ... and deserted some post that was in jeopardy was assigned [by Durruti] to trench-digging."[17] Anyone lying or feigning illness in order to secure leave faced "two days on pick-and-shovel duty."[18] Finally, before going to the lengths of capital punishment, there was still the option and the outright intimidation of their being punished according to their offenses. *España Libre* reported the case of one bunch of young militians who had gone AWOL and were keen to get back to Barcelona: "Durruti came upon them en route, stopped his car, climbed out, and headed them off with his pistol unholstered. He had them line up, backs to the wall. Another militian passing by asked him for a pair of shoes. 'Have a good look at the shoes these guys have on. Pick out a pair that suits you. Why should we bury shoes and let them rot?'" Of course, Durruti didn't shoot the deserters.[19] "Of course," the author of the article wrote, because Durruti never went to those lengths, or at any rate we have no testimony that he did.[20] It looks as if every time that a militian was executed it was as a result of a collective decision and not because of any order issued by Durruti.[21] All of which allows us to assert that Durruti was quite measured when it came to enforcing discipline and was able to retain a sense of proportion, which is no mean feat in situations of the sort.[22] Likewise, in the words of Jesús Arnal, when it came to "comrades from the Column, [Durruti] was unbending, strict, and at the same time scrupulous, earning everyone's respect."[23]

Even so, the introduction of strict discipline and a command structure clashed with traditional anarchist thinking and triggered a degree of ideological resistance. The article "The Notion of Discipline," published on October 9, 1939, appears to indicate that some views or attitudes critical of the new arrangements still lingered. The article was primarily intended to disentangle discipline from authority, as if the latter was non-existent within the Column: "There are a lot of comrades who lamentably mix up discipline with authority. The notion of authority, or authority per se, is clear cut and roundly rejected in our anarchist circles. There is no way that authority can be squared with Freedom, which is our 'leit-motif,' or the essential principle underpinning our every act. Freedom and authority are mutually repugnant and opposed and, if one of them gains the upper hand, the other perishes." The piece then went on to champion a discipline rooted in equality:

> Every war implies military organization and, for this, discipline. The point is that every individual effort is coherently subordinated to the goal being pursued: VICTORY. Here we are all equal. Though we have no higher-ups in the old sense, we do have comrades who direct the war, we do have a Military Command.... Every conscious comrade is disciplined. But these lines are addressed to those who, most likely confusing the ideas of authority and discipline, respond sourly and extravagantly to the very mention of the latter. Organization, always. Then, discipline. And now, more than ever, DISCIPLINE![24]

Denying the existence of authority within the Column was obviously an embellishment. However, it is true that all its members were equals in the sense that a command position entailed no distinctions or privileges of any sort. As leader, Durruti always took pains to set an example by behaving as just one among the many; he lived with his people, wore the same clothing and footwear, ate the same food and—this was undoubtedly what most endeared him to them—fought alongside them.[25] So that his militians looked upon him as one of them, a comrade.

In short, Durruti reorganized his column by imposing a firm discipline, which he managed to enforce with a modicum of tact while abiding by its main revolutionary characteristics: specifically its internal democracy—confined, naturally, to periods of rest whereas in combat its delegates had to be obeyed without complaint—and the absence of any privileges attendant upon positions of command, as well as of any other outward, barrack-style displays like saluting, stripes, marching in formation... all of which were despised by anarchists. Besides, in order to facilitate unity of action, the columns raised in the rearguard and dispatched to the front "were completely assimilated" by adapting to the prevailing discipline.[26] Contrary to what happened in other columns such as the Torres-Benedito column, which, "in actual fact it was [made up of] seven columns, each having its own military arrangements."[27] One can easily imagine the negative impact that might have upon coordination. And to take charge of the different sub-sectors (Pina, Osera, etc.) a series of lower-level war committees was formed that enjoyed a measure of autonomy and were empowered to suggest and discuss military strategy.[28] The outcome was something of a success in that it turned the column into an effective military unit. One indication of this—in addition to the clash with Urrutia's forces that October—was the aforementioned secret document from consul Antonov-Ovseenko, which contended that the Durruti Column was "in addition to the Karl Marx Division, arguably the one with the greatest fighting ability."[29] Likewise, Jaume Miravitlles, an ERC politician and thus someone with no reason to sing Durruti's praises, told Ronald Fraser that "with the notable exception of Durruti on the front, the persistent blemish on the CNT was the indiscipline within its own ranks."[30]

The circumstances of the war, along with the fact that broad swathes of the population were not supportive of revolutionary ideas, also forced the anarchists to resort to forms of coercion and imposition when it came to starting to build their new order in the realms of economics and society.[31] The process of collectivization in the Aragonese countryside, rather than coming about freely and unsolicited—which is not to say that there were not segments of the peasantry driving and supporting it—took place under the overall auspices and sometimes the direct management of the militia columns.[32] There was no need to force the peasants into the collectives at gunpoint; all it took was the climate of coercion in which "fascists," real or alleged, were being shot.[33] The upshot was that alongside the "unsolicited" collectives there were other "enforced" ones, just as, within them, willing collectivists coexisted with others who were there against their will.[34] The aim of this agrarian collectivization process was an attempt to lay the foundations for more communitarian and harmonious forms of coexistence, but also to thrash out an organizational arrangement that would facilitate the control of production and consumption, with an eye to ensuring food supplies to the columns.[35] Essentially—as the rationalist school-teacher José Alberola retorted to Francisco Carreño at the September 1936 Regional Plenum of the Anarchist Groups of Aragon, Rioja, and Navarra—it amounted to a policy that had more in common with a War Communism dictated by circumstances than with libertarian communism proper.[36]

In this regard, what has come to be known as the "Bujaraloz Decree" represents the ultimate example of collectivization from above. On August 11, 1936, the Column's War Committee issued a proclamation endorsed by Durruti in which, after describing the harvest "as something sacred in terms of the interests of the working people and antifascist cause," instructions were issued for harvest work to start "without the slightest waste of time." It did away with the big landowners' private ownership of the land, fruit, livestock, means of transport, work tools, tractors, threshing machinery . . . which from then would be the people's property overseen by the local committee, and it concluded that "the antifascist militias' armed struggle being the safeguard of the interests and lives of the working people, the citizens of Bujaraloz are to afford these their enthusiastic and unstinting material and moral support."[37]

Durruti must have known that this move, and others like it, such as the assignment of a bunch of right-wingers and Romanis to work on a road between Pina and Monegrillo were contrary to the anarchist ideal.[38] But as he stated in *El Frente* on September 2, 1936, "ideological musings" had to be set to one side. "This is not exactly the right time to be probing theories for a solution to the problem that fascism and the reaction to it have created. . . . Let us put aside essays and statistics and let us wage war. . . . We will have time enough for delving into the plans and tactics of the new social order that is burgeoning in the recaptured villages."[39] The subordination of the rearguard to the war effort, to the war, was necessary; if this could be achieved voluntarily, great, otherwise it would be done with some degree of force. The general mobilization order on November 4 pointed in more or less the same direction. Durruti raised the point in blunter terms at the conference of Political and Military Chiefs on the Aragon front on October 13, 1936. I would highlight the following extract lifted from a couple of his contributions:

> A mobilization is called for with the war bring interpreted as the circumstances require. Let any who protest overnight be shipped off in trucks to the front. I remember that, during the Great War [sic] when panic broke out . . . as a result of the use of gas, everyone claimed to sick and Clemenceau came up with a solution: that lists be drawn up of those wishing to head for Paris on leave. Whereupon he had them all rounded up and dispatched to the most dangerous front. War is to be taken seriously. Let the villages wage war for us, on the front, with or without weapons; everyone moving up to the front, with the remainder mobilized in their factories. But unless they take it seriously, they are a bother to us. . . . [We need] to have mobilization lists without age restrictions for when danger looms on the front. . . . Even if it is only trench-digging, mining, and all that, people must serve on the front.[40]

The aim was to defeat the rebels, and as quickly as possible, because that brutalizing circumstance of war had to be brought to an end and, equally importantly, the revolution needed to break out of the impasse in which it found itself.[41] So, when a reporter from *L'Espagne Nouvelle* asked Durruti: "Don't you think that if the war drags on for long militarism might become embedded and pose a threat to the revolution?" The latter replied: "Right! For that very reason we need to win this war as quickly as we can!"[42] Which brings us back again to the importance credited to Zaragoza as a means of boosting both the war and the revolution. Its capture needed to be accomplished. Durruti, who was rather "child-like" despite the dire situation in which his column had been left—with the Ebro looming ahead—intended to be the main player in so doing.[43] Saturnino Carod, who, together with Ortiz had several meetings with Durruti for the purpose of coordinating a joint operation, points out that he always refused to have his arm twisted and was "determined to be Zaragoza's 'liberator' ... and to play the highest profile role."[44] The rather less trustworthy Koltsov also testified to this.[45] During his meeting with Durruti on August 14, Durruti supposedly told Koltsov, "It may well be that only a hundred of us survive, but that hundred are going to enter Zaragoza, crush fascism, hoist the banner of the anarcho-syndicalists and proclaim libertarian communism ... I'm going to be the first one into Zaragoza and I will proclaim a free commune there." Shortly after that, he is alleged to have replied sourly to an offer made by Trueba (a communist) to wait in Huesca to back up his push on Zaragoza on his right flank, if and when a serious attack would be mounted: "Help, if you want to; if you don't want to, don't. The Zaragoza operation is mine, in military, political, and politico-military terms. I am answerable for it. Do you think that just by giving us a thousand men you're going to share Zaragoza with us? Zaragoza will know either libertarian communism or fascism. Help yourselves to the whole of Spain but give my head peace about Zaragoza!"[46]

Not that Durruti lived to see his dream of becoming Zaragoza's liberator. A few months after his death, in order to ease the way for a militarization process that had run into quite a bit of resistance from within the anarchist militias, the libertarian movement's leadership committees dusted off an ambiguous statement credited to him: "We renounce everything, save victory." Which may well have been coined by Ilya Ehrenburg based on the statement that "now we are setting everything aside, except the war," which was reported by Ricardo Rionda—the implication being that Durruti would have been prepared to embrace militarization. His name was subsequently even hitched to the notion that he would have renounced the revolution and its gains for the sake of winning the war and defeating fascism first. Nothing could be further from the truth. How Durruti's thinking might have evolved, we have no way of knowing: but at the time of his death, he had not given up on maintaining the militias' revolutionary features—whether these could have been maintained is a different matter—let alone the revolution as a whole. Instead, he stood out as one of its staunchest champions. Ricardo

Rionda, no less, who was on that balcony alongside Durruti, recounts that, taken aback by that announcement, he had pressed Durruti: "What was that you said? . . . That we are to set everything aside? Is that what things have come to? If you are leaving the revolution to one side, I'll go home right now. What does the war matter to me?" To which Durruti had replied: "You misunderstand me. . . . What are you thinking? For years my mind has been filled with the making of the revolution, but we were unarmed then, and now that we have the arms, do you think that I am about to set everything to one side? You don't know me."

IV

Militarization of the Column and the Eclipse of the Libertarian Movement: The End of the Dream

> "The comrades standing watch on the Aragon front have long demanded to fight and advance. They want to ease the pressure on Madrid at all costs. They are not listened to. That front languishes behind the veil of a deceptive silence and threatening discouragement. Why does no one want to deal decisively with this front?"
>
> —Carl Einstein

In entering the central government, the libertarian leadership was aiming—among other things—to find a resolution to the dramatic dearth of arms and munitions afflicting their forces and, likewise, take a hand in the process of molding a brand-new army that was just finding its footing; they also wanted to prevent it from being left exclusively in the hands of their rivals—and looming as "the instrument of a single faction"—and the fact that they had reached the conclusion that it was time to move beyond the party and trade union militias format.[1] Here, the proposal of the National Defense Council already incorporated into its program the establishment of "mandatory war militias" and a "unified military leadership," which would by itself have amounted to an army, albeit that due to ideological scruples it chose not to refer to them as such.[2]

We can divine in the declaration made by the CNT National Committee's representative at the Plenum of the Levante Regional, held just a few days after the entry into the government, how confident they were that they still had the power to oversee the raising of armed forces more attuned to their principles and interests. From now on, the representative declared, "there will be no more anarchist columns, nor any belonging to the CNT or the UGT; they will only be revolutionary antifascist militias overseen by the Higher Council of War," a body on which García Oliver was serving.[3] But, having been relegated to secondary ministries, it was clear that they had little or no say in that or other military affairs.[4] The only concession they would wring out of Largo Caballero was a guarantee that anarchist units would not be touched, would not be disbanded and blended with units of different ideological outlooks and their officers would be drawn from the CNT.[5] The upshot was that the Republic's People's Army stuck to organizing along traditional lines as if it was just another regular army, with the supply of war materials by the Ministry of War restricted to the troops under its remit.[6]

Faced with this situation, the main libertarian leaders, on their own authority and at their own risk, reluctantly decided to militarize their columns and integrate them into that army. As Julián Casanova points out: "Taking advantage of this militarization, which is to say, ensuring that the CNT would emerge with as little possible loss in this battle under way for leadership of the republican army, was the single preoccupation of those rearguard and front-line leaders. . . . That being the way things were, there was nothing at all odd about those leadership circles being seized by a sudden haste to comply with 'the requirements imposed by the war.' The timing also required that they set aside the jumble of committees, meetings, and plenums that might jeopardize speedy decision making."[7] That decision, though, not surprisingly, was about to run up against opposition from a sizable part of the membership and above all from their militians annoyed at not having been consulted about something that so directly affected them and—this is the essential point—they were not inclined to resign themselves to this latest backward step that this "resurrection of the old army" meant for the revolution.[8] And all this for the chance, the promise—though not the certainty—of securing arms. And so began a traumatic process that was to tear apart and weaken the libertarian movement even more.

Militarization of the Column and the Eclipse of the Libertarian Movement

As for those militias opposed to militarization, we emphasize that it was not the building of an army per se that they were against—no matter that they were so still repulsed by the word, what with its discipline and its unified command, these being things that the broader membership at the grassroots had come to accept was inescapable—but the enforcement of a barracks-style discipline with its corpus of salutes and parades, the subordination to an alien War Ministry and Central High Command from which they could expect little comradery and support, the removal of all channels for oversight and democratic participation by the rank-and-file and the introduction of different pay-scales depending on rank. Which is to say: the actual direction and character of this so-called Peoples' Army, the banishment of all of the revolutionary features that had set the militias apart. As we shall see as we focus on the Durruti Column, more than one voice would even call openly for an authentic revolutionary army to replace it. However, with the benefit of hindsight, when was there any alternative to incorporation into the republican army? In my opinion, there wasn't one; the time for different approaches had passed, never to return. Much of the tragedy they faced could be traced to that. As at any other point in history, it was not just a matter of what this or that actor wanted to do but also of what they *could* do. And by then, following that initial rejection of a seizure of power or at least to seize part of the Bank of Spain's gold reserves, the Spanish anarchist movement's strength and ability to maneuver were very limited. Having now become bit players in the republican rearguard, lacking either the power or influence to foist the formation of a revolutionary army on other antifascist factions, and bereft of economic assets and foreign allies of note, what actual alternative did they have? Should they stay the outsiders they had been this long? The better option was to secure a foothold inside that army, even if only in the attempt to gain some supplies. But I say again that this is a lot easier to do and say with the benefit of hindsight; back then, what those militias could see and sample at close hand was the reality of a revolution that was retreating, that was fighting in retreat in a process that, if not stopped at some point, would inevitably lead to complete defeat. In which case winning the war on fascism would have little point.

Opposition from militians took the form of resistance to accept militarization, varying in degree and persistence between one column and the next and, ultimately, as desertions. In the Durruti Column, militarization, plus the negative impact made by the death of its leader and Lucio Ruano's authoritarian leadership, was about to break out as a crisis of such dimensions that at times it even threatened to lead to its disintegration.[9] In the end, "after laborious, prolonged and endless overtures," about 60 percent of its former militians would consent to serve in the new Division.[10] If true, this leads us to estimate that some 2,800 of the 7,000-odd militians who made up the column in late November 1936, left the unit over the course of this process.[11]

Durruti's death had, as indicated earlier, come as a tremendous blow to his militians.[12] Not only in terms of loss but also because there was the firm suspicion, if not conviction, that he had been murdered by the communists.[13] Especially strong within the contingent that had accompanied him to Madrid was the feeling that they had been thrown into the battle by the High Command without their having been afforded time to rest or to familiarize themselves with the new battlefield after several days of fighting without rest or relief and that they had sustained losses in excess of 50%.[14] "Utterly exhausted and sleepless," those who survived felt like rats caught in a trap, surrounded by enemies and the majority of them lobbied for a return to Aragon.[15] Ricardo Sanz, Durruti's successor in Madrid, recounts how, on arrival, he found that "huge unrest prevailed. Besides Durruti's death the previous day, another two comrades from the column had been killed while walking down the street. The militian clamored: "No, Sanz! This cannot go on!" when he asked one of them: "What's happening?," one of them replied:

> Comrade Sanz, don't be surprised to find us altered. We are all convinced that it was not the fascists that killed our Durruti. It was enemies from within our own ranks, enemies within the Republic. They killed him because they knew that Durruti was incorruptible and would countenance no questionable compromises. The same will happen to you if you are not careful. They

are out to liquidate those who stand for our revolutionary ideas. That is what is going on here. There are those who fear the revolution might go too far. Yesterday two comrades out for a stroll were murdered from behind. They'll kill you too if you stay in Madrid. We want to get out of here as soon as possible, we want to head back to Aragon. There we know whom we are fighting and there are no enemies there to attack us from behind.

And Sanz concludes: "Pretty much all of them thought that. A sizable part of the column returned to Aragon in fact. The rest stayed behind in Madrid."[16]

In Aragon, the column had been left under the command of Lucio Ruano, a person given to violence and a man of few words. It is telling that as early as November 11, at a gathering of the higher committees in Catalonia, the Regional Committee had suggested "to Santillán that somebody needed to be sent in there [to the Durruti Column], because Ruano is not given to negotiation"—something that was not done.[17] Which then raises the question, given that he was known for his authoritarian temperament, why Durruti left him in charge. Joan Llarch explains that Lucio Ruano and his brother, who followed him everywhere as if he was his shadow, were[18]

> two Argentinean nationals who had relocated to Spain from their homeland.... The Ruanos were two of the sorts of undesirables that tend to stick their noses into every movement and organization.... Their interest was in carrying out expropriations [hold-ups] to line their own pockets, using a revolver at every opportunity. The Ruanos's father had sheltered Buenaventura Durruti from the law during the latter's activities over in Argentina, when he robbed the San Martín Bank with Francisco Ascaso and Gregorio Jover. Buenaventura Durruti was the sort of man to repay favors received.... The welcome he afforded the Ruanos in Aragon by placing his full trust in them, was recompense for the help that he had received from their father as he therefore looked upon them as close friends.[19]

Zaragoza Bound

We can only imagine how Durruti's presence might have acted as a brake upon their worst instincts.[20] Or, to rephrase that, might have forced them to disguise or hide their true faces—in part at any rate, unless we call to mind the doubts that may have arisen regarding that failed attack on Perdiguera. With Durruti off the scene and with nothing to restrain them, "the two Ruanos, like many another of their kind," Joan Llarch goes on, "ruled the roost . . . [Because also] when he left, Durruti selected his best men and left behind in Aragon a contingent of decent militias, interspersed by more dubious types with very shallow ideological beliefs, if any at all."[21]

It was not long before the first cracks showed because of the differences with Durruti in terms of character and the way subordinates were dealt with. One nameless militian dubbed "militiaman X" by the Gimenologues, explains that: "Durruti never had a fighter from his column shot for retreating in the face of the enemy or for desertion. . . . There was no need, if one may say so, because he managed to sustain a high degree of cohesion among his miliciens and most of them had every confidence in him. Ruano, on the other hand, was not in control of the situation and lacked stature."[22] That same unnamed militian points out that, on an unspecified date, "he had shot a young militiaman who had left the front without permission to seek out his family. The Libertarian Youth swore to avenge him, but Ruano was not afraid of them and just laughed at their threat: 'Let them come! The moment they see me they'll take to their heels like rabbits!'"[23] Moreover, in late November, as a result of a rout during an attack in Fuentes de Ebro in which somebody lost his rifle, Headquarters—meaning Lucio Ruano and his adjutants—issued a proclamation threatening punishment or even shooting for anyone who left his post. In response to which Antonio Campos tells us that Ángel Sáez, the political delegate from the artillery battery in which he served in Bujaraloz, ordered him to train his guns on Headquarters and, unless issued with countermanding orders by eight o'clock, to open fire.[24] In the end this did not happen because Ruano, on that occasion, caved in and withdrew the proclamation before the fateful hour.[25]

Prolonged military inaction due to lack of arms and ammunition—interrupted only by artillery duels, sniping, and periodic attempts at raids—was another factor that helped conjure up a morbid state of discontent, as the militias who had, remember, signed on as volunteers, were mostly eager to fight and defeat the rebels as a way of promoting the revolution.[26] In mid-November 1936, there had been a couple of attacks on Quinto, thwarted by the lack of coordination with the Ortiz Column.[27] And in late November and early December, an attack on Villafranca and Nuez de Ebro was frustrated by a failure to coordinate with other columns. The operation was to have been accompanied by diversionary attacks in other sectors along the Aragon front, but these failed to happen, and the rebels were presented with an opportunity to marshal their forces in order to stem the onslaught.[28] This latter failure helped undermine the militias' morale, because, according to a report by Manzana, the attack had suffered from "lack of leadership during the prosecution of the fighting and the utter lack of concrete orders regarding the objectives to be occupied," this having led to an "excitement of minds that must have lowered our fighters morale" as well as a "loss of confidence in their leaders."[29]

Such incompetence on the part of Ruano, moreover, did not give him pause for thought on December 10, when he shot two militians for abandoning their post and the machine-gun they were manning.[30] This triggered a great scandal among the centurias because those two militians had distinguished themselves by excellent service on previous occasions.[31] In an ignominious follow-up the next day, a proclamation was posted in which, after it was claimed that in certain operations a number of militians had behaved like "gays" a disciplinary code was imposed under which—among other things—withdrawing from any position without orders from their delegates or jettisoning arms, munitions, or gear would be punishable by shooting "unless the circumstances are such as to make the offense ineluctable."[32] Those unwilling to embrace this code could leave the Column, as some groups of militians did, judging from the remarks included in an article in *La Noche* on December 15.[33] On the other hand, on December 8, Jaime Boguña—formerly delegate with the Statistics Section (in other words, the Column's bookkeeper)—who had been dismissed with those who worked alongside him in that service about a month before, had been shot after he was charged with having claimed the pay of some militians and keeping them.[34]

The first steps toward militarization were taken in December: this adopted a special format among the troops on the Aragon front who were answerable to Catalonia, since the so-called "Exèrcit de Catalunya" (Army of Catalonia)—the new military organization replacing the militias system—had different structures from the rest of the People's Army and answered to the Generalitat's Defense Department rather than the Central High Command.[35] The intention behind this brand of autonomous Catalan army, very possibly driven by mutual agreement between the Catalanists and anarchists, is easily guessed: to conform to the militarization that Largo Caballero required for procuring weapons while retaining a measure of independence and oversight of its troops.[36] That stratagem, however, was not about to produce the desired outcomes. In April, the Generalitat—within which the CNT still held important departments, especially Defense—agreed to reconfigure the army using the rest of the republican army as the model, whilst retaining some measure of control over it.[37]

Juan Giménez Arenas, a young libertarian who served in the Durruti Column, recounts how Ruano—whom he wonders how he ever "reached a position of such responsibility"—embarked that December on action designed to further that militarization. The Column's members, though, gathered together and decided to appoint a three-man delegation to inform Ruano of their opposition.[38] However, on arrival at Headquarters, the delegation was still speaking when Ruano retorted: "Get back to your centurias with all possible haste, unless you want me to line you up against the wall. Remember that I command here and what I say, I do."[39]

Militian José Blanco's December 5, 1936, article is indicative of the demands and criticisms of many of the militians: "Not all of us on the front lines embrace this barrack-style militarization, over [which] would-be commissars swoon. Marshaled within this people's army, whether specifically voluntarily or under compulsion, we do not find saluting acceptable and will not indulge in it as it is an action repugnant to our libertarian consciousness. We agree to unified command,

Militarization of the Column and the Eclipse of the Libertarian Movement

technical discipline, but nothing more. . . . The army of obligatory service is the people's army and thousands of us men who accept that it is at present imperative, that it represents life or death for the people's liberties will join it: but we accept it without hierarchies, or salutes, or bended knees toward none, since we find every one of these things repugnant."[40]

Another token of this resistance is the resolution passed by the Germans from the International Group on December 22 in Vilella: after criticizing the fact that the basis for militarization had been drawn up without any contact with those serving in the front lines, it suggested a list of demands regarding the drafting of a "new military code":

1. Abolition of salutes.
   2. Equal pay for all.
   3. Freedom of the press (front-line newspapers).
   4. Freedom of discussion.
   5. A Battalion Council (three delegates elected per company).
   6. No delegate shall wield command functions.
   7. The Battalion Council is to summon a general meeting of all soldiers, should two-thirds of the company delegates see fit.
   8. The soldiers from each unit (regiment) are to elect a delegation of three men trusted by the unit. These will have the power to convene a general meeting at any time.
   9. One of them shall be seconded to the (brigade) High Command by way as an observer.
   10. This structure ought to be extended to cover general representation of the Soldiers Councils across the entire army.
   11. The General High Command should include a representative from the soldiers' General Council.
   12. Field court martials shall be made up entirely of soldiers. In the event of charges brought against officers, one officer shall be added to it.[41]

That list of demands would be accepted and adopted also by a plenum of the Barcelona FAI on December 29 but remained a dead letter, in that the measure went no further, nor did it get the libertarian leaders to amend their position by one bit.

On December 18, 1936, along with other commanders from the anarchist columns on the Aragon front, Ruano traveled up to Barcelona to give an account of his actions, regarding which a delegation of militians had complained to the Regional Committee.[42] In the course of this gathering, Ruano, allowing his frivolity to shine through, declared: "I HAD TWO BEINGS SHOT AND NOT SPECIFIC INDIVIDUALS: IT IS THE FACT ITSELF THAT I WAS OUT TO SHOOT [because] if certain acts of cowardice are permitted, they can have very damaging consequences for a huge number of other comrades who are in as much or even more danger than the ones that took to their heels. ANYONE WHO DOES NOT LIKE THIS IS FREE TO LEAVE. HE IS WITHIN HIS RIGHTS SO TO DO."[43]

Alongside Ruano's corrosive efforts, militarization continued to sow divisions. Edi Gmür, a member of the International Group wrote in his diary entry for December 31: "There was a meeting for all the internationals during the early afternoon hours. Topic: Militarization. The debate was somewhat heated. It is primarily the French and the Spaniards who oppose the militarization of the militias.[44] The Germans and the other internationals are for it, but they have a few stipulations. The meeting ended in chaos."[45]

The straw that broke the camel's back and what may well have induced the libertarian upper echelons to decide that Ruano would be replaced by Manzana was the discovery that, without leave, he had pocketed a huge sum of money from the villages where the Column operated and there was every suggestion that he had been out to line his own pockets.[46] The leader who had been so harsh in judging his subordinates was himself exposed for his own immorality and corruption. Which also raises a question if the dismissal and subsequent shooting of Jaime Boguña had not in fact been just a ploy to get rid of someone who might have been a hindrance to him and/or exposed his misappropriation of funds, but given that according to the proclamation announcing his shooting had been "roughly one month" earlier, it may well have occurred after Durruti's departure.[47]

Militarization of the Column and the Eclipse of the Libertarian Movement

On arrival back from Madrid on January 8, 1937, Manzana found an extremely strained situation that was about to trigger a flurry of fresh desertions.[48] Straight off, the replacement of Ruano meant that he and, in solidarity, a bunch of his loyalists quit the Column.[49] Nevertheless, militarization remained the number one burning issue and source of friction. As Juan Giménez Arenas goes on to recount, Manzana summoned together the militians "in Pina, Gelsa, Osera, and Farlete and briefed them on the situation and need for us to organize militarily in order to face up to the war-time satiation that was emerging as well as to respond to the politicians of every persuasion who were campaigning against the Column."[50] That campaign revolved mostly around the press, especially the communist newspapers, which maliciously depicted not just the Durruti Column but the entire Aragon front due to the libertarians ascendancy there, as disorganized and lazy and whimsically inactive.[51] The communists, theoretically revolutionaries but in practice inimical to any revolution beyond their control and dictatorial ideological schemes, were plugging away at anti-revolutionary watchwords like "enough with the try-outs and schemes" or "first win the war and then make the revolution."[52] Juan Giménez closes by recalling: "From that point on, a lot of comrades headed back into the rearguard to await conscription into the ranks. Among them was a band of gypsies that said that they had no desire to be soldiers as they were revolutionaries."[53]

By the beginning of January 1937, the International Group had been formally militarized and changed its name to the First International Company. Foreign volunteers who accepted militarization had gone off to their base in Pina, but the ones who rejected it stayed on in Gelsa. On January 8 the latter published a statement together with the Fourth Agrupación, the War Delegation, and the "Acción y Alegría" Group in which, after pointing out that "all we are missing is the attack materials that make victory feasible," they attacked militarization on the grounds that it was likely to give rise to a brand new "militarism."[54] On the other hand, the group of internationals that had moved to Pina, after Manzana refused to recognize the representatives chosen by them to serve as their officers—a concession that had apparently been agreed to by Ruano—came together in assembly on January 10 and endorsed the following list of demands, a truncated version of what had been agreed in Velilla:[55]

> 1. Each section chooses a soldiers' council. The four soldiers' councils in each company have the following entitlements:
>
> a) The right to take part in all military and administrative business related to the International Group.
> b) They are authorized, on the basis of documents issued by headquarters, in the event of urgent matters, always to make direct approach to all the pertinent places to resolve an issue.
>
> 2. Free choice of all officers with the above-mentioned exceptions [regimental commander, High Command and Column Commander]
> 3. Equal pay for all combatants in the confederal columns (…)
> 4. No obligation to give military salute.
> 5. No obligation for a fixed term of service.
> 6. The comrades we appoint to present these requests to the Regional Committee have no authority to alter them. They are duty-bound to return within 48 hours, even should it be the case that they have no written response from the Regional Committee. If no response to our demands is forthcoming, we will assume that they have been rejected.
> 7. In the event of our just requests being rejected or left unanswered, each of the under-signed persons [signatories] recover his complete freedom of action.[56]

With Manzana refusing to let the chosen delegates go, on January 11, forty-nine fighters stood down so that they could deliver their statement to the Regional Committee of the CNT of Catalonia.[57]

January 16 saw the appearance of another manifesto, drafted in Gelsa and endorsed by the International Group posted there, the Fourth Agrupación, the "Acción y Alegría" Group, the artillery batteries, machine-gunner sections, and other centurias. The text started out by insisting yet again that the main reason for the paralysis on the Aragon Front was the shortage of war materials and it cautioned that, even if they were to militarize themselves, the State would have no reason to furnish them with more arms, and, finally, it suggested an alternative military organizational format that made provision for delegates and soldiers' councils that "should it be accepted," would "rescue many of the essences of our ideas from foundering."[58]

In the wake of the Plenum of Confederal and Anarchist Columns held in Valencia in February, militarization moved on to its final stages. There, for all the discontent and initial opposition of many of the delegations, the representatives of the CNT National Committee succeeded in imposing its own viewpoint on the majority; they had to abide by militarization if they were to have access to the state's armaments stores, since the only other option was to "storm the place where the arms were being stored . . . [but that] might bring about a situation where our disturbances might provide fascism with a chance to find us weak and to pull off its triumph."[59] The Iron Column, which had convened the plenum, suggested that they threaten to withdraw from the front lines and head back into the rearguard "to bring pressure on the government to furnish us with arms without having to resort to militarization," fell on deaf ears.[60] Deep down, looking past opinions as to the greater suitability of one or the other propositions, what they both hinted at, all in all, was the libertarian movement's position of dependency and weakness on the crucial issue of supplying war materials. No consideration was given to alternatives other than the channels of the central state.

This final phase of militarization would be anything but clear sailing in the case of the former Durruti Column, by then formally renamed the Durruti Division.[61] On the one hand, the ongoing desertions had made it necessary to fill the gaps with members of other political organizations who were, for the most part, armed with the rifles that those who had left had had to leave behind.[62] That, plus the fact that the newcomers had been equipped completely by the quartermasters "with their appropriate bedrolls, whereas our men, even though they had been six months in the fight, had to sleep on straw sacks and we barely had some blankets." This created great discontent among the older hands and threatened "to destroy the trust that the comrades had placed in us," Manzana warned in his report.[63] Moreover, the frictions between those who embraced militarization and the oppositionist Gelsa contingent were growing in bitterness, to the extent that they were threatening to culminate in bloodshed.[64]

At a gathering of committees on February 12, Manzana explained that the Gelsa comrades, who would not accept militarization,

> are handing out manifestos [to] the other sectors, explaining the grounds for non-acceptance of militarization. . . . He mentioned a few of the incidents that had occurred . . . and ended by stating: Said comrades have assured us that if they are forced to abandon their base, they will do with arms and all. Another extremely serious issue . . . is the killing of a comrade from the "Sons of Night," murdered, it is believed, by the men from Gelsa who contend that he was drunk. . . . Furthermore, he complained . . . that the Gelsa comrades had stolen rifles and other sort of munitions such as bombs and the like, and he closed by saying: If no solution is found to the Gelsa matter, he would have to hand in his final resignation, and his departure will be followed by all of his militians because they have assured him of that."

Later, at the same meeting, Manzana was to take the floor again to lay out the horrific shortages of weapons they were facing, not having enough to face up to the offensive that he feared would shortly be coming. And finally he spelled out his fears that the Libertarian Youth "are not only organizing in the rearguard but are also organizing by setting up groups in the trenches themselves, and in all likelihood it may come to pass that he [or the] UNIFIED COMMAND might issue some order, only to have the organized youth REFUSE TO OBEY IT."[65] That claim gives some sense of the discontent spreading through one segment of the rank-and-file membership and the gap that had opened up between them and their main leaders.

A report from the Liaison Committee of the FAI Anarchist Groups in Catalonia noted that it had been agreed that the Gelsa militians would be invited to a meeting to hash out a solution to the situation once and for all. "Those comrades took up the invitation issued by the organization's committees and after lengthy consideration, they agreed that two weeks after that meeting, they would leave the front, surrendering their weapons to the other comrades arriving as their replacements."[66] Toward the end of February and in contravention of this arrangement, the Gelsa militians—some seven hundred of them—left the front, taking their weapons with them.[67] Once in Barcelona, they and other anarchists critical of the collaborationist policy, launched the Friends of Durruti *Agrupación* that March: its goal was to reclaim and resurrect the revolution and fight those aiming to bring back the situation that had been in place prior to the army mutiny, and they adopted the figure of Buenaventura Durruti as their reference point.[68] This was when, as previously indicated, Durruti was beginning to be invoked by the leadership committees for ideological purposes.

That March, furthermore, Manzana did as he had warned and resigned with no further explanation. In addition to events in Gelsa, just a few days earlier he had had a showdown with José Mira, during which it appears they may have gone so far as to reach for their pistols.[69] That clash may be related to Mira's suspicions that the bullet that ended Durruti's life had come from his [Manzana's] gun.[70] Without a doubt, this incident must have weighed heavily on the already delicate frame of mind and prompted Manzana to quit the unit. In a letter to Helmut Rüdiger on March 28, Rudolf Michaelis, the International Company's political delegate, referred to Manzana's having suffered a mental breakdown.[71] The belittling and boycott he was subjected to by the central government and the High Command of the Aragon front might have contributed to the breakdown.[72] And he concluded with the explanation that at a meeting attended by two delegates from the Catalonian CNT's Regional Committee and one representative from the Generalitat's Defense Department, headed at the time by the CNT's own Francisco Isgleas, he had been persuaded to return for a while until such time as a replacement could be found for the then head of the High

Command in Aragon, Alfonso Reyes, a soldier close to the communists.[73] Which also bought time for them to come up with a replacement for Manzana, who was at that point regarded as indispensable as head of the Durruti Division.[74]

Alongside this, over the early months in 1937, war action in the central sector of the Aragon front had been very scarce. Which does not mean, of course, that the anarchists did not carry on focusing their gaze and hopes upon the city on the Ebro. The operation planned by Antonio Ortiz at around this time was particularly outstanding. The main thrust of it was for 1,000 of 1,500 fighters to be smuggled into Zaragoza to launch street-to-street fighting; together with an attack from without by the Durruti and South Ebro or Luis Jubert divisions (which is to say, the old Ortiz Column), this was expected to lead to the capture of the city. The operation was to have been accompanied by diversionary attacks in the Teruel area and a resolute push in the direction of Calatayud that would seek to overrun that area. The final aim was to link up with the confederal forces from the center of the peninsula in order to leave Teruel isolated in a large pocket. Again, the importance credited to Zaragoza was evident in the fact that Ricardo Sanz associated that operation with "going for broke" in what was a very optimistic sense, given the balance of power at the time. That said, there is no denying that had it come off successful, it would have made a huge impact on a libertarian movement that was clearly in retreat. However, the operation ran into the usual obstacle: lack of armaments. Which seems, according to Ortiz, to have led to "failure of the talks in Barcelona" and it had to be called off.[75]

What did take place over those months was a series of minor attacks and counterattacks, mainly in the northern and southern sectors of the Aragon front. On February 18, the rebels launched a big push that enabled them to overrun Vivel de Río and push on towards Utrillas. To assist, a force made of troops from other sectors, including a battalion of the recently constituted Durruti Division was raised and sent in; the counterattack started on the 23rd. By the beginning of March, after Portalrubio was abandoned and after some back and forth, the front was re-established and liaison with forces from Valencia operating against Teruel was assured.[76] On the other hand, the Generalitat's Defense Department, at the request of the republic's Central High Command, which lobbied for more action on the Aragon front in order to take some of the pressure off Madrid, mounted a series of operations over March and April.[77] As part of these operations, on March 19 and 20, the Durruti Division attempted to close off the Villafranca de Ebro area and the adjacent hills. It started out successfully and a series of hills were overrun, but due to a fierce enemy counterattack and the overwhelming superiority of their air force, it was forced to halt and dig in in the recently captured positions.[78] Troops from the Division were also to take part in the operations designed to tighten the noose on Huesca. On April 12, the International Company arrived to assist in efforts to capture the Santa Quiteria hermitage in the Tardienta sector. The attack started well, and the hermitage was captured, but, with back-up from their air force, the enemy counterattacked and evicted them after inflicting heavy losses. Meanwhile, despite its having promised assistance, the republic air force never left the airfield, allegedly due to technical problems. Rightly or wrongly, the militians construed this as yet more sabotage, and it triggered further desertions.[79]

Things were even worse in political terms. The libertarian representatives in the various regional governments and central government operated very sluggishly and ingenuously, having no clear course or policy of their own and they were obsessed with holding together the antifascist front at any cost, stumbling from one concession to the next and surrendering morsels of the revolution each time.[80] Every new concession simply undermined the foundations of their power; in other words, it weakened their hand in negotiations; which gave wings to their rivals who replied with fresh demands. In Catalonia, in particular at the time of the March campaign, the offensive by the counter-revolutionary entente made up of Catalanists and communists, having applied the screws to the supplies committees and collectives through a series of economic-financial measures, then turned their sights on what armed power the libertarian rank-and-file in the rearguard could still command.[81]

On March 4, with the acquiescence of its CNT councilors, the Generalitat published a battery of decrees.[82] They endorsed, notably: disbanding the Home Security and Defense Departments at municipal levels; the withdrawal of frontier monitoring from all patrols, militians, and Investigation or Control committees and their replacement by government personnel and, most important of all, the disbandment of the Assault Guard, Republican National Guard, Control Patrols (a sort of revolutionary police force set up by the CAMC and operating in Barcelona: a majority of their members were drawn from the CNT) as well as of all bodies operating within the field of public order, and setting up an Internal Security Corps to replace them. It was assumed that entry into this single security corps, which was to have a monopoly on "legitimate" violence in the rearguard, was open to all, especially to all members of the aforementioned corps and agencies that were being disbanded. However, the inclusion within this flurry of decrees of one decree that not only disbanded the Workers' And Soldiers' Councils—bodies made up of trusted officers and CNT and UGT delegates and designed to oversee and purge the various traditional law-and-order agencies—but banned personnel from the new agency from having any trade union or political affiliations. This was a clear signal that the intention was to exclude most patrolers as well as members of revolutionary bodies generally.[83] Meaning that it was to be made up solely of the "apolitical" traditional forces of order who were by nature dyed-in-the-wool conservatives and pro-Catalanists.[84] A couple of weeks after publication, Francisco Isgleas, on whom an attempt had been made to pin the blame for implementation of a campaign to disarm the rearguard—plainly targeting the libertarian rank-and-file—handed in his resignation, irked by the ridiculous role that he and his comrades were acting out inside the Generalitat.[85] The remainder of the libertarian councilors, under pressure from an alarmed membership and in keeping with an agreement reached at a meeting held with the higher committees and delegates from the comarcas—who had also come to the conclusion that these public order decrees represented a menace—followed suit and also resigned, leaving the decrees hovering in the air and thereby ushering in a period of negotiations and provisional governments.[86] The aim was to fend off those decrees or at any rate to tidy up their damaging features.

However, among the libertarian grassroots the notion of going further and ending collaboration and pressing on with the revolution was making headway.[87] Outstanding here was the Friends of Durruti Agrupación, within whose ranks an interesting process of theorization and ideological revision was under way. This was based on the firm belief that power could and should have been taken, back in July.[88] Essentially that was the original sin to which every other subsequent misstep and the ugly overall situation of the time could be traced. The *agrupación*'s members were to embark upon an intense campaign of agitation in the form of newspaper articles, manifestos, leafleting, and rallies, which resulted by late April in posters laying out their program being stuck up all over Barcelona.[89]

Their list of proposals included, notably: 1. The immediate formation of a Revolutionary Junta, construed as a revolutionary government made up of workers, peasants, and combatants. 2. Trade union direction of the economy and oversight of distribution. 3. Establishment of a revolutionary army. 4. Absolute working-class control of public order. 5. Proletarian justice. And it concluded with the triple watchword: "All power to the working class. All economic power to the unions. A Revolutionary Junta instead of the Generalidad."[90] Swords had been drawn.

Alongside this, a series of incidents was adding to the already rather tense atmosphere.[91] On March 5, a communist commando operating out of the Voroshilov barracks tried to steal twelve light tanks from the war materials depot controlled by the CNT, producing a requisition order bearing the forged signature of Eugenio Vallejo, who was in charge of Catalonia's War Industry and belonged to the CNT; even though the barracks political commissar disowned the actions of his subordinates, the intention behind them—making ready for an upcoming clash—was unmistakable.[92] On April 14, Camillo Berneri, the director of *Guerra di classe*, published in that weekly newspaper an "Open Letter" addressed to Federica Montseny highlighting the contradiction between the duties imposed by the revolution and the handiwork of the CNT ministers inside the government. The letter also included a fragment from the December 17, 1936, edition of *Pravda* that left not one shadow of a doubt as to the communists' intentions: "As for Catalonia, the mopping up of Trotskyist and anarcho-syndicalist personnel has begun and this task will be carried out with the same vigor as it has been in the USSR."[93] On April 25, an important PSUC-UGT representative (and former CNT member) Roldán Cortada was mowed down in a hail of bullets at a makeshift roadblock. The blame for his death was pinned on a bunch of CNT members, although no proof was forthcoming. At his funeral, which was attended by armed forces and police, there were anti-anarchist chants.[94] On April 27, Antonio Martín, the anarchist chairman of the revolutionary committee in the border town of Puigcerdá was killed along with three more CNT members in a clash with the Assault Guards and Republican National Guard in the nearby town of Bellver. Shortly after which, three truckloads of carabineros were sent from Valencia by the moderate socialist Finance minister, Juan Negrín, and started to take over the border posts previously controlled by revolutionary committees.[95]

Which brings us to May 1, which had been declared an ordinary workday. All demonstrations had been banned for fear of clashes on the streets. That darkened workers' day, Carl Einstein, spokesman for the internationals in the Durruti Division, published an article in which, after giving a brief run-down of the anarchist columns' early actions and accomplishments, he denounced the forced idleness of the Aragon front: "Why will nobody take this front resolutely in hand?" he asked. And then he offered this answer:

> Deployed in these mountains are the columns of the CNT, the spearhead of the revolution and collectivization. Those anarchists have hardly any international support of note, nor any effective propaganda abroad. They are known and judged according to the opinions of their enemies. They are known about through vulgar, antiquated literature, which in all too many occasions speaks only about the gunman. Scarcely any foreigner has offered a European assessment of constructive

anarcho-syndicalism. We have highlighted the CNT's constructive endeavors. But it seems—and this is crucial—that it comes under criticism from influential quarters because of that very merit. The whole of Spain is dominated by the "democracy or socialism" debate.[96]

[Meaning whether to revert to a capitalist liberal democracy or establish a revolutionary regime once and for all.] Einstein went on to express his full confidence that the rebels would be defeated: "It has become clear today that fascism cannot embed itself in Spain. Hitler and Mussolini will lose this war." And he closed by arguing in favor of the revolution, antifascist unity, and giving the neglected Aragon front a boost:

> Foreign colonialist capitalism must never be able to return. I cannot believe a single Spaniard would dare to sell the life and labor of the Spanish proletariat to foreign speculators, no matter how democratic they may be. Young Spanish capitalism—moreover—has collapsed in on itself during the war.... 'First the war!,' you say. Yes, first the war but a war understood as a revolution. And to that end, a war on all fronts and consequently a war in Aragon. There is a duty upon us to exploit all the opportunities the battle offers us and to mobilize every effort to press ahead with our war and shorten it and win it.... No one wants to see Aragon and Catalonia being in jeopardy any longer. When all is said and done, thus far the CNT's columns have been defending themselves from the enemy, inseparable with the other divisions. None of these militians ever haggled over life or death. The war in Aragon is doable. And can be cut short if all the fronts are coordinated. We can and we must capture Zaragoza. The government is duty-bound to bring about the antifascist front's victory by every means.... Friends, let these divisions fight and let them win in Aragon.[97]

Meanwhile, far removed from this craving for antifascist harmony, the Republic National Guard and Assault Guards were fully committed to carrying out searches on the streets of Barcelona, with numerous libertarian militants being disarmed and arrested.[98] Clashes and mutual seizures of weapons had become more frequent over recent days.[99] In light of which, the May 2 edition of *Solidaridad Obrera* issued the following cautionary note: "THE GUARANTEE OF THE REVOLUTION IS THE PROLETARIAT IN ARMS. ATTEMPTING TO DISARM THE PEOPLE IS TANTAMOUNT TO MANNING THE OTHER SIDE OF THE BARRICADES. COUNCILOR OR COMMISSAR THOUGH YOU MAY BE, YOU CANNOT ISSUE AN ORDER TO DISARM THE WORKERS WHO ARE FIGHTING FASCISM MORE SELFLESSLY AND HEROICALLY THAN ALL THE POLITICIANS IN THE REAGUARD WHOSE INEPTITUDE AND IMPOTENCE ARE KNOWN TO ALL. WORKERS, LET NO ONE SUBMIT TO BEING DISARMED ON ANY GROUNDS! THAT IS OUR WATCHWORD. LET NO ONE ALLOW HIMSELF TO BE DISARMED!"[100]

In this explosive climate, Companys and the communists were about to raise the stakes and escalate their offensive. On May 3, Rodríguez Salas, Public Order Commissioner and a member of the PSUC, showed up at the Telephone Exchange in Barcelona with three truckloads of Assault Guards and a seizure warrant issued by Aguadé, the ERC-affiliated Councillor for Homeland Security. Lawfully collectivized and controlled by a joint CNT-UGT committee, on which the anarcho-syndicalists were the majority, the exchange was also a symbol of the revolution as well as a significant power lever of the libertarian movement, as it allowed it to intercept and eavesdrop on communications in the region. Which in fact, they did. The CNT members on the lower floors, caught off guard, submitted to being disarmed: but on the floors above staunch resistance was offered as the guards' way was barred.

News of what was going on spread like wildfire. The war Defense Sections (or Committees) rallied to the defense of the Telephone Exchange, throwing up barricades at various strategic points and calling a general strike, stepping up and spreading the fighting. The entire city was filled with the sounds of gunfire and explosions. This was the beginning of five days of bloody fighting in Barcelona, spilling over into other points around Catalonia: the so-called May Days. On one side there was the counter-revolutionary bloc made up of Catalan nationalists and communists who were reliant on the traditional forces of order. On the other, championing the revolution, were much of the libertarian grassroots, joined by POUM members and the odd other tiny faction of left-wing anti-Stalinist communists.

On May 3 itself, the revolutionaries, who could also count on backing from the toiling masses of Barcelona, had taken control of the entire cordon of outlying barrios, with the counter-revolutionaries confined to a small area in the city center where the main government buildings were located. The battle was tilting in the favor of the insurgents. In spite of this, the insurrection found itself struggling—or rather, leaderless—due to opposition coming from the libertarian leaders themselves. For one thing, not only had these issued no mobilization call or call to uprising, but they had tried to restrain and hold back the membership, only to be overwhelmed. Once things were under way, they were to espouse a conciliatory approach, trying to calm minds and seek a negotiated solution, which very quickly became brazen compromise. So, over the ensuing days, while they were issuing repeated calls for a ceasefire and a withdrawal and for provocations to be ignored . . . they embarked upon disgraceful negotiations and a tug of war over various issues regarding which, as was their wont, they ended up caving in. On May 5, they agreed that the central government should take over Public Order and Defense duties from the Generalitat, allegedly to try to pacify the situation (even though that Defense Department had done everything in its power—and largely successfully—to keep the troops on the front out of the fighting. On May 6, in a "goodwill gesture," they ordered armed militants to withdraw from the Telephone Exchange which was then swiftly and treacherously taken over by police personnel. The fact that it had no clear-cut political objectives helped undermine the insurrection even further as it was, more than anything else, an anger-fueled, world-weary defensive reaction in the face of the latest assault on the revolution.

Only the minuscule Bolshevik-Leninist Section of Spain on the afternoon and evening of May 4, and The Friends of Durruti on

May 5 each produced a leaflet trying to offer guidance to the uprising and invest it with some content. The Friends of Durruti leaflet, in keeping with their posters in late April, called for the establishment of a Revolutionary Junta, for those culpable in the storming of the Telephone Exchange to be shot, for the disarming of all the armed police agencies, and the disbandment of the political parties alleged to have attacked the working class. It concluded: "Let us not give up the streets.—Revolution ahead of all else. Hail to our comrades from the POUM who fraternized with us on the streets. LONG LIVE THE SOCIAL REVOLUTION! DOWN WITH THE COUNTER-REVOLUTION!"[101]

Distribution of the leaflet helped reinvigorate the uprising, but it was just the swan song: with the passing of time and with the repeated appeals coming from the libertarian leaders, libertarian activists were losing heart and withdrawing. The remainder of the revolutionary fighters would follow suit. By May 7, the clashes were as good as over. That afternoon Assault Guards drafted in from Valencia, paraded down the Diagonal, and proceeded to occupy the city.[102] Although the insurgents had not been beaten in military terms, the final outcome represented a stark defeat that was about to plunge the libertarian movement into demoralization and crisis. In the short term, this meant the loss of the Telephone Exchange and the Defense Department: nevertheless, the most significant point was that the libertarian leaders had displayed absolute faint-heartedness.

In line with what I have been pointing out, it is not my view that the circumstances at the time were ripe for the seizure of power, for ending the Generalitat, and establishing a Revolutionary Junta as the Friends of Durruti were pressing for. There was certainly a chance of seizing power in Catalonia, but then what?[103] Of course, clashes had erupted in other regions where the anarchists and or revolutionaries in general might have had a different fate. The revolutionary euphoria of the previous summer was a distant memory, there could be no reliance on unanimous popular support and, besides, the counter-revolutionary forces and above all the communists had carved out solid positions with the reconstituted armed corps of the state. Even in the hypothetical situation in which they might have emerged victorious without triggering a collapse of the front lines, how would the USSR have reacted? One can easily imagine the arms supply being cut off and the gold deposited in Moscow being impounded, making it all but impossible to carry on with the war successfully. So, I discount as wishful thinking the chances, for which some argued, of success of the revolution within Spain's triggering a tide of solidarity and support among workers elsewhere.[104]

I personally believe that the best solution was to repay the provocation with force of arms, hitting hard and deep, wherever necessary, but while simultaneously negotiating from a position of strength rather than seizing power.[105] That could only have been the ultimate escape in the event of the enemy's not giving in on a basis more temporary than permanent. Of course, what should never have been countenanced was that disgraceful stand-down, that half-surrender that merely left the door wide open to utter surrender and defeat.

The first strike back would not be long in following: capitalizing upon the recent events, the communists pushed for the removal of Largo Caballero who was much too leftist and independent for their liking, and a government with no anarchist presence was formed under Negrín.[106] Emanating from this new brazenly counter-revolutionary government, there followed a campaign to crack down on the POUM—which was flatly outlawed—and on the libertarian movement, especially its more revolutionary elements. That campaign would be accompanied by a push to mop up the last remaining vestiges of anarchist power; on June 5, the Public Order chief appointed by the central government did away with the Control Patrols once and for all.[107] At the same time, a number of Ward Committees and their Defense Sections-Committees were overrun and shut down. Shortly after that, on June 29, the CNT was ousted from the reshuffled Generalitat executive, with not a single CNT councilor remaining.[108] Finally, that September, one after another, all of the remaining Ward and Defense Committees were raided.[109] The only response from the libertarian leaders was to demobilize their rank-and-file and avert a violent backlash, confining themselves to the odd token protest.[110] Such was the extent of their moral and political collapse. In fact, that there was no split within the CNT during the civil war was in part due to this tide of repression, which saw the bulk of the more discontented membership, critical of their leaders, murdered, jailed, or forced into hiding or on the run; this too partly accounts for the timidity of their response.[111]

In matters military, the central government's take-over of the Generalitat's Defense responsibilities implied that the forces on the Aragon front would now be fully absorbed into the Republic's People's Army and answerable directly to the Central High Command. Among them was the Durruti Division which had been rechristened as the 26th Division in late April—that title would survive until it crossed over the Pyrenees in early 1939.[112] On May 15, 1937, Ricardo Sanz, along with the remnants of the Column that had marched off to Madrid, arrived in Bujaraloz to take over command of the Division from Manzana.[113] This may be taken as the conclusion to the militarization process. Inevitably, it made no great changes in terms of equipment, but in those circumstances, it flagged up the nose-dive in the fortunes of the libertarian movement. As a rule, absorption of the erstwhile anarchist columns into the Republic's army did not mean that in future they would be issued with the same equipment as any other unit. When it came to supplies of war materials, they would still receive second-class treatment, especially in comparison with units in which communists ruled the roost.[114] We might point to a couple of concrete examples in the case of the 26th Division. First, Antoine Gimenez recounts: "There was a lot of talk among us regarding Russian aid in terms of arms and munitions, but I must concede that, by late July 1937, on the sector of the front where I was serving, we had seen none of it. There was just one difference: the hunting rifles were shipped off to the museum and replaced by Winchester and Lebel rifles. The former coming from Mexico and the rest from France. Our machine-guns were left-overs from the First World War."[115] Secondly, a report, possibly dating from July–August 1937 and submitted to the CNT Regional Committee for Catalonia, points out that the anarchist divisions were "utterly ignored by the Quartermaster Corps, so much so that the 26th (erstwhile Durruti) Division still has no summer clothing and there are those who have no trousers to wear. As for food rations, not only is the food poor but it even falls short of what is needed."[116]

The first operation in which forces originally answerable to Catalonia were to operate as integral parts of the republican army would come that July. Its aim was to capture Huesca and help ease the pressure on the Basque front, which was crumbling at the time. Outstandingly novel was the fact that this was the first time that troops drawn from other fronts had rather more gear available than had been directed to Aragon on previous occasions.[117] However, as usual, the operation was a failure. As Maldonado Moya notes, "What that targeting of Huesca showed was that the rebels' defense of the city and along much of the Front was highly organized, and for serious consideration to be been given to an attack with any serious prospects of success, a lot more troops than had previously thought would have been required. The blame for the 'inaction' on the Aragon Front had quite a few more explanatory factors than any passivity credited to the republican [and let it be said, mostly anarchist] troops deployed there. And those in command were well aware of it."[118]

So, for the August 1937 offensive against Zaragoza, a huge army of maneuvers was mustered, made up of several divisions under almost exclusively communist commanders. Once again, in addition to overrunning the city, the operation was out to ease pressure on the northern front, specifically to try and hold up an attack on Santander once the Basque Country had fallen. Nevertheless, there was also an unspoken political purpose as it was part of an onslaught on the last remaining morsels of anarchist power: that concentration of troops would be used to disband the Council of Aragon, the autonomous governing agency set up in October 1936, and to target the collectives in the area.[119] This was done just ahead of the launch of the operation. Now, with the Catalan and Aragon rearguards under the thumb, the central government embarked upon a push against Zaragoza that it had hitherto done nothing but impede. From the make-up and leadership of the troops cast in the leading role in this we can divine that it was also out to teach the anarchists a lesson. By showing that where they had failed, the republican army headed by communist divisions would succeed, and that if they had failed to capture the Aragonese capital, it had been due to their own ineptitude and disorganization.[120] Therefore, as Ricado Sanz has it, it dispensed "initially with the commanders and troops occupying positions along the Aragon front via which it intended to push forward . . . troops familiar with the terrain and what was required," these being held back as reserves or deployed on auxiliary tasks.[121] As we know only too well, the upshot was that the attack quickly became bogged down and distracted by secondary targets, with the operation directed against Zaragoza turning into the Battle of Belchite.[122] The very costly capture of Belchite came as a pyrrhic victory that altered nothing. A few months after that, with the collapse of the north a fait accompli, Aragon would become the main theater of operations as the civil war entered a brand-new phase. But that is another story: yet no scheme designed to radically transform society was at stake, nor was one dependent upon its success.

The social revolution had been utterly defeated. Of the new world that, a little over a year before, as the Durruti Column set off, was being created, little remained beyond its ruins, its memory. By then the plan to capture Zaragoza and proclaim libertarian communism looked a far-off and fantastic prospect. This was the end, the final end of the libertarian dream. From now on, the only option left was to survive as best one could, as individuals and as a movement, in the context of an increasingly authoritarian bourgeois republic under the sway of the communists and to try to draw some sort of lessons from what had happened. If that was possible.

Epilogue: A Hard Lesson to Swallow

"What happened was what inevitably had to happen. The CNT was devoid of revolutionary theory. We did not have the right program. We did not know where we were going. There was lots of lyricism, but in the final analysis, we were clueless as to what to do with those enormous masses of workers."
—**Jaime Balius,** *Towards a Fresh Revolution*

The libertarian movement's main leaders and leadership committees always justified their policy of collaboration, as well as their backsliding and concessions generally, on the basis that the army revolt's had opened up a hiatus during which, if fascism was to be defeated, anarchist principles had to be temporarily set aside. Once the war was over, the debate would polarize around those who believed that the aforesaid policy line should be maintained until such time as Franco was no more and those who disavowed it and categorizing it as a huge historical mistake, calling for a reversion to orthodoxy and ideological purity.[1]

Few of them stated the obvious, and then usually only timidly and ambiguously: what was needed was a thoroughgoing doctrinal rethink; because traditional anarchist theory, in its anarcho-syndicalist version, had failed spectacularly in the task of offering a response to the many challenges posed by the revolution. Broadly speaking, there was a startling absence of self-criticism. It was much easier to stick to the false certainty and security proffered by the same old cant, even at the expense of ideological contradictions and contortions, even if it meant parking them for a time. One noteworthy exception, as indicated, was the Friends of Durruti.[2] This *agrupación*, which had begun its own process of ideological rethink back in March–April 1937, was to launch its own newspaper, *El Amigo del Pueblo*, after the May Events in 1937; there it would persist in and delve deeper into its proposals and analysis. Finally, by way of an afterthought and summation of its theory, in January 1938 it published a pamphlet written by Jaime Balius, one of its chief ideologues and spokesmen.[3] Aside from its literary merits, *Towards a Fresh Revolution* stands out for the lucidity of many of the issues it raised.

The text opens with comment regarding the establishment of the Republic and how it developed, before fully engaging with an account of the army revolt and its defeat across much of Spain, something which it pointed out had opened the door to revolution. However, having arrived at that point—and this was the keynote idea—a theory or program up to the challenge was missing. The CNT had neither guide nor guidelines:

> Despite having the strength, it failed to chisel out the feat that had been played out on the street in a spontaneous way. The leaders themselves had been startled by events, which as far as they were concerned needed to be filed under "unforeseen." Nobody knew what course to follow. A theory was missing. We had spent a number of years fussing around abstractions. What do we do? The leaders back then would have been asking themselves. And the revolution was allowed to slip away. In such ultimate moments, one cannot vacillate. But one has to know where one is headed. This is the vacuum we wish to fill.[4]

And how did they intend to do so? By introducing what they termed "a slight tinkering within anarchism," the establishment of a Revolutionary Junta or National Defense Council the members of which would be democratically elected by the unions and not just the CNT unions but revolutionaries in general, in which those comrades away at the front would have to be taken into account.[5] Once the bourgeois government of the day had been removed, it would fall to that Junta or

Epilogue: A Hard Lesson to Swallow

Council to direct the war, watch over the revolutionary order and handle international affairs and propaganda. Its actions would be subject to oversight by the trade union assemblies and "in order to forestall anyone's forming an attachment to them," posts would be subject to periodical renewal.[6] Meaning, no matter how hard they tried to steer clear of such jargon, operating as a revolutionary government. In accordance with the traditional line, direction of the economy would be left to the care of the unions and local organization to that of the Free Municipalities, which would federate at regional and national levels.[7]

Other innovations relating to defense of the revolution included the unashamed acceptance of the need for a revolutionary army and worker-monitored law and order agencies.[8] And, most important of all, the acknowledgment that revolutions are totalitarian "despite all claims to the contrary."[9] Being all-encompassing, they had to grapple with every sphere—economic, political, cultural, military—unless they wanted to fail; and in addition to authoritarianism, they were required to monitor and crack down on various hostile segments of society and impose their authority.[10] This was the most controversial claim, no doubt about it. It should be added that, of course, the aspiration should always be to transform society by peaceful means, but the fact is that they must also not be so naïve as to seek to abjure the use of force in self-defense. The two were not mutually exclusive. For the time being, the only irrefutable fact was that history cannot show any example of a revolution of any hue that had not had to face up to violent backlashes and sabotage from within and without.

Furthermore, the pamphlet also included a range of minor details and sections dedicated to the May Events, about Spain's independence and collaborationism and the class struggle. And it closed by pointing to the patently counter-revolutionary scenario in place at the time and by calling for a fresh revolution. "Let us get on with laying the groundwork. And in the heat of this new feat we will again find on the streets the comrades who are today fighting in the front lines, the comrades who languish behind bars and the comrades who, right now, have still not abandoned hope in a revolution that will do right by the working class. Building a fresh revolution to offer complete satisfaction to the workers of city and countryside. Achieving an anarchist society that meets human aspirations. Onwards, comrades!"[11]

All in all, it was a program that came quite close to the classical Marxist approaches. On which basis the Friends of Durruti, even though they always thought of themselves as anarchists, were labeled as Marxists or authoritarians by the libertarian leadership.[12] However, looking past the ideological tags or the details that are open to debate, the essential point was the great timeless lesson that was being offered. The lesson of the failed Spanish Revolution, that might be summed up as the inescapable obligation to take political power and establish some sort of a democratic revolutionary government, complete with its corresponding specialist armed agencies—army or police, or howsoever one might prefer to label them—unless one was prepared to doom the revolution in advance; during the early stages at any rate. The anarchist movement's great tragedy had been that it had right on its side when it came to warning of the perils of power and authority—including power and authority exercised in the name of the people, as the Russian experience had shown—but erred in trying to dismiss them out of hand. Which was simply impossible and unrealistic.

That, ultimately, was the legacy of the Friends of Durruti. Let us be clear on that point. Because today as in the past the fight between Capital and Labor, between a society driven by unalloyed personal advantage and another riven by the common good, continues. And there is no better tribute to the memory of that group, as well as to the generality of all the honest revolutionaries who gave their lives in the Durruti Column—and most especially its leader—than to learn from the events and experiences it fell to them to live through: from where they got things right and, above all, from their mistakes. Only that way will we be in a position to avoid repeating them.

"The difference between a soldier giving out orders and a revolutionary who leads resides in the fact that the former rules by force, whereas the latter commands no authority beyond that derived from his own conduct."

This book was put together in the autumn of 2018, a hundred and thirty years since the birth of Nestor Ivanovitch Makhno, the Ukrainian anarchist revolutionary and ataman of the Black Army which for nearly three years managed to run the Vilna Terytoriya (Free Territory), one of the most interesting experimental libertarian societies history has to show. In 1927, by which time that dream had been crushed, Makhno, harried by the Bolsheviks and driven into exile in Paris, had a face-to-face meeting with some young Spaniards by the names of Francisco Ascaso, Juan García Oliver, and Buenaventura Durruti.

Notes

Introduction

1 Even Ángel Pestaña, so critical of the use of violence, see Pestaña's *Lo que aprendí en la vida* (Madrid: Zero, 1972) regarding his views on *pistolerismo* and armed robberies and despite his eventual decision to engage with politics through the elections, regarded it as inevitable. Ángel Pestaña "chose to participate in politics, whilst nonetheless being of the belief that the people, as a basic principle cannot fundamentally forego violence if it really wants to see its emancipation. And not because it is the people that should cultivate it, no; because its eternal enemies will never willingly give up the privileges they enjoy and if the people should ever want to do away with or be rid of them, they will resort to violence in defense of them. It is from that vantage point that I reckon that the people, as a basic principle, cannot abjure violence. Even should it forego it, a time would come when its adversaries themselves would compel it to have recourse to it," Ángel Pestaña, *Por qué se constituyó el Partido Sindicalista* (Madrid: Zero, 1969), 19.

2 Among those anarchists who argued that revolution was achievable by completely peaceful means, two factions deserve singling out: 1) Those who trusted in the victory of a general strike that would bring society to a standstill and force rulers and capitalists to concede defeat; a couple of accounts of how this was conceivable can be found in José Álvarez Junco, *La ideologia política del anarquismo español (1868–1910)* (Paracuellos de Jarama, Spain: Siglo veintiuno editors, 1991), 569–70. And 2) The Tolstoyans contended that it was futile trying to do away with violence by using violent methods and that the path to the betterment of society was through a withholding of all support from the State (paying taxes, performing military service, etc.) and for everyone to work on his own moral perfection. For more details of their political teachings, see Leo Tolstoy, *Cristianismo y anarquismo*, I.

3 It should be made clear that the term "libertarian movement" to designate the anarchist movement overall, or at least its main organizations (the CNT, the

FAI, and the Libertarian Youth) was coined during the early days of the Civil War, albeit that in this book it is occasionally used also in reference to the Republican era.

4 Hannah Arendt, *Sobre la violencia* (Madrid: Alianza Editorial, 2005), in English as *On Violence* (New York: Houghton Mifflin, 1969), 66.

5 To further add to the confusion, this also included all those armed criminal gangs which, hiding behind some alleged libertarian (or other brand of) ideology, were out for nothing more than personal gain and/or revenge. As Eric Hobsbawm points out: "The underworld is an anti-society, which survives by turning the values of 'respectable' people upside down in a world 'gone wrong,' whilst also living as a parasite upon it. A revolutionary world is also an 'upright' world, except maybe in especially apocalyptic times when even anti-social criminals succumb to impulsive patriotism or revolutionary hot-headedness. Thus, as far as the bona fide underworld is concerned, revolutions are little more than unusually good opportunities to perpetrate crime." Eric Hobsbawm, *Bandidos* (Barcelona: Crítica, 2011), 118–19 (in English as *Bandits* [New York: New Press, 2000]).

6 José María Maldonado Moya, *El Frente de Aragón: La Guerra Civil en Aragón (1936–1938)* (Zaragoza: Mira Editores, 2007), 45–46: prior to that a range of small armed bands such as the ones led by Manuel García Prieto or Miguel García García and Francisco Subirats had been raised and marched off their own bat. The July 24, 1936, edition of *La Vanguardia* for instance recounts the departure on the 23rd—a day ahead of the Durruti Column—of a small group of forces. On the other hand, the first column as such to arrive in Aragon from Catalonia was the so-called Hilario-Zamora column from Lérida.

7 Ricardo Sanz recounts the reasons for this: "At one of the meetings called by the Barcelona Local Federation of Anarchist Groups, there was a little surprise waiting for us. One of the recently formed groups there had chosen to name itself 'Los Solidarios.' No one representing the old 'Los Solidarios' group pointed out that the new Local Federation was itself of recent vintage and, furthermore, there being no patent on the name, it was allowed to pass." Ricardo Sanz, *La política y el sindicalismo* (Barcelona: Petronio, 1978), 191. As for the date, the context suggests that this was in 1931, shortly after the proclamation of the Republic: Abel Paz specifically states that it was in May 1931, Abel Paz, *Durruti en la revolución española* (Madrid: La Esfera de los Libros, 2004), 264. Nevertheless, a letter from José Peirats to Fidel Miró states: "The fact that there may have been another 'Los Solidarios' group in the Barcelona L[ocal]F[ederation] may have been down to the real owners of the name not being . . . under its control. The change of name to 'Nosotros' may have been due to their re-entry come the avalanche in 1934 when they could not force the other group to change its name." Fidel Miró, *Catalonia, los trabajadores y el problema de las nacionalidades* (Mexico, 1967), 62. This is backed up by Juan García Oliver: he mentions no specific date but from what he says it can be inferred that entry into the FAI and the change of name came some time in late 1933 or early in 1934, Juan García Oliver, *El eco de los pasos. El anarcosindicalismo en la calle, en el Comité de Milicias, en el gobierno, en el exilio* (Barcelona: Fundació d'Estudis Llibertaris i Anarcosindicalistas, Llibrería La

Rosa de Foc y CNT Catalunya, 2008), 133. Furthermore, in "Letter from José Peirats to Frank Mintz," of June 7, 1985, cited in Stuart Christie's ¡Nosotros los anarquistas!: "As for the involvement of the FAI in the uprisngs, José Peirats, who was secretary of the Barcelona Local Federation of Anarchist Groups at the time, recalls that in the wake of the January 1933 revolt, his local federation asked the Nosotros group to attend a clandestine meeting on Monte Horta to give an accounting for its conduct.... They contended that, even though they did not belong to the organization, they had decided to take part [in the meeting] as a courtesy, nothing more." Peirats added: "As general secretary of the Barcelona groups up until mid-1934, I am in a position to guarantee that neither Durruti, nor García Oliver were members of the specific organization." Stuart Christie, ¡Nosotros los anarquistas! Un estudio de la Federación Anarquista Ibérica (FAI) 1927–1937 (Valencia: Universitat de València, 2010), 144; in English as *We the Anarchists! A Study of The Iberian Anarchist Federation (FAI) 1927–1937* (Oakland: AK Press, 2008).

8 Following his return from exile after the proclamation of the Republic, Ascaso was to join the Los Indomables group.

9 The leading exponents of whom were Federica Montseny, Diego Abad de Santillán, and Pedro Herrera. Agustín Guillamón, *Barricadas en Barcelona: La CNT de la Victoria de Julio de 1936 a la necesaria derrota de Mayo de 1937* (Ediciones Espartaco Internacional, 2007).

I. Armed Agencies and Debates Around Defense of the Revolution During the Second Republic

1 César M. Lorenzo points out that Los Solidarios, during their time in exile in France in the 1920s, formed a group calling itself Los Treinta (nothing to do with the 'Manifesto of the Thirty' and its signatories) for which García Oliver often acted as the spokesman, arguing the need for a "revolutionary army." César M. Lorenzo, *Los anarquistas españoles y el poder 1868–1969* (Paris: Ruedo Ibérico, 1972), 46–48. That claim seems somewhat of a stretch given where they stood at the beginning of the Republic; besides, no mention is made in García Oliver's autobiography, *El eco de los pasos*, of his having pushed that stance for years. Nevertheless, the fact of the matter is that the Arshinov Platform was drafted during that time, specifically in 1926 and may have had some influence on them; even though García Oliver denies any influence on his thinking by that Platform in his interview with Freddy Gómez, *Colección de Historia Oral: El movimiento libertario en España*, 2. (Madrid: Fundación Salvador Seguí, 1990), 14–15.

2 José Álvarez Junco, *La ideología política del anarquismo español (1868–1910)* (Paracuellos de Jarama, Spain: Siglo veintiuno editors, 1991), 255.

3 For instance, in the November/December 1932 and January 1933 issue of the *Boletín de la CNT de España*, dated April 1932 and signed off by the National Committee, one reads: "So the defense of the revolution, sticking to just that, will consist of proper organization of producers of serviceable age, into a regular

army which, after training, will carry out the tasks asked of or assigned [sic] to it.... Domestic threats will be banished once and for all by ensuring that the producers do not give up their arms, not for a single moment, until time has moved on and circumstances dictate otherwise. Only a call sent out to individuals in any locality, or through the free municipality, could be up to to snuffing out any counter-revolutionary intent that some groups might entertain, and a general mobilization call would, in just a few short hours, muster enough manpower and material on the borders to nip foreign interference energetically in the bud. The producers of the future must reject even the slightest suggestion redolent of a predisposition to maintain a standing army for domestic defense." No doubt the failure to go into detail about organization and discipline, which might have been more controversial but at the same time substantial, was deliberate: "Going into a lot of considerations as to the many essential details and [transformations] in order to answer that question would have us transcribing the formulas inherent in Libertarian Communism for resolving issues and might be better dealt with in the appropriate place, which is not in a report which should stick strictly to the essentials drawn from overall reflection upon the matters under consideration." See also in the following footnote for what Bakunin reckoned the "revolutionary army" would look like.

4 "10. This association starts from the conviction that revolutions are never the handiwork of either individuals nor even of secret societies (...) All that a well-organized secret society can do is, first, act as a midwife to the revolution by spreading among the masses ideas that mirror the instinct of masses and organize, not the army of the revolution—the army should always be the people— but a sort of a revolutionary general staff made up of committed, energetic and intelligent individuals and, above all, honest friends of the people, neither ambitious nor vain and capable of acting as conduits between the revolutionary idea and the people's instincts," Mikhail Aleksandrovitch Bakunin, *Estatutos secretos de la Alianza: Programa y objeto de la Organización Revolucionaria de los Hermanos Internacionales* 1868, http://miguelbakunin.wordpress.com. Bakunin said: "the sole purpose of the secret society should be, not to constitute an artificial force outside of the people, but to arouse, marshal, and orchestrate the people's spontaneous forces. In which conditions, the army of the revolution, the only one capable and real, is not separate from the people but the people itself." Mikhail Aleksandrovitch Bakunin, *Carta de Bakunin a Nechayev*, June 1870, http://miguelbakunin.wordpress.com.

5 José Álvarez Junco, *La ideologia política del anarquismo español (1868–1910)* (Paracuellos de Jarama, Spain: Siglo veintiuno editors, 1991), 487–88.

6 Chris Ealham, *La lucha por Barcelona. Clase, cultura y conflicto 1898–1937* (Madrid: Alianza Editorial, 2005), in English as *Anarchism and the City* (Oakland: AK Press, 2010).

7 For an account, see Abel Paz, *Durruti en la revolución española* (Madrid: La Esfera de los Libros, 2004), 284–86. For a taste of the scale of it, see Ramón Salas Larrazábal, *Historia del Ejército Popular de la República* (La Esfera de los Libros, Madrid, 2006), 106: "General Ruiz Trillo's troops sorted the situation out with

cannon-fire: thus the 'Casa Cornelio' in which the anarcho-syndicalists had taken cover was demolished."

8   For a few snippets of their thinking, see Julián Casanova, *De la calle al frente: el anarcosindicalismo en España (1931–1939)* (Barcelona: Crítica, 1997), 87: "The revolution could not be left in the hands of 'more or less daring minorities.' It would grow out of 'a steam-roller movement by the people en masse, by the strides towards final liberation made by the working class, the unions and the Confederation.' Rough-housing and rioting and 'rudimentary preparations' were to give way to forward-planning, discipline, and organization." In the realm of the economy, the plan for National Federations of Industry deserves highlighting: "Joan Peiró . . . had offered a forestaste of his reasoning in the Vigo-based newspaper *¡Despertad!* . . . The national federations of industry would *help* 'focus the proletariat's initiatives and action . . . on a nationwide level of opposition to capitalism' and laying the groundwork for 'the structuring of the economic machinery of the future.'" Julián Casanova, *De la calle al frente*, 25.

9   García Oliver, interviewed in *La Tierra* on October 3, 1931: "Without specifying a date, Oliver went on, we advocate the act of revolution, careless as to whether we were or were not prepared for the making of the revolution and the introduction of libertarian communism. . . . Without at all under-estimating revolutionary preparedness, we see it as secondary because, on the basis of the Mussolini phenomenon in Italy and the fascist experience (Hitler) in Germany, it has been shown that any sort of propaganda and ostensible preparedness for revolutionary action entail parallel preparedness and backlash from fascism. . . . As for revolutionary construction, the CNT should not, on any pretext, postpone the social revolution because in fact some preparations have already been made. Nobody is going to imagine that in the wake of the revolution the factories are to run in reverse, nor will there be any contention that the peasants are going to have to work their fields by using their feet." Stuart Christie, *¡Nosotros los anarquistas!*, 123–24.

10 *Solidaridad Obrera*, April 25, 1931.

11 Paz, *Durruti en la revolución Española*, 333–34.

12 Similarly, Juan García Oliver points out that this proposition emanated from his affinity group. Juan García Oliver, *El eco de los pasos. El anarcosindicalismo en la calle, en el Comité de Milicias, en el gobierno, en el exilio* (Barcelona: Fundació d'Estudis Llibertaris i Anarcosindicalistas, Llibrería La Rosa de Foc y CNT Catalunya, 2008), 129.

13 Alexander Shapiro said: "That National Defense Committee as well as the Regional Defense Committees and the local defense committees are bi-partisan agencies made up of an equal number of representatives from the appropriate confederated bodies plus representatives from the FAI's corresponding organizations. These defense committees . . . had as their sole purpose stockpiling of the arms needed in the event of a uprising, organization of shock groups in the various popular districts, the organization of resistance from troops in their barracks, etc. The Defense Committees had no executive authority. They were to hold themselves solely at the disposal of the CNT once their preparatory efforts had concluded." Alexander Schapiro, *Association Internationale des Travailleurs:*

Notes to pages 8–12

Rapport sur l'activité de la Confédération National Du Travail d'Espagne, 16 December 1932–26 Février 1933.

14   Horacio Martínez Prieto, for instance, points out "The understanding is that once there are no further outside threats, once the world revolution has become a happy fact, we will entirely dismantle the militaristic machine as being inimical to peace between peoples." Horacio Martínez Prieto, *Anarcosindicalismo: cómo afianzaremos la revolución* (Bilbao, 1932).

15   Thus, the very organization that holds the document—the Fondation Pierre Besnard—attaches to it the following note of explanation: "Just as Isaac Puente's libertarian communism spelled out the aspirations of the workers from 1933 to 1939, so this pamphlet from Horacio Prieto set the mold for the top echelons, especially in 1936–1939." The pejorative implication is plain.

16   Martínez Prieto, *Anarcosindicalismo*.

17   Jean Marestan, "Open Letter regarding 'Defense of the Revolution,'" *Tierra y Libertad*, September 2, 1932.

18   Marestan, "Open Letter."

19   Sébastien Faure, "My Reply to Marestan," *Tierra y Libertad*, September 9, 1932.

20   The text within quotation marks comes from the Dielo Truda Group, 113. Grupo Dielo Trouda (Nestor Makhno, Ida Mett, Piotr Archinov, Valevsky, and Linsky), "Plataforma de Organización de la Unión General de Anarquistas (proyecto)" 1926, in *Germinal. Revista de Estudios Libertarios*, October 8, 2009, 112–35, in English at https://libcom.org/article/organisational-platform-general-union-anarchists-draft.

21   Grupo Dielo Trouda, "Platforma." See the section headed "Organizational Part," 132–35.

22   Grupo Dielo Trouda, "Platforma."

23   Self-discipline was one of the principles underpinning the Makhnovist Army, as explained in Piotr Arshinov's *Historia del Movimiento Makhnovista*: "All of the army's disciplinary rules were drawn up by commissions of guerrillas before being endorsed by the army in general and strictly observed as the responsibility of every single revolutionary and every single fighter." Piotr Arshinov, *Historia del Movimiento Makhnovista* (Buenos Aires: Tupac Ediciones-La Malatesta, 2008), 94.

24   In this text, the Group of Russian Anarchists in Exile clarified how this third point was translated into practice: "this army must . . . be utterly subordinate to the workers and should be guided by them, politically speaking. (We stress politically speaking because when it comes to its strategic and military direction, this could only be defined by the military bodies within the ranks of the army itself, which are answerable to the workers' and peasants' organizations.)" Grupo de Anarquistas Rusos en el Extranjero (*Dielo Trouda* editorial committee) *Suplemento a la Plataforma Organizativa (Preguntas y Respuestas)*, November 1926, http://www.nestormakhno.info/spanish, in English at https://libcom.org/library/supplement-to-the-organisational-platform.

25   Matters relating to defense of the revolution. Grupo Dielo Trouda, *Germinal*, 130–32.

Notes to pages 12–14

26   For more about the Platform and its influence in Spain, see Juan Gómez Casas, *Historia de la FAI* (Zero, Madrid, 1977), 108–16. In English as *Anarchist Organization: The History of the F.A.I.* (Montreal: Black Rose Books, 1986).

27   *Suplemento de Tierra y Libertad*, No. 4, November 1932.

28   *Suplemento de Tierra y Libertad*, No. 5, November 1932.

29   According to García Oliver, this strategy was of his devising. See Juan García Oliver: "I had set myself a line to follow inside the Organization [the CNT]: to deem the recently established republic as a bourgeois entity that was to be outstripped by libertarian communism, to which end its stabilization and consolidation had to be frustrated by means of pendulum-style insurgent activity mounted by the working class on its left, which would inevitably be countered by the rightward onslaught from the bourgeois, until the collapse of the bourgeois republic came to pass." Juan García Oliver, *El eco de los pasos*, 115. The accuracy of his prediction suggests that such a strategy may well not have been a notion devised after the fact, one conjured up for the purposes of self-aggrandizement and showing him as a man of great intellect and insight. Nevertheless, there are other sources that show that within the Los Solidarios-Nosotros group at any rate there was a fear that the Republic might achieve stability and thus gain in strength. And that action had to be taken to forestall that. In addition to the quotation at the opening of this chapter, we ought to highlight Hans Magnus Enzensberger and his interview with Federica Montseny on April 21, 1971: "Within days of the proclamation of the Second Republic . . . Durruti, Ascaso and García Oliver came to my home. . . . According to them the Republic should not be afforded time to embed itself . . . that would jeopardize the further development of Spanish society and interrupt the process of revolutionary structural change." Hans Magnus Enzensberger, *El corto verano de la anarquía: Vida y muerte de Durruti* (Barcelona: Anagrama, 2002), 76.

30   Alexander Shapiro: "They wanted to try their hand at a coup d'état, they were out to 'make the social revolution' and had not a care in the world as to whether the conditions in place were suitable or otherwise and above all had not the slightest consideration for the interests of the National Confederation of Labour." Shapiro, *Association Internationale des Travailleurs*.

31   This notion of revolutionary gymnastics has certain connections with the more classical idea of "propaganda by deed," based on the proposition that in order to awaken the rebel potential of the people, the impact of an act of violence is a lot more effective than the spoken or written word, to borrow the definition offered by Juan Avilés Farré. *Francisco Ferrer y Guardia: Pedagogo, anarquista y mártir* (Madrid: Marcial Pons, 2006), 21. (For more about the shaping of the notion, see Juan Avilés Farré and Ángel Herrerín López, *El nacimiento del terrorismo en Occidente: anarquía, nihilismo y violencia revolucionaria* [Torrejón de Ardoz, Spain: Siglo XXI, 2008], 1–4.) Initially, the written word envisaged only insurrections as a method of propaganda rather than individual attentats, but following the rash of anarchist terrorist attacks in the late-nineteenth century and early-twentieth century, it finished up being taken as almost exclusively synonymous with the latter type of activity. García Oliver, *El eco de los pasos*, 115.

Notes to pages 14–15

32 García Oliver, *El eco de los pasos*, 130: "In terms of the purposes of revolutionary gymnastics, failure was non-existent."

33 In *Tierra y Libertad*, March 25, 1932: "in the revolutionary upheavals that we will undoubtedly witness in the future, in the course of which, the bourgeois journalists would have us believe, Spanish anarchism will go on playing its last card. Plainly those bourgeois journalists must be referring to the last card in some never-ending shuffle of the deck."

34 For a detailed description of the preparations and circumstances surrounding the outbreak of revolution, as well as those recriminations, see Shapiro, *Association Internationale des Travailleurs*.

35 This is also pointed out by José Peirats in his article "Did the Spanish libertarian movement, in 1936–1939, foreswear the making of revolution?" and García Oliver, *El eco de los pasos*, 23: "it also requires the emergence of the revolutionary inclinations that were apparent within the Spanish libertarian movement prior to July 1936 . . . for a start, the inclinations of the group headed by García Oliver, Ascaso and Durruti. . . . Theirs was a classically romantic notion along Bakuninist lines. Based on the stroke of daring and taking popular contagion as read. The people carried an innate revolutionary being latent within its subconscious. That had simply to be awakened through the selfless example set by the minorities."

36 Casanova, *De la calle al frente*, 20: "In the words of Manuel Balbé 'the rulers of the republic were incapable of tailoring the administration of public order to the principles of democratic rule', and Casanova, *De la calle al frente*, 22: "The republican authorities displayed a remarkable inability to distinguish between social strife and 'acts of aggression against the Republic.'" Casanova, *De la calle al frente*, 125: "If we burrow into specific, well-documented instances, the profile of the instigator of the uprising and that of those who backed it, were very different. The former was usually over 30 years of age, active in the CNT and affinity groups and was generally nomadic, albeit that he might have had close ties to the locality of which he was headed. The latter were almost always young—or very young, most of them being less than 20 years of age—field hands or construction workers and unmarried, which is to say that, at most they were risking their own lives and rarely those of their families."

37 Julián Casanova, *Anarquismo y revolucion en la Sociedad rural aragonesa, 1936–1938* (Madrid: Siglo Veintiuno Editores, 1985), 2–3: exemplified and buttressed by Ealham, *La lucha por Barcelona*, 165: "During the mobilizations in the summer of 1932, hundreds of thousands of workers joined the Confederation, persuaded that it was the best vehicle for the achievement of their day-to-day material aspirations, which bears out just how much the membership was moulded by the confederal unions' ability to take on the bourgeois, sometimes successfully."

38 José Bonet was a pseudonym of Julián Merino Martínez: see Agustín Guillamón, *La Guerra del pan. Hambre y violencia en la Barcelona revolucionaria. De diciembre de 1936 a mayo de 1937* (Barcelona: Aldarull-Dskntrl-ed!, 2015), 47. "Let's win the people over to the revolution," *Tierra y Libertad*, June 16, 1933.

39 Casanova, *De la calle al frente*, 129. A little earlier, on the same page, he points to

how inhibited the bulk of the trade union membership showed itself when it came to the fighting in the 1933 uprisings.

40   "Revolutions are not decreed from on high: they emanate from below." Shapiro, *Association Internationale des Travailleurs*.

41   Shapiro, *Association Internationale des Travailleurs*: "what is more, the NC, basing itself on the measures that the government was taking, briefed the regionals in a letter of December 29 that, in the event of some region's hoisting the flag of revolt, every other region should follow suit and also revolt."

42   Shapiro, *Association Internationale des Travailleurs*: "Secondly, the responsibility of the CNT's NC is at stake. It allowed itself to be overridden by the Defense Committees and let itself be swayed by various anarchist comrades, personal friends of most of the members of the National Committee. The NC should have prized the Confederation's interests higher than the personal leanings of certain of its members. The NC ought to have deployed all its moral authority to forestall haste at any cost, even at the cost of the gear stockpiled by the Defense Committees."

43   Shapiro, *Association Internationale des Travailleurs*: "The CNT should announce categorically that it will recommend that no agency should remain outside it and, as a result, escape its direct and permanent supervision, and that regardless of the high moral worth of the individuals making up any such agency when it comes to embarking upon revolutionary action on a grand scale."

44   "In Response to a Timely Survey," in *Suplemento de Tierra y Libertad*, No. 7, February 1933.

45   "For the *Tierra y Libertad* Survey," in *Suplemento de Tierra y Libertad*, No. 8, March 1933.

46   Anatol Gorelik "How Anarchists Construe Defense of the Anarchist Social Revolution," *La Revista Blanca*, September 15, 1933. Italics in original.

47   Bari, "Sheer Fascism," *Tierra y Libertad*, October 6, 1933.

48   For more detail on the abstentionist campaign and the arguments used, see Casanova, *De la calle al frente*, 115–17.

49   Joaquín was cousin of Francisco Ascaso, the renowned member of the Los Solidarios-Nosotros group. Joaquín is also remembered for having headed up the Aragon Regional Defense Council.

50   Paz, *Durruti en la revolución española*, 364.

51   Manuel Salas, *20 de noviembre,* Ed. CNT, 1936: his testimony was reinforced for the author by Cipriano Mera: see Paz, *Durruti en la revolución española*, 373: "at a gathering of militants from Zaragoza, doubts were raised as to which groups should be launching the fight. It had been agreed in principle that it should be Zaragoza, promptly backed by the remainder of Lower and Upper Aragon . . . it fell to Durruti's turn to parley with them . . . and he said . . . that if, in that event, Aragon held back, the CNT's entire credibility would be shredded since there was no other region in Spain capable of tackling the fight that they meant to unleash. . . . But—he told them—if it was their view that they should not take part in the uprising, they were free to make that decision. Nevertheless, the CNT and the FAI had made a commitment to the people to go for a trial of strength

and that would proceed, with or without Aragon"; José Peirats, *Los anarquistas en la crisis política española* (Madrid: Ediciones Júcar, 1977), 86: "In the run-up to the elections, in the Monumental Bullring in Barcelona, one of those so-called 'monster' rallies was held with a hundred thousand people in attendance, with the speakers most heeded by the toiling masses: Domingo Germinal, V. Orobón Fernández, and Buenaventura Durruti. The theme was: 'Social revolution versus the ballot box.' Once again, the CNT had to keep faith with the commitment it had given."

52   Paz, *Durruti en la revolución española*, 364: "Durruti was minded that a defeat—which would be no defeat at all from the practical point of view of 'revolutionary gymnastics'—was preferable to standing idly by." Likewise, Enzensberger, *El corto verano de la anarquía*, 80, in his interview with Federica Montseny on April 21, 1917: "Durruti played an active part in all the rebellions and struggles during the time of the Republic. He was of the view that he had to be constantly geeing up the process"; This special emphasis on action within the Los Solidarios-Nosotros group can plainly be discerned in the article "Our Anarchism" by Francisco Ascaso (published by the FAI Peninsular Committee, 1937 and cited in Christie, *¡Nosotros los anarquistas!*, 103: "I have never imagined nor agreed that the issue of intellectual betterment can be resolved by filling one's head with a huge number of theoretical formulas or philosophical notions that will never be put into practice. Even the most beautiful theories only have value if they are based on practical experiences and if they bear upon those experiences in an innovative fashion.... We are in the throes of construction and in order to build we need brawn, maybe more so than mental agility in expressing opinions. I agree that we cannot build without first knowing what it is that we want to do. But I believe that the Spanish proletariat has learnt more from its practical experiences than anything the anarchists put them through and than the latter's publications, which the former have not read.... Our people stand ready to go into action. It will only be able to advance if it moves ahead. Let us not hold it back, not even for the purpose of teaching it prettier theories."

53   As is pointed out by Leon Trotsky, *Historia de la revolución rusa* (Paris: Ruedo Ibérico, 1972), 113: "The vast majority of soldiers feel themselves all the more able to sheathe their bayonets or transfer over to the side of the people, the more convinced they become that the rebels actually are such and that this is not a drill, after which they will have to return to barracks and answer for their actions, that this actually is the struggle in which everything is at stake and that the people can win if they join with it and that its victory will not merely guarantee them impunity but will improve everyone's lot."

54   We might well label this Blanquism, as Diego Abad de Santillán did: "There were enthusiastic and valiant groups who dreamt that they could speed up the process of social change by placing their own sacrifice on the balancing scales: a touch of revolutionary Blanquism with a soupçon of youthful euphoria. But within the CNT there were also men with long records of struggle, who could not countenance zealous, ardent minorities' compromising the entire organization in reckless adventures." Diego Abad de Santillán, *Contribución a la historia del*

Movimiento Obrero Español, VOL. III, Del advenimiento de la Segunda República (1931) a julio de 1936 (Puebla, Mexico: José M Cájica, 1971), 92.

55 For instance, Peirats cautioned: "The revolution should not be a play in several acts. The intervals in the revolution are the breeding grounds of every reaction, from the Napoleonic through to the latest fascist model." "Incitement to Perseverance," *Tierra y Libertad*, February 16, 1934.

56 Cited in Agustín Guillamón, *Los Comités de Defensa de la CNT en Barcelona (1933–1938) De los Cuadros de defensa a los Comités revolucionarios de barriada, las Patrullas de control y las Milicias populares* (Barcelona: Aldarull Edicions, 2011), 1. Actually in libertarian circles there was a double-edged interpretation of the October Revolution. See Casanova, *De la calle al frente*, 138: "On the one hand, there was a sort of an inkling that they had let slip an historic opportunity [as the motion from the DCNC lamented]; on the other there was confirmation that it was not going their way because 'government by the right versus government by the left is not the dilemma; bourgeois republic or libertarian communism is.'" Nevertheless, it seems clear that there was a firm belief that acting through attempted uprisings could not go on: "The socialists were traveling a road that was new to them and even the most radical anarchists suggested that they had given that up already, due to exhaustion: 'We cannot carry on as we have thus far with trial and error. All trials are limited and as far as the FAI is concerned, that limit was reached on December 8, 1933,' declared *Tierra y Libertad* on October 11, by which time everything had ended," Casanova, *De la calle al frente*, 138.

57 As Agustín Guillamón happily phrases it. Guillamón, *Los Comités de Defensa de la CNT*, 20.

58 Guillamón, *Los Comités de Defensa de la CNT*, 11–12.

59 Guillamón, *Los Comités de Defensa de la CNT*, 12.

60 Guillamón, *Los Comités de Defensa de la CNT*, 13.

61 Guillamón, *Los Comités de Defensa de la CNT*, 15.

62 Guillamón, *Los Comités de Defensa de la CNT*, 13–15.

63 Guillamón, *Los Comités de Defensa de la CNT*, 15–16.

64 As would be acknowledged in the submission to the January 1935 Plenum of the Barcelona Federation of Anarchist Groups: "Just as the defense committees have hitherto been primarily shock teams, so from now on they must be bodies capable of scrutinizing the realities of modern warfare." Guillamón, *Los Comités de Defensa de la CNT*, 24.

65 Regarding the CNT at large, see Julián Casanova: "There was organizing and mobilizing capability. However, the National Committee was just a 'correspondence bureau' that found itself incapable of coordinating 'confederal activity across the entire country.' So true was this that if we are to credit its own claims it learnt of disputes, strikes, and protest movements whenever 'The press points them out to us.' In part this was because of the CNT's federal structure as such where, moving from its basic unit, the trade union, up to the apex, i.e. the National Committee, things were processed through a network of local, comarcal, and regional committees that was very hard to oversee." (Casanova, *De la calle al frente*, 70–71).

Notes to pages 21–23

66 Guillamón, *Los Comités de Defensa de la CNT*, 18.
67 Guillamón, *Los Comités de Defensa de la CNT*, 19.
68 Guillamón, *Los Comités de Defensa de la CNT*, 21.
69 Guillamón, *Los Comités de Defensa de la CNT*, 23–24.
70 Guillamón, *Los Comités de Defensa de la CNT*, 22.
71 Guillamón, *Los Comités de Defensa de la CNT*, 22–23.
72 For the decisions of the Congress, see Casas, *Historia de la FAI*, 188–208.
73 Gómez Casas, *Historia de la FAI*, 199.
74 Such as those from Federica Montseny in "Towards a New Dawn for Society" in *La Revista Blanca*, February 15, 1932: "It is a crass mistake to think that fighting in large masses is more effective and powerful in dealing with the enemy than fighting by means of ambush and guerrilla warfare.... Just think of the example of Sandino who managed to hold off the United States for over two years through the use of guerrilla warfare.... Napoleon, victorious around the world, dug the grave of his own empire by wearing himself out in an unequal fight with Iberia's guerrillas who, exploiting the lay of the land, decimated his troops by attacking them from behind.... Spain, the traditional homeland of guerrilla warfare, from Viriatus up to our own day, from Roncesvalles through to San Cornelio, should launch and has already launched into this approach for the sake of the imminent revolution. The fighting needs to be relocated from the cities. There, all we see are only total stoppages that bring business to a standstill or raids that pin troops down. The revolution needs to proceed from the countryside into the city." And in "Andalusia's Red Hour" in *El Luchador* on May 27, 1932, she wrote: "If Andalusia happens to be the first place in Spain where the fire breaks out and the masses there display a modicum of instinct and tact and manage to launch the struggle on the basis of two primitive procedures, *the laudability and uniqueness of which resides in their simplicity*—guerrilla warfare and arson—which will allow them to fight the fight without many losses and spread out across a front that will encompass every province, then the revolution's chances of succeeding in Spain will be that much greater" [italics in the original].
75 It is worth pointing out that at the time of the preparations being made for that uprising, the Los Solidarios-Nosotros group does not seem to have been part of the FAI yet. See Introduction, note 7.
76 See *El Congreso Confederal de Zaragoza* (Bilbao: Zero, 1978), 150.
77 See note 39 above. Also Julián Casanova: "the scant or mis-directed attention that the CNT paid to agrarian matters, an essential issue in a society like Spain's at that time, thwarted its solid expansion in country areas, as compared with the UGT-affiliated National Federation of Land Workers (FNTT). That anarcho-syndicalism during those years, and earlier, had no foothold in country areas is a claim that cannot be contested," Casanova, *De la calle al frente*, 86.
78 As pointed out by Eric Hobsbawm: "Traditionally associated with bandits, 'noble' and otherwise, the Andalusia area turned, one or two decades after their demise, into an area traditionally associated with rural anarchism." Eric Hobsbawm, *Bandidos* (Crítica, Barcelona, 2011).
79 Thus, for instance, for the December uprising, leaflets were printed up containing

a basic revolutionary program and proposing the raising of "an armed worker militia that would render the enemy *hors de combat* and organized along the lines of small, mobile guerrilla bands." Paz, *Durruti en la revolución Española*, 373.

80 One instance of this idea was the plan put forward by J. Puente in "What Our Revolution Should Be Like," *Tierra y Libertad*, April 22, 1932; and further explored by Bernabé Villambiste in "Towards Libertarian Communism" in the same paper on June 10, 1932. Prominent among the "agrarian" school of thought was the Urales family. For Federica Montseny, see note 74 above, as well as Alexander Shapiro: "I remember a conversation I had with Federica Montseny, the elderly militant F. Urales's daughter, who was at the time a public speaker very much in fashion at anarchist and labor meetings and who, whilst not herself a member of the FAI, has boundless admiration for it. Federica Montseny was saying that she had no interest in the towns and that the social revolution would emerge first, and successfully, in the countryside among the peasants without any need for the slightest prior preparation. But when it was drawn to her attention that the peasant revolution was worthless unless it boosted the well-being of the peasant and that that well-being was dependent on the farm machinery that would be furnished to him by the towns, which is to say the industrial working class and that, as a result, the revolution needed making in the towns as well, she was lost for words, the thought never having entered her head before." Shapiro, *Association Internationale des Travailleurs*.

81 Both quotations lifted from José Peirats, *De mi paso por la vida* (Barcelona: Flor del Viento Ediciones, 2009), 366.

82 For an overview of the maquis, Secundino Serrano's *Maquis: historia de la guerrilla antifranquista* (Barcelona: Círculo de Lectores, 2002) is particularly recommended.

83 For the factors and circumstances that facilitated the success of the revolutionaries in Asturias and the so-called "Asturian differences," Paco Ignacio Taibo II's essay in Gabriel Jackson's *Octubre 1934* (Madrid: Siglo Veintiuno, 1985), 231–41, is especially interesting. In addition to the Workers' Alliance, the author flags up the importance of a hitherto overlooked factor: the patient prior effort by the socialists, and, to a lesser but not negligible extent, by anarchists and communists to stockpile arms and organize shock cadres. It was this that created the possibility, once the revolution began, of relying upon a "paramilitary" force which, in confronting and defeating the forces of order, allowed the capture of further arms with which more sympathizers could be armed.

84 "Once Again on the Impossible Union between Anarchists and Socialists," *La Revista Blanca*, June 7, 1935.

85 "For Comrade M. Ramos," *La Revista Blanca*, June 14, 1935 [capitals in original].

86 "For a United Front of the Working Class," *La Revista Blanca*, June 28, 1935.

87 Ricardo Sanz, *La política y el sindicalismo* (Barcelona: Petronio, 1978), 251.

88 Paz, *Durruti en la revolución española*, 450.

89 Evidence from Liberto Callejas cited in Paz, *Durruti en la revolución española*, 450–51. According to Jacinto Toryho, during a plenum of Barcelona anarchist groups held in 1935, Durruti is supposed to have stated: "We will shortly have

a civil war in Spain and we are going to need to rely on militias and even on an army—yes, don't be shocked, let me say it again—with a disciplined, well-organized, and well-armed army if we are going to be able to win." Jacinto Toryho, *No éramos tan malos* (Madrid: G. del Toro, 1975), 72. However, the likeliest proposition is that Toryho in making this claim was out to justify the way in which, from the columns of *Solidaridad Obrera*, as the editor-in-chief of which Toryho had served from November 1936 through to the spring of 1938, the figure of Durruti had been manipulated until, after his death, he had been represented as the "champion" of militarization.

90   García Oliver, *El eco de los pasos*, 137.

91   For the full text see "The Manufacturing and Textile Union of Barcelona on the issues of reconstruction. Motion passed for presentation to the Congress of the National Confederation of Labor," *Solidaridad Obrera*, April 19, 1936.

92   Given that the minutes of the Zaragoza Congress do not record the full proceedings and that García Oliver himself says barely anything in his autobiography regarding his proposal of a revolutionary army, I have, in order to reconstruct it, had to look to the following two sources: the first being Abel Paz (*Durruti en la revolución española*, 431): "The CNT action groups and the anarchist groups were to set up a nationwide defense organization which, starting off from the group, would move on to the centuria as the main unit of the Proletarian Army"; this evidence appears to have come from Liberto Callejas, although that is none too clear from the manner in which it is cited. The second source is the comments about the Local Plenum of Barcelona Anarchist Groups held in July 1936 in Agustín Guillamón's *Los Comités de Defensa de la CNT*, 51–52, where the use by the Nosotros group of the notions of "taking power" and "revolutionary army" come in for criticism: "According to García Oliver the organizing of defense cadres, coordinating as barrio defense committees across the city of Barcelona, was the model to be followed and spread to the entirety of Spain with this structure being coordinated at regional and national levels in order to establish a **revolutionary army** of the proletariat. That army was to be complemented through the setting up of hundred-man guerrilla units" [bold type in the original].

93   Sanz, *Los que fuimos a Madrid*, 252.

94   Sanz, *Los que fuimos a Madrid*, 253.

95   Symptomatic of this approach and the embarrassment at calling a spade a spade was the article by El Pájaro Rojo, "In Defense of the Revolution," in *Solidaridad Obrera* on May 29, 1936: "in the face of the danger of foreign invasion or a capitalist backlash, the people must be armed for the purpose of defending the new regime and, ultimately, armed proletarian battalions raised which, whilst not a regular army, are the guarantors of anarchist ideals. In today's age, resurrecting a guerrilla war is completely out of the question. Given the modern fighting tools available these days, that tactic has nothing positive to offer. In succeeding articles, we shall study the history of the Bulgarian, Russian, Greek, German, Austrian, and Italian revolutions, and the insurgencies in the countries of South America. In every instance we shall find that ultimate success required the adoption of an overall plan involving the materials available." Meaning that he was

Notes to pages 29–31

        suggesting a conventional style of war whilst at the same time denying that the battalions raised to wage it amounted to a regular army: nor does he say they add up to a revolutionary army with certain idiosyncrasies of its own.

96   Ironically, Cipriano Mera would become one of the greatest champions of militarization within the libertarian camp during the civil war. García Oliver, *El eco de los pasos*, 138. See also Sanz, *Los que fuimos a Madrid*, 253: "Comrades Ascaso and García Oliver can let us know which color of general's braid they want."

97   *Congresos anarcosindicalistas en España, 1870–1936* (Toulouse/Paris: Ediciones CNT, 1977), 173.

98   *Congresos anarcosindicalistas en España*, 174.

99   Here *Solidaridad Obrera* did try to inject a note of common sense in the form of its May 26, 1936, article, "Revolutionary Defense: Capitalism throws down a gauntlet to the working class. As revolutionaries let us accept that challenge and, starting here and now, get our forces ready to defend and attack." Relying upon a range of historical examples and quotations from respected anarchists, it championed the existence of a measure of discipline in the groups or battalions raised with an eye to the "general mobilization" referred to in the motion from the recent congress in Zaragoza, albeit that it pointed out that this might be incompatible with the "theory of freedom."

100 *Congresos anarcosindicalistas en España*, 168.

101 César M. Lorenzo, *Los anarquistas españoles y el poder 1868–1969* (Paris: Ruedo Ibérico, 1972), 78. See also, in this connection, the remarks made by Julián Casanova regarding Helmut Rüdiger, the IWA secretary in Spain between 1936 and 1938 who, in his "Materials for discussion on the Spanish situation at the IWA Plenum on June 11, 1937" dubbed "the notion of libertarian communism that the CNT had prior to July 1936 'romantic.'" Casanova, *De la calle al frente*, 156–57. He was to expand upon these arguments in *El anarcosindicalismo en la Revolución Española*, published by the CNT National Committee in Barcelona in 1938, from which Julián Casanova picks out the expression "subversive lyricism," and goes on that, "at the end of the road there was always some great cataclysm imagined, after which an age of bliss would be ushered in" which explains why he identified such thinking as romantic.

102 A particularly eloquent paean to spontaneity during the early period of the war can be found in the article "Findings: The Army and the People" in *Solidaridad Obrera*, August 2, 1936. "The response to the militaristic strategy of having some wretched marionettes, all moving in the same direction, was to have thousands of strategies [the reference is to the fighting in Barcelona against the army rebels]. Each champion of freedom was a strategist. In that action on the part of determined minds prompted by the common good every initiative was explored. The entire military strategy collapsed and roundly failed once the untutored and intuitive strategy of the masses came into play and by adapting their actions to the moment and to each situation, they were able to respond to every attack and operate with unprecedented agility and surefootedness where every move was subordinated to one voice, one order, one bully."

II. Zaragoza Bound: The Revolution Awaits

1. There is a wide-ranging historiographic debate on the term to be used to define the movement initiated on July 17–18, as well as the dictatorship established as a consequence of it. According to Julián Casanova, fascism is identifiable not solely in terms of its outward forms or paraphernalia and it matters that we do not lose sight of the historical context in which it surfaced and the "social function" that it served: bringing a violent end to a crisis of legitimacy for the ruling classes, a crisis ushered in during the period between the wars. "In all three instances [Spain, Italy and Germany] fascism's social function was to stabilize and reinforce capitalist property relations and ensure the social and economic ascendancy of the capitalist class which, at a point of deep-seated crisis, felt itself under threat and was divided and doubtful as to the right means to overcome the crisis and it was ready to forego some of its political power in order to cling to its privileged position." Julián Casanova, "La sombra del franquismo: ignorar la Historia y huir del pasado" in Julián Casanova, et al, *El Pasado oculto, fascismo y violencia en Aragón (1936–1939)* (Zaragoza: Mira, 2001), 35.
2. See *Gaceta de la República*, July 19, https://www.boe.es/buscar.
3. Grandizo Munis, *Jalones de derrota, promesas de victoria: crítica y teoría de la revolución española (1930–1939)* (Bilbao: Zero, 1977).
4. In most instances the coming together of the forces of order and the militias from the left-wing organizations was the key factor in the defeat of the revolt: as is pointed out by Julián Casanova: "The concerted resistance from security forces loyal to the Republic and activists from the political and trade union organizations was crucial in the crushing of the revolt in Barcelona, Madrid, Málaga, Valencia, Gijón or San Sebastián. By contrast, where no such union came about (as in the cases of Seville or Córdoba) or where the Civil Guard and Assault Guard supported the actions of the mutineers (Zaragoza and Valladolid, for instance) the fight was so one-sided that it very soon tilted in the direction of the rebels." Julian Casanova, *De la calle al frente: el anarcosindicalismo en España (1931–1939)* (Barcelona: Crítica, 1997), 155. Even so, every author places a differing emphasis on the importance of such partners. In the case of Barcelona, Agustín Guillamón in *Barricadas en Barcelona* (Ediciones Espartaco Internacional, 2007), 11–69, and *Los Comités de Defensa de la CNT en Barcelona* (Barcelona: Aldarull Edicions, 2011), 54–93, and Abel Paz in *Durruti en la revolución española* (Madrid: La Esfera de los Libros, 2004), 471–79, go into a detailed examination of the clashes, highlighting the pre-eminence of the Defense Committees in the fighting. Whereas Vicente Guarner, as head of the Generalitat's Public Order agencies, plays down the importance of the popular forces, reducing these to a secondary role, and highlighting instead the efforts of the Assault and Civil Guards. Vicente Guarner, *Cataluña en la Guerra de España* (Madrid: G. del Toro, 1975), 103–32.
5. For a couple of accounts from two important public order chiefs in Catalonia that illustrate this situation perfectly, see Guarner, *Cataluña en la Guerra de España*, 139–145; and Frederic Escofet, *Al servei de Catalunya i de la República, Vol. II, La victoria, 19 de juliol 1936* (Paris: Edicions Catalanes de Paris, 1973), 400–03.

6   García Oliver, in a letter to Abel Paz, as cited in Paz, *Durruti en la revolución española*, 510.
7   Allow me to single out the two following reports, one from the trade union organization and the other from the FAI, *Informe y resoluciones de la delegación de la CNT al congreso extraordinario de la AIT, Barcelona, Diciembre 1937* (IISH-CNT-61C1), 96: "A Regional Plenum of Local Federations and Comarcal Committees was held in Barcelona on July 21, 1936, convened by the Regional Committee for Catalonia. It analysed the situation and determined unanimously that there was to be no talk of libertarian communism until the part of Spain that was in the hands of the faction [the rebel military] was recaptured. The Plenum decided therefore that it would not proceed with totalitarian practicalities because it was faced with the dilemma of either imposing its dictatorship, using violence to trample all over those who, alongside it—Guards and militants from other parties—had aided and abetted the victory over the rebel troops on July 19 and 20, which dictatorship would in any case have been overwhelmed from abroad even if imposed at home." And *El Anarquismo en España. Informe del Comité Peninsular de la Federación Anarquista Ibérica al Movimiento Libertario Internacional, 1937* (BPA), 2–3: "How appropriate is it for us to embark upon an experiment in libertarian communism in Catalonia when the war and all the dangers of foreign intervention that all implies are not yet over? . . . It was decided that the antifascist bloc should be preserved and the word went out across the whole region: there is to be no proclamation of libertarian communism. See to it that we retain our hegemony on the antifascist militias committee and postpone any totalitarian pursuit of our ideas."
8   For a collation and analysis of the debates and the arguments raised, see Guillamón, *Barricadas en Barcelona*, 51–76.
9   Julián Casanova, *Anarquismo y violencia política en la España del sglo XX* (Zaragoza: Institución Fernando el Católico, 2007), 74.
10 Here see the following comment in Paz, *Durruti en la revolución española*, 512: "the way for the revolution to succeed was through an effective revolutionary alliance between the CNT and the UGT, meaning—in geographical and social terms—Madrid and Barcelona marching in step with each other. . . . The whole drama of the Spanish revolution resides in the fact that . . . anarchism carried a lot of clout on the one hand and that on the other there was an equally powerful social democracy."
11 The difference between what Companys wanted that committee to be and what the libertarian movement's representatives imposed can be readily understood by comparing the Generalidad decree that introduced it into law (see *Butlletí Oficial de la Generalitat de Catalunya* of July 21, and published in *La Vanguardia* in Castilian the next day) and the foundation decree passed on July 21 by the committee itself and issued as a proclamation (in *La Vanguardia* on July 22 as well), which completely ignored the earlier order and, from item one, introduced "a revolutionary order." Quite a statement of intent.
12 For a fuller exploration of this contradictory body, Agustín Guillamón's overall oeuvre and Enric Mompó's *El Comité Central de Milicias Antifascistas de Cataluña*

Notes to pages 35–36

y la situación de doble poder en los primeros meses de la Guerra civil española (1994), https://www.somnisllibertaris.com/libro/El_Comite_Central_de_Milicias_Antifascistas.htm) are especially interesting.

13 This was the very same decree-proclamation referred to in note 11 above. It literally reads: "Sixth: For the purpose of recruiting personnel for the Antifascist Militias, the organizations making up the Committee are authorized to open appropriate recruitment and training centers."

14 Paz, *Durruti en la revolución Española*, 518–19: "Up until July 21, the barracks and army forts were in the hands of men who had stormed and captured them, meaning, in the hands of the CNT and FAI. When the principle of representation on the Central Antifascist Militias Committee was agreed, a serious mistake was made, to wit, it was left up to each political party to raise its own troops, meaning its own militias, with their own delegates from those parties. This meant that the barracks and the weapons were at the disposal of the political parties. . . . [This] represented the first step in the disarming of the working class." Mompó, *El Comité Central de Milicias Antifascistas*, Section 4.2.1: "The barracks in the possession of the anarcho-syndicalists were later handed over once the Central Antifascist Militias Committee had embraced the principle of representation within its ranks for the various parties and trade unions. . . . At first, the Pedralbes barracks was readied to serve as the nerve center for the organizing of the anarcho-syndicalist militias. The rest of the organizations made up their minds to raise their own militia columns which would be overseen solely by themselves. The barracks and military installations in Barcelona were allocated for that purpose."

15 César M. Lorenzo, *Los anarquistas españoles y el poder 1868–1969* (Paris: Ruedo Ibérico, 1972), 141. It may well be a minor detail, but Juan J. Alcalde points out that the so-called militia battalions "had no centurias, but abided by the same standard scheme for all battalions regardless of their ideologies." Juan J. Alcalde, *Milicias y unidades armadas anarquistas (FAI, FIJL) y anarcosindicalistas (CNT) en la Guerra civil española 1936–1939* (undated), 186, http://www.enxarxa.com/biblioteca.htm.

16 Here we have an interesting comment from a participant in the war on the Francoist side: Ramón Salas Larrazábal, *Historia del Ejército Popular de la República* (La Esfera de los Libros, Madrid, 2006) I, 310–11: "On the opposing side [meaning the rebel side] which was also a motley political bunch, the factions were forced to unify, in terms of military action at any rate, by the Army. . . . There too there was a fragmenting of authority and cantonalism, but in this instance, that was due more to the complete absence of centralizing agencies, than to any craving for dispersion. . . . The Army was to assume power by arrogating to itself both civilian authority and the direction of the war. Any political solution was banished to the future. In the present term, the winning of the war consumed most attention. The political organizations, thwarted from doing anything else, tacitly endorsed this arrangement. Within the Nationalist zone politically distinct armed militias were also formed, but they remained under the absolute control of military commanders."

Notes to pages 37–38

17   "On the Organization of Militias" in *Solidaridad Obrera*, August 5, 1936.

18   Not so much duplication, as Agustín Guillamón points out, as a duality of powers or the existence of a dual power situation brings with it "a ferocious, no-quarter struggle between **two competing poles** out to destroy the rival power" [bold type in the original], something that did not occur. Guillamón, *Barricadas en Barcelona*, 84. Moreover, there never was, as such, a pole around which revolutionary power was centralizing. Agustín Guillamón, *La Revolución de los comités. Hambre y violencia en la Barcelona Revolucionaria. De junio a diciembre de 1936* (Barcelona: El Grillo Libertario-Aldarull, 2012), 491. Besides this term—duplication—was the one used by the CNT delegation in its report to the Extra-ordinary Congress of the IWA to characterize the situation that existed. See *Informe y resoluciones de la delegación de la CNT al congreso extraordinario de la AIT, Bacrelona, Diciembre 1937* (IISH-CNT-61C1), 97: "The thinking was that in order to avoid duplication of powers in the shape of the CAMC and the Generalidad government." Enric Mompó on the other hand, in line with Grandizo Munis (*Jalones de derrota*) does talk about dual powers but places it in the context of the multitude of revolutionary powers that emerged as a result of the defeat of the army revolt and those bodies that championed the republican order, even though he points out that initially the crumbling of the republican State was such that "the duality was not to be found between the ashes of the republican government and the multitudes of committees' governments . . . but between the latter and the leadership committees of the Popular Front workers' organizations." Mompó, *El Comité Central de Milicias Antifascistas*, Section 1.1. In this regard and apropos of the CAMC, he points out: "The Central Militias Committee was a contradictory sort of a body. Born in the heat of the revolution, it was also the product of victorious anarcho-syndicalism's foregoing of power and the inability of the Generalidad government to retain its grip upon it. Captive to this situation, the Central Militias Committee would reflect the duality of powers that existed in Catalonia and throughout the republican zone. Throughout its existence, those two factors would make their impact felt. Having become the ultimate authority in Catalonia, within its ranks it would mirror the evolution, growth and also the demise of the revolutionary process." Mompó, *El Comité Central de Milicias Antifascistas*, Section 6.4.

19   It was rather cynical that, having let slip the chance to organize when he was at the head of the CAMC, García Oliver was, months later, to declare in a talk (*La Noche*, January 25, 1937): "The Spanish proletariat is never going to be independent and will not be able to make a reality of its ideals, unless it can be assured of the independence of the country through the setting up of a revolutionary army. . . . Not that I see this as anything new. When the CNT held its last national congress in Zaragoza, I . . . made the case for the raising of a revolutionary army in the service of our ideals. . . . The guarantee of the Revolution . . . is the raising of the revolutionary army. Had we but had one, the fascists' foolhardy venture would not have lasted this long."

20   During the FAI plenum in June 1936, invoked in note 192 of ch. 1, García Oliver "set out his concept of taking power"; in essence, he stated that once the

Notes to page 38

revolution was under way, the spreading unrest had to be channelled so that it might be boosted and to pre-empt others' exploiting it. Nothing too concrete, we may say. For further details see Guillamón, *Los Comités de Defensa de la CNT*, 46–47.

21   See note 6 above.
22   Albeit that he is mistaken in saying that it took place on July 23; García Oliver, *El eco de los pasos . El anarcosindicalismo en la calle, en el Comité de Milicias, en el gobierno, en el exilio* (Barcelona: Fundació d'Estudis Llibertaris i Anarcosindicalistas, Llibrería La Rosa de Foc y CNT Catalunya, 2008), 185.
23   This characterization turns up repeatedly in libertarian documentation related to this matter.
24   Abel Paz "Against bureaucracy and 'natural leaders,'" quoting from García Oliver, *El eco de los pasos*, 33–37, points out that prior to July 1936 there had been a theoretical ambiguity surrounding the role that the CNT and FAI would play during the revolution and in practice a Bolshevik understanding of it prevailed, because if the thinking was that "these organizations [and most especially the CNT] were to hold sway after the revolution, we would find ourselves with a Bolshevik single party, albeit the party belonging to the anarchists."
25   Mompó, *El Comité Central de Milicias Antifascistas*, Section 3.11.3: "The anarcho-syndicalist leaders were forgetting that, at best, the unions included only the most pugnacious and advanced portion of the labour movement and landless peasantry. The anarcho-syndicalist and socialist trade unions were not channels for the political aspirations of a vast tranche of the workers who had only just arrived on to the political stage with the July revolution. The refusal to expand and democratize the committees left a significant segment of the population with no channels through which to articulate its interests."
26   Mompó, *El Comité Central de Milicias Antifascistas*, Section 3.11.3: "The bewilderment of the CNT at the revolutionary turn that the reaction to the army revolt had taken was accompanied by a deep-seated puzzlement at the popular bodies that had arisen from it. Bodies that had cropped up in the heat of the July revolution were not part of the libertarian model that had been debated at the Zaragoza Congress. . . . If the revolutionary committees were just temporary bodies doomed, sooner or later, to fade away, there was no need to democratize them or turn them into the authentic voices of the workers through democratic election of their members. Nor was there any need to orchestrate and organize them by creating pyramidal power structures, organized from the bottom up. In other words, in denying the need for soviet-type organizations in the Spanish revolution, anarcho-syndicalism, even though it would end up defending the committees from their most impatient adversaries, were condemning them to under-development and thus to decline and extinction." Mompó, *El Comité Central de Milicias Antifascistas*, Section 5.3: "Even as the organizations tied to the Popular Front were agitating for their swift dissolution, the CNT-FAI was looking askance at them. When all is said and done, the libertarian view was that it was the trade unions and not the committee-governments that were the proper channels through which the working classes could express themselves."

27 The quotes are from García Oliver, *El eco de los pasos*, 182.
28 Ricardo Sanz, *La política y el sindicalismo* (Barcelona: Petronio, 1978), 74.
29 He had served as commander of the *Mozos de Escuadra* and was the person appointed to serve as military commander of the aborted Civilian Militias (see the *Butlletí Oficial de la Generalitat de Catalunya* of June 21, reproduced in Castilian in *La Vanguardia* the next day).
30 José María Maldonado Moya, *El Frente de Aragón. La Guerra Civil en Aragón (1936–1938)* (Zaragoza: Mira Editores, 2007), 45, for the words inside quotation marks. For a more detailed exposition of the entire argument, see Maldonado Moya, *El Frente de Aragón*, 41–45.
31 In the further exploration of the army plot and how the revolt went in the Aragonese capital as well as the reasons for its success, these are of interest: José Borrás, *Aragón en la revolución española* (Barcelona: César Viguera, 1983), 86–104; Julián Casanova, *Anarquismo y revolucion en la Sociedad rural aragonesa, 1936–1938* (Madrid: Siglo Veintiuno Editores, 1985), 75–89; Francisco Carrasquer, *Ascaso y Zaragoza. Dos pérdidas: la pérdida* (Zaragoza: Alcaraván, 2003), 11–26.
32 See testimonies in Ronald Fraser, *Recuérdalo tú y recuérdalo a otros. Historia oral de la Guerra civil española* (Crítica, Barcelona, 1979), Vol I, 161 in English as *Blood of Spain: An Oral History of the Spanish Civil War* (New York: Pantheon, 1979).
33 García Oliver, *El eco de los pasos*, 190.
34 See Federica Montseny, letter to the author, cited in Paz, *Durruti en la revolución española*, 509; Gaston Leval in Josep Alemany "On the revolution, July 19, and a famous dilemma," cited in García Oliver, *El eco de los pasos*, 13–22; and José Peirats in *Noir et Rouge. Cahiers d'études anarchistes* 38 (June 1967), in *Historia Libertaria* 4, (March–April 1979); and in the interview included in the *Colección de Historia Oral: El movimiento libertario en España*, 1, (Madrid: Fundación Salvador Seguí, 1989), 35. On the other hand, Juan García Oliver's account is backed up by the testimonies of Antonio Ortiz in José Manuel Márquez Rodríguez and Juan José Gallardo Romero, *Ortiz: general sin dios ni amo* (Barcelona: Editorial Hacer, 1999), 108; and of Ricardo Sanz and Félix Carrasquer in Ronald Fraser, *Recuérdalo tú y recuérdalo a otros*, I, 147–50. On the other hand, though, César M. Lorenzo—based on the report of a contribution by Agustin Souchy at the VIIth IWA Congress as published in *España Libre* on June 3, 1951—points out that, at a Plenum of Local and Comarcal Federations of the Libertarian Movement of Catalonia held in late August 1936, García Oliver had declared himself a "'supporter of the CNT's taking power' … and wanted to see the political parties eliminated, the UGT brought to its heels, the Generalidad abolished and the Militias Committee overhauled with its powers boosted so that it might emerge as the supreme authority," Lorenzo, *Los anarquistas españoles*, 98. Nevertheless, this does not imply that he must necessarily have championed taking power or "going for broke" in July. There is a chance that after gauging the depth of the revolutionary experiences that attempts were being made to pursue, he may have changed his mind. Federica Montseny's testimony points in that direction. Besides, by early August the expedition to Majorca was under way—an operation organized by the Generalitat behind the back of the CAMC and that this too may have

Notes to pages 41–42

impacted on his change of mind; because the operation was tantamount to an outright ignoring of the CAMC's authority and his own as the man in charge at its War department. But none of this is certain. The only documents, if there ever were any, that might cast more light on this matter and perhaps help us discard our doubts once and for all, were the (since vanished) minutes of the Plenums of Local and Comarcal Union Regionals on July 21 and 26 and the joint CNT and FAI Plenum on July 23.

35   Sanz, *La política y el sindicalismo*, 259: "Yes, that was the last gathering of the 'Nosotros' group, that tragic gathering at the Atarazanas where Francisco Ascaso perished. After that, nothing. Absolutely nothing except ingratitude and lack of understanding on every side. We—Paco's closest friends—found it impossible to gather together one single time during the entire war after that. We were not even able to accompany Paco one last time on the day he was buried."

36   Márquez Rodríguez and Gallardo Romero, *Ortiz*, 109. Similarly, Ortiz places the meeting in Gregorio Jover's home whereas García Oliver places it at the Sailing Club, then headquarters of the CAMC.

37   "Ac[ta] de la reunión del Comité Nacional celebrada el día 29 de julio de 1936, a las 10 de la mañana" (IISH-CNT-79B1), 1.

38   Guillamón points out a two-sided change in the defense committees: into militias "which shaped the Aragon front during the early days, promoting the collectivization of the land in the liberated Aragonese villages" and into revolutionary committees which "in every barrio in Barcelona and every village around Catalonia, imposed their 'new revolutionary order.'" Guillamón, *Los Comités de Defensa de la CNT*, 94–96.

39   Paz, *Durruti en la revolución española*, 525. To get a rather less shallow grasp on what such training consisted of and how it worked, see Guarner, *Cataluña en la Guerra de España*, 180: "Inside the premises of the organizations or outside on the streets these people were offered makeshift training by someone who might have been an officer or NCO in the Army; it consisted of a few marches and maneuvers in close order and three abreast, in the launching of guerrilla attacks, in adjusting the sights of rifles and shotguns and how to load and empty the weapon, which many of them were seeing for the very first time. Automatic weapons and mortars were generally operated by those who had handled or seen these arms at close quarters during their military service. Using slings, there was practice in grenade-throwing, with not much attention's being paid to the weight of the stone's matching the actual weight of the grenade. The spectacle was such as to stun any professional soldier." Apart from the bit about marching in formation, this would have applied also to the libertarian columns' training.

40   *La Vanguardia* of July 24 for instance shows Durruti on a visit to a barracks along with Pérez Farrás and exhorting the troops present—actually the Alcantara Infantry Regiment—to come with them to Zaragoza.

41   For the text of his address, see *La Vanguardia*, July 25, 1936.

42   For the Generalitat's possible attempt, see the evidence of Jaume Miravitlles in Fraser, *Recuérdalo tú y recuérdalo a otros*, I, 192: "The idea was raised of involving all of the Civil Guard units still out in the villages. The anarchists got wind of this

Notes to pages 42–43

plan. He [Miravitlles] and Tarradellas, representing the Generalitat, met with Durruti, García Oliver, and Mariano Vázquez from the CNT, who showed up armed. "Try and bring in the Civil Guard and we will call a general strike on the spot. There will be a massacre of Generalitat and Esquerra leaders." The CNT personnel were fully aware that the plan was directed against them, that the Civil Guards would be deployed against them to regain control of the situation."

43 Diego Abad de Santillán, *Por qué perdimos la Guerra* (Madrid: G. del Toro, 1975), 84.

44 Abad de Santillán, *Por qué perdimos la Guerra*, 85.

45 Manuel Grossi Mier, *Cartas de Grossi* (Sariñena, Spain: Sariñena Editorial, 2009), 140.

46 Figures such as the four thousand quoted by Grossi Mier, *Cartas de Grossi*, 35, or José Mira's unbelievable twelve thousand, *Los guerrilleros confederales* (Barcelona: Comité Regional de la CNT, Sección de Propaganda y Prensa, 1937), 73. A year later this latter author, assuming of course that *La 26 División* was actually written by him, slashed this figure to "around two thousand," José Mira/Anónimo, *La 26 División* (Barcelona: Sindicato de la Metalurgía CNT, 1938), 9. See also Vicente Guarner, *Cataluña en la Guerra de España* (Madrid: G. del Toro, 1975), 161; and Paz, *Durruti en la revolución española*, 531.

47 See, for instance, the evidence of José Gabriel in *La vida y muerte en Aragón* (Buenos Aires: Edicions Imán, 1938), 25–26; José Colera, *La Guerre d'Espagne vue de Barcelone. Mémoires d'un garde civil républicain (1936–1939)* (Paris: Editions du Cygne, 2008); and the interviews with Valeriano Conde Ferrer and Pablo Ruiz in *La Noche* of August 26, 1936 and March 24, 1937, respectively. As well as the register in a Lérida hospital of the entries and exits of members of the Column (note 48 below). The July 24, 1936 edition of *La Noche* reported the Assault Guards departing with the column. There is another mention and footage of them in the documentary *Aguiluchos de la FAI. Por tierras de Aragón*, Pt1, minute 12, "*Archivo cinematográfico de la Revolución española. CNT 1936–1939*," Vol. 1, DVD1; Grossi Mier, *Cartas de Grossi*, 35.

48 As is evident in several fragmentary documentary series held at the CDMHS. For a start, there are thirty-nine war credentials from the Column dating back to the CAMC days: one at PS Aragon R4/35 of a CNT militian; another in PS Aragon R52/26 of a CNT member who was also a member of the Unión Republicana Youth, and finally, another thirty-seven at MF/R731—Leg.340/2 (digitalized as PS Barcelona_Generalitat,340,2). Twenty-four of these would be CNT militians, three were from the UGT, and ten have their trade union affiliation records left blank. Secondly, there is a series of pages containing the particulars of members of the 26th (Durruti) Division (see PS Aragon C.138): if we take the ones who had joined between July 24 and October 31, 1936—the latter being the date of the publication by the Generalitat of an order enlisting four contingents using the old traditional recruitment list system (it is worth pointing out that that order was largely ignored as demonstrated by the repeated call-up issued to those contingents in a further decree later on March 20, 1937)—that makes twenty-three fighters from the CNT, one from the UGT, and four unaffiliated. Finally, a listing

of entries and exits from a Lérida hospital where serious illness unrelated to war wounds were treated (also affording us a broader insight into the entire front and not just the sectors where fighting was under way): between November 14 and 30, 1936, (MF/R729-Leg.338/2) some 197 members from the Column were admitted: 167 from the CNT-FAI, ten from the UGT, four from the ERC, three from the GNR (presumably the Republican National Guard, formerly the Civil Guard), five servicemen, two with no particulars recorded and six labeled as foreigners or internationals. Furthermore, http://anarquismo.jimdo.com/carnets-1907-1944 shows a card belonging to a CNT militian still displaying the stamp "Durruti-Farrás Column"; to see it full-scale the image needs to be downloaded and opened.

49 Some anarchist historians such as Abel Paz or Miguel Amorós describe Durruti as a "Delegate" rather than "Commander." But the fact is that Durruti, like every other column commander, signed his paperwork as "Column Commander" (*Jefe*). See his column reviews and payments lists, held at CDHMS (PS Aragon C.85 and 95).

50 Jesús Arnal states: "Within the column, Farrás was barely the equal of a militian in terms of his status," *Por qué fui secretario de Durruti* (Andorra la Vieja, Andorra: Edicions Mirador del Pirineu, 1972), 91; Paz, *Durruti en la revolución española*, 526–27, 538. Particularly enlightening is the complaint recorded by Manuel Grossi Mier: "Once in Barbastro and having met up with Pérez Farrás, the latter said to me: 'I despair entirely about what is going on in our column. . . . We are falling down badly in terms of any sort of discipline. There isn't even the merest hint of orchestration. Everywhere you look there is a group with a captain appointed by itself. They refuse to listen and when confronted come out with the canard that they are a free force with a free command and freedom of action." Grossi Mier, *Cartas de Grossi*, 84. José Mira: "In September 1936, Major Farrás from the *Mozos de Escuadra* and Military Chief of the Column tendered his resignation" (Mira, *La 26 División*, 14). It needs to be added that this resignation must have come after mid-September, since *La Noche* reported on September 16: "Pérez Farrás completes fifty days on the front."

51 Márquez Rodríguez and Gallardo Romero, *Ortiz*, 109–10; and Maldonado Moya, *El Frente de Aragón*, 51.

52 See the documentary *Ortiz, Général sans dieu ni maître* by Ariel Camacho, Phil Casoar, and Laurent Guyot, 1996, Pt. 1, minute 27–28, https://www.youtube.com/watch?v=OnF1POWI6CA. Abel Paz says, apropos of this, that "seventy per cent of the men making up his column were the finest flower of Barcelona's young anarchists," Paz, *Durruti en la revolución española*, 532.

53 For a listing of these detachments, see José Manuel Martínez Bande: although he offers no figures for how many personnel they had, it is clear that, altogether, they represented a sizable force. José Manuel Martínez Bande, *La invasión de Aragón y el desembarco en Mallorca* (Madrid: Editorial San Martín, 1989), 45–46.

54 Abad de Santillán, *Por qué perdimos la Guerra*, 85.

55 Abad de Santillán, *Por qué perdimos la Guerra*, 42: "what preoccupied virtually the entirety of the high command of our organizations' leaders [he means the anarchists] was a preoccupation shared by the leaders of all the parties, none of

Notes to pages 44–46

whom wanted to dispatch their most representative figures to the front, subscribing to the same poor understanding that they needed to keep their wits about them for the carve-up. An undercurrent of politicking surfaced in the rearguard that might disgust the professional pliers of the old political trade." Guarner, *Cataluña en la Guerra de España*, 141: "This mass and the proletarian organizations and even their leaders were all equal believers that the war was all but won and every trade union or party was beavering away on the stockpiling of arms so that they could gain the upper hand in the post-war period."

56 Abad de Santillán, *Por qué perdimos la Guerra*, 90.

57 Maldonado Moya, *El Frente de Aragón*, 48–49: for a broader view of the columns that arrived in Aragon from Catalonia and Valencia.

58 The expression comes from Vicente Guarner: "The spirit of revolution had infiltrated into the Public Order forces, which it seems were still organized, and the military units that, from the very outset, headed off to Aragon and had been 'dispersed as militians' throughout the popular columns." Guarner, *Cataluña en la Guerra de España*, 158.

59 For an example bearing on the Durruti Column, see Hans Magnus Enzensbeger: the April 23, 1971, interview with Ricardo Rionda Castro, a member of the columns' War Committee and future political commissar of the Division: "Yes, we went to Madrid. And what did we see on the streets? Some cretin ordering four or five guys to go right, go left, every one of them brandishing a rifle. It was too much! We soon put a stop to that situation. 'What? Have you lost your mind? We haven't come here to square-bash. We're off to the front lines!'" Hans Magnus Enzensberger, *El corto verano de la anarquía: Vida y muerte de Durruti* (Barcelona: Anagrama, 2002), 229.

60 Pelai Pagès i Blanch, "Manuel Grossi and the POUM's militias" in Grossi Mier, *Cartas de Grossi*, 15. For instance, George Orwell, a volunteer with a POUM column, pointed out that "within the militias an attempt was made to establish a sort of temporary model of a classless society. Of course, there was no perfect equality, but it came as close to that as I have ever experienced or that struck me as conceivable in war-time." George Orwell, *Homenaje a Cataluna* (Barcelona: Virus Editorial, 2003), 46.

61 As acknowledged by Guarner, *Cataluña en la Guerra de España*, 178.

62 Juan García Oliver, *El eco de los pasos*, 194.

63 There is a striking example from the Durruti Column from Simone Weil: "Orders [from Durruti]: Obey the 'military expert.' Heated arguments. Organization: elected delegates. Devoid of competence. Devoid of authority. Not enforcing respect for the military expert's authority." Simone Weil, *Escritos históricos y políticos* (Editorial Trotta, Madrid, 2007), 512.

64 Grossi Mier, *Cartas de Grossi*, 39–40.

65 Equally revealing here is the interview "Two Million Anarchists Fighting for the Revolution, Declares One Spanish Leader," *Toronto Star* August 18, 1936, cited in Abel Paz, *Durruti en la revolución española*, 529: "Van Paassen asked whether he [Durruti] reckoned that the rebel military had already been beaten: 'No, we have not beaten them yet. . . . Two or three weeks from now we will be committed to

143

decisive battles: 'Two or three weeks?,' the journalist asked, intrigued. 'Two or three weeks, or maybe a month,' Durruti argued. 'The struggle will last for the entire month of August, at least.'" Even though the latest research suggests that this interview was fictitious—see for instance, "Pierre Van Paassen, in *Toronto Star* (Canada) August 18, 1936, and Durruti on the Aragon Front" by Manel Aisa Pàmpols in *Orto. Revista cultural de ideas acratas*, No. 202, July–September 2021—it still captures the atmosphere of the times and the most widely held view.

66   The account of a Caspe native who was an eyewitness to the events: Agustín Camón, *Crónicas del 36* (Zaragoza: Mira Editores, 2000), 27–39. Another account of the Durruti Column's involvement in the taking of Caspe, differing in some particulars from the former can be found in José Mira, *Los guerrilleros confederales* (Barcelona: Comité Regional de la CNT, Sección de Propaganda y Prensa, 1937), 107–08. For the group of militians that were first to reach Caspe, see Paz, *Durruti en la revolución española*, 535; and Los Gimenólogues, *En busca de los Hijos de la Noche. Notas sobre los Recuerdos de la Guerra de España de Antoine Gimenez* (Logroño, Spain: Pepitas de calabaza, 2009), 242.

67   Mira, *Los guerrilleros confederales*, 108. On what happened during the first few days after the rebellion and before the arrival of the Durruti Column in the area, see Borrás and therefore somewhat after it reached Bujaraloz. Borrás, *Aragón en la revolución española*, 112–14.

68   Paz points out that it reached Bujaraloz on July 27 (*Durruti en la revolución española*, 535): however, an act of homage offered to Durruti in Bujaraloz on April 4, 1937, indicates that it was a day earlier than that, since a plaque was unveiled that read: "Bujaraloz remembers the courageous Buenaventura Durruti. His headquarters were established on these premises on July 26, 1936," *Solidaridad Obrera* and *Via Libre* of April 6 and 17, 1937, respectively. As for La Almolda, José Luis Ledesma gives the date of July 25, José Luis Ledesma, *Los días de llamas de la revolución. Violencia y política en la retaguardia republicana de Zaragoza durante la Guerra civil* (Zaragoza: Institución Fernando e Católico, 2002); but given the date of arrival in Bujaraloz, it would make more sense to think that he entered that village on the 26th, as pointed out by Borrás, *Aragón en la revolución española*, 113.

69   For differing accounts of this episode, see Paz, *Durruti en la revolución española*, 536; Grossi Mier, *Cartas de Grossi*, 41; García Oliver, *El eco de los pasos*, 197; Sanz, *La política y el sindicalismo*, 260; Mira, *Los guerrilleros confederales*, 110; and Arnal, *Por qué fui secretario de Durruti*, 86–87.

70   Paz, *Durruti en la revolución española*, 536: Los Gimenólogues, *En busca de los Hijos de la Noche*, 243: in this regard, Miguel Amorós mentions that "it was at this point that the Durruti Column proper was born."

71   Paz, *Durruti en la revolución española*, 539: reconstructed on foot of the testimonies of Liberto Ros and Pablo Ruiz.

72   Mercedes de los Santos Ortega and Javier Ortega Pérez, *El devenir revolucionario de Buenaventura Durruti. Durruti y las tradiciones del antimilitarismo* (Estella, Spain: Hiru, 1997), 129.

73   We should mention in passing that on August 3, the CAMC, at the instigation of

Vicente Guarner, sent the Durruti Column its congratulations "upon its discipline and sense of organization." Minutes in *Various Authors, Ordre public i violència a Catalunya (1936–1937)* (Barcelona: Edicions DAU, 2011), 58.

74   *Solidaridad Obrera*, August 14, 1936.
75   Paz, *Durruti en la revolución española*, 532.
76   Mira/Anónimo, *La 26 División*, 9.
77   Alejandro Soteras Marín, *Mis memorias* (Zaragoza: Asociación Casa Libertad de Gurrea de Gállego, 2003), 49.
78   In "Fighting Capability and War Tactics" in *Solidaridad Obrera* of August 14, there was already reference to twenty-five-man groups. Likewise, Abel Paz, in his description of the column in mid-August, also indicates that the centurias were broken up into twenty-five-man groups and not ten-man teams (Paz, *Durruti en la revolución española*, 542). Finally, in "Notes from the Front" in *Solidaridad Obrera* of September 6, we can again read of the Durruti Column's centurias being split up into twenty-five-man groups.
79   "The Column's structure or organization was being worked out on the hoof with whatever did not work being discarded and replaced by a different approach that did the job better. It was a process of trial and error that had begun as early as July 22, when the first adjustments were being made to the volunteers reporting to the unions. Authorship of it could not be credited to anyone, because it had been a collective effort, with everyone contributing whatever came to mind." Paz, *Durruti en la revolución española*, 544.
80   For further details of the column's organization, see Paz, *Durruti en la revolución española*, 542–45.
81   Not that such imitation was wholesale and the various libertarian columns differed from one to another: for instance, the Iron Column had no agrupacións, only centurias, the aim being to foster a more direct sort of internal democracy in that the delegates from the *centurias* dealt directly with the War Committee. Abel Paz, *Crónica de la Columna de Hierro* (Barcelona: Virus Editorial, 2004), 94.
82   Mompó, *El Comité Central de Milicias Antifascistas*, Section 4.4.1.
83   Los Gimenólogues, *En busca de los Hijos de la Noche*, 288.
84   *Los guerrilleros confederales* contains some information regarding La Banda Negra, which was made up of metalworkers (Mira, *Los guerrilleros confederales*, 112). It represented a sort of a flying assault team, but it also stood out on account of its involvement in the repression carried out in the rearguard (Ledesma, *Los días de llamas de la revolución*, 107, 142). Furthermore, it looks as if the name "Sons of Night" was a generic title bestowed upon guerrilla groups of the sort that customarily mounted raids under cover of darkness: see Ramón Rufat, *Espions de la République* (Paris: Allia, 1990), 27–28; and Los Gimenólogues, *En busca de los Hijos de la Noche*, 287.
85   See the report in *Solidaridad Obrera* on August 9; for a more detailed description of how these villages were captured, see the August 11 edition of the same paper.
86   *Solidaridad Obrera*, August 13. For a description of the entry into the village written by one of the militians involved, see Manuel Ramos, *Una vida azarosa. 44 años de exilio en Francia* (Sant Feliu de Guixols: self-published, 1993), 49.

87 *Solidaridad Obrera*, August 15.
88 Guarner, *Cataluña en la Guerra de España*, 162.
89 Mira, *Los guerrilleros confederales*, 111.
90 Federica Montseny tells of a meeting held at the Casa CNT-FAI in late July or early August 1936 (albeit that she incorrectly refers to García Oliver's being in post as secretary of the Generalitat's Defense Department at the time), at which García Oliver and the Catalan CNT overall opposed Durruti's plans regarding an effort to capture Zaragoza, see Federica Montseny, *Mis primeros cuarenta años* (Esplugues de Llobregat, Spain: Plaza & Janés Editores, 1987), 109. Hans Magnus Enzensaberger, in his interview with Federica Montseny on April 21, 1971, also appears to be referring to the same episode: he points out "Durruti was out to attack Zaragoza from Yelsa [Gelsa]" and "García Oliver, the then secretary of the Militias Committee in Catalonia, was against that." Enzensberger, *El corto verano de la anarquía*, 174.
91 Paz, *Durruti en la revolución española*, 542–45 and Mira/Anónimo, *La 26 División*, 9–13.
92 Maldonado Moya, *El Frente de Aragón*, 87. According to Vicente Guarner there were "between 2,000 and 2,500" of them (Guarner, *Cataluña en la Guerra de España*, 162).
93 In "Escapee from Zaragoza Speaks" in *Solidaridad Obrera* on September 26, 1936, the fugitive in question recounts how "the general strike lasted for a fortnight." Francisco Carrasquer points out that the strike held out for ten days, which is still a reasonable length of time (Carrasquer, *Ascaso y Zaragoza*, 26). "Comrade Durruti" in *La Noche*, September 10, 1936: in this interview Durruti explained that he had brought up some barges, since the bridges had been blown up and that he would shortly be trying to cross the river in order to operate on the far bank.
94 Abad de Santillán, *Por qué perdimos la Guerra*, 138.
95 The best available assessment of his strategic capabilities may well be that coming from Ricardo Sanz, his fellow group member who was to take over command from him. In an interview on April 22, 1974, with Hans Enzensberger, he states: "He was no general; none of us was. We had had a pretty good grasp of urban guerrilla warfare in Barcelona and elsewhere, of streetfighting surrounded by a population familiar to us and where we knew there is a hiding place there, that yonder news vendor on the corner was a comrade and that's the police station across the street; arms dumps, the warehouses down by the docks, we knew the terrain well. But out in the countryside, at altitude, what with the trenches and ordnance maps, we did not have much of a clue; that was not our strongpoint and, besides, why would it have been? Prior to the army's coup attempt we had not needed any of that. No, we were no great strategists. And neither was Durruti." Enzensberger, *El corto verano de la anarquía*, 133–34.
96 It is unclear whether such cooperation from the Marine Transport Union was secured by trickery, by leading it to believe that the CAMC was behind the operation or whether it was simply acting off its own bat. García Oliver even insinuates that it may well have been a plot in which his leading enemies within the libertarian movement—Federica Montseny, Abad de Santillán, and his group—were

involved, the purpose being to discredit the CAMC and García Oliver. García Oliver, *El eco de los pasos*, 238–46.

97 Particularly interesting on this expedition is the summary and analysis offered by Mompó, *El Comité Central de Milicias Antifascistas*, Section 4.4.5. Likewise, see the expedition commander, Alberto Bayo's statement to the CAMC following his return after it was defeated. Agustín Guillamón, *La Revolución de los comités*, 184–85.

98 There is no question but that the headlines in the press over the first few days largely contributed to this feeling of failure and of disappointed expectations. For instance, on July 24, *Solidaridad Obrera* reported: "The murderous fascists in Zaragoza will shortly be in the clutches of the proletariat": on July 27, the headlines screamed: "At the very gates of Zaragoza!... The Aragonese capital will very shortly be free of its executioners"; and on August 4: "Zaragoza on the verge of surrender."

99 Juan García Oliver gives no date for when that plenum took place; all that we can glean from his account is that it was prior to the setting up of the Aragon Front War Committee, which occurred around mid-August. García Oliver, *El eco de los pasos*, 265–68.

100 *Informe y resoluciones de la delegación de la CNT al congreso extraordinario de la AIT, Barcelona, Diciembre 1937* (IISH-CNT-61C1), 97.

101 For more detail, see Guillamón, *La Revolución de los comités*, 141–44; and the extract from the "*Acta del Pleno Regional de Grupos Anarquistas de Cataluña, celebrado en Barcelona el 21 de Agosto de 1936*" (SA-PS Bilbao 39/25) in which the decision made by the plenum on the 17th to disband the CAMC was endorsed and there was some more discussion of the Councils and Commissions arrangement that was due to replace it.

102 Julián Casanova, *De la calle al frente*, 177.

103 Lorenzo, *Los anarquistas españoles*, 199: "The CNT had to share in political power, not in order to take control of it, but to thwart others from so doing and using it against anarchism." This notion was very present in all of the reports and debates turning on the taking of power and whether or not to participate in government. For some examples and further details, see Burnett Bolloten, *La Revolución Española. Sus origenes, la izquierda y la lucha por el poder durante la Guerra civil 1936–1939* (Barcelona: Grijalbo, 1980), 288–90. Likewise the following extract from the *Informe y resoluciones de la delegación de a CNT al congreso extraordinario de la AIT, Barcelona, Diciembre 1937* (IISH-CNT- 61C1), 60, deserves highlighting: "with capitalism overthrown and being obliged to direct and manage a very considerable portion of the nation's assets, we were in no position to dispense with the extraordinary powers of the State if we were to hold onto our gains, be able to regulate the operation of the factories, the collectives, transportation."

104 Lorenzo, *Los anarquistas españoles*, 181.

105 As acknowledged in *El anarquismo en España. Informe del Comité Peninsular de la Federación Anarquista Ibérica al Movimiento Libertario Internacional, 1937* [BPA], 7: "The new government established was dubbed the Generalidad Council to make it more palatable to us and circumnavigate the last shibboleth we needed

to overcome. We soon saw, though, that in Catalonia we had forced the dropping of the word Government—ultimately, childishness, since, call it whatever you like, the purpose it served was that of a government—elsewhere in loyalist Spain things did not go the same way."

106   Lorenzo, *Los anarquistas españoles*, 183–85; and Julián Casanova, *De la calle al frente*, 178–81.
107   As pointed out by Francisco Largo Caballero himself, *Mis recuerdos. Cartas a un amigo* (Mexico City: Ediciones Unidad, 1976), 175.
108   Julián Casanova, *De la calle al frente*, 193.
109   For more detail regarding this governing body, see Casanova, *Anarquismo y violencia política*.
110   Take for instance, the Durruti Column militian Francisco Carrasquer (*Ascaso y Zaragoza*, 63–64).
111   See "Durruti in Madrid" in *Solidaridad Obrera*, October 8, 1936.
112   Abraham Guillén, commissar with Cipriano Mera's Army Corps and a prestigious military analyst and theoretician of urban guerrilla warfare, posits that the path to victory entailed waging a revolutionary form of warfare combining conventional operations and large-scale guerrilla operations, the former mounted by the units of a regular army and the latter by more informal popular forces. Agustín Guillamón, *La Revolución de los comités*. Given the enemy's numerical superiority, what should never be done is taking him on in a sheerly conventional war. Anthony Beevor, *La Guerra Civil Española* (Barcelona: Crítica, 2006), 679, and Michael Alpert, *El ejército republican en la guerra civil* (Paris: Ruedo Iberico, 1977), 294–96, do not go quite so far, but do agree that the so-called republican side generally failed to cash in on the opportunities offered by guerrilla warfare.
113   Márquez Rodríguez and Gallardo Romero devote a brief aside to talking about the Ortiz Column's guerrilla teams (*Ortiz*, 124–26). Regarding one of the best known of these groups—Los Iguales—and especially its leader, Agustín Remiro, see Antonio Téllez Solá, *Agustín Remiro. De la guerrilla confederal a los servicios secretos británicos* (Zaragoza: Diputacion Provincial de Zaragoza, 2006).
114   Bear in mind the oft-cited Confidential Order No 1 issued by Mola on the eve of the army revolt: "It is to be borne in mind that the action has to be of extreme violence in order to break the enemy, who is strong and well-organized, as early as possible. Naturally, all of the leaderships of the political parties, societies, or trade unions not supportive of the Revolt are to be jailed, with exemplary punishment inflicted upon said persons in order to snuff out attempts at rebellion or strikes." See also the testimony of the Marqués de Marchelina in Fraser, *Recuérdalo tú y recuérdalo a otros*, I, 215: "Repression is a military tactic that, unfortunately, has been replicated in every war, a way of asserting authority, a dismal law of warfare. For the military, the problem boiled down to their forces initially being quite few, and therefore discipline had to be enforced. At the outset, the outcome of the war did not seem all that certain and the slightest vacillation might have proved fatal: sabotage attacks, bombings, even guerrilla campaigns might have erupted."
115   During a talk transcribed in *Acracia* of October 23, 1936, José Peirats had this to say: "Our classical guerrilla tactics are no longer of use in the war. Our warfare

is characterized by its being identified with every war. . . . Past the enemy's advance positions, after three months of relentless 'mopping-up,' we ought not to expect to hear a single friendly voice. The enemy is not easily attacked from his rear. . . . So guerrilla warfare is an anachronism these days. We must use military expertise against the fascists' military tactics."

116 Paz, *Durruti en la revolución española*, 565–67: the author reconstructs that interview on the basis of a number of eye-witnesses, including Francisco Subirats. For the correspondent's own version, see Mikhal Koltsov, *Diario de la guerra de España* (Barcelona: Planeta, 2009), 41: "He stated [Durruti] that the column is well-armed and has access to lots of ammunition"; very different, as one can see. However this testimony, like lots of others in his book, was not designed for verisimilitude. Koltsov, out to praise the communists and discredit their political enemies, engaged in manipulation and concoction on such a scale that even his pro-communist compatriot Ilya Ehrenburg was moved to say of his book that "it is of no historical merit." Ilya Ehrenburg, *La nuit tombe*, cited in Paz, *Durruti en la revolución española*, 565. It is also worth highlighting the following testimony concerning late August, Mira/Anónimo, *La 26 División*, 10: "For a long time, the very deficient and incomplete supply of arms was [sic] an ongoing and basic preoccupation. Had arms been available in abundance, the number of men joining the Column as volunteers might have been doubled. Ammunition remained in short supply and on occasion plumbed critical depths with some operations that had been launched superbly foundering for that very reason." Likewise, Alejandro Soteras Marín: "One day, prompted by an irrepressible urge to press on to Zaragoza, another two lads and I were moved to have a word with Durruti . . . Durruti welcomed us and explained the reasons behind those fighters' untoward inactivity: "One cannot fight bare-handed against a better armed enemy who is waiting for us. We are short of munitions and we are even short of weapons for a lot of people." Alejandro Soteras Marín, *Mis memorias* (Zaragoza: Asociación Casa Libertad de Gurrea de Gállego, 2003), 50.

117 The quotation comes from Diego Abad de Santillán, *Por qué perdimos la Guerra*, 138. Similarly, in keeping with the testimony above see Ricardo Sanz, *Buenaventura Durruti* (Toulouse: 1945), cited in Enzensberger, *El corto verano de la anarquía*, 152–53.

118 As José Mira says: "During the month of August . . . our forces were left to stagnate for want of ammunition and other war materials. . . . Thwarted from launching ventures of note, our Durruti took the initiative of implementing war on a small scale, or guerrilla warfare," Mira, *Los guerrilleros confederales*, 118.

119 Los Gimenólogues, *En busca de los Hijos de la Noche*, 287, as they point out: "Antoine Gimenez used the characterization of 'black bonnets' to refer to his group [but] there is every indication that he was one of the 'Sons of Night.'" For another couple of that group's later operations see Mira, *Los guerrilleros confederales*, 119, and *El Frente* of February 15, 1937. These operations are recounted in abundant detail in Antoine Gimenez, *Del amor, la Guerra y la revolución. Recuerdos de la Guerra de España del 19 de julio de 1936 al 9 de febrero de 1939* (Logroño, Spain: Pepitas de calabaza, 2009), 71–77.

Notes to pages 55–57

120   The first related to the proclamation covering the "commandeering of all manner of weapons of war and munitions," issued by the CAMC and published on August 25 in the press, in, say, *La Vanguardia* or *Solidaridad Obrera*. Previously, a Regional Plenum of the Anarchist Groups of Catalonia had decided to ship all available weapons up to the front, more details in "Acta del Pleno Regional de los Grupos Anarquistas de Catraluña, celebrado en Barcelona el 21 de Agosto de 1936" (SA—PS Bilbao 39/25) cited in Guillamón, *La Revolución de los comités*, 145.

121   See, for instance, *La Noche*, September 5, 1936, and *Solidaridad Obrera*, September 12, 1936.

122   *El Frente*, August 27, 1936: "Arms are needed in the front lines for the fight against the fascist scum and not for military parades in the city. At this singular time [every] weapon denied to those who give their lives to crush the fascists is an act of betrayal of the revolution." On October 9, 1936, *El Frente* called for: "FEWER CEREMONIAL MARCHES AND MORE ATTENTION TO THE IMPERATIVE OF THE DAY: ALL ARMS TO THE FRONT!"

123   For more details of this incident see Paz, *Durruti en la revolución española*, 579–80; Abad de Santillán, *Por qué perdimos la Guerra*, 91; Miguel Amorós, *Francisco Carreño y los arduos caminos de la anarquía* (Vitoria, Spain: Asociación Isaac Puente, 2013), 37; and Fraser, *Recuérdalo tú y recuérdalo a otros*, I, 182.

124   See the *Manifesto* published by the Barcelona Defense Committees that September, cited by Paz: "While the Revolution has yet to resolve the issue of political power and there is an armed force obedient to the orders of the Madrid Government which is not subject to the oversight of the workers, the *defense groups* [italics in the original] will not lay down their arms because these constitute the defense and guarantee of revolutionary gains." Paz, *Durruti en la revolución española*, 579. Meaning the Civil Guard (relaunched as the Republican National Guard under a decree published in the *Gaceta de la República* on August 31, 1936—the Assault Guards and the *Mozos de Escuadra*. See "Reunión del Comité realizada el día 22 de Agosto de 1936" (IISH-FAI-CP-17- B10); "Reunión de Comités, celebrada el día 30 de octubre de 1936" (IISH-CNT-94-D11); and "Acta del Pleno de Grupos anarquistas celebrado el día 13 de los Corrientes en la Casa CNT-FAI (Barcelona. 13 noviembre 1936)" (IISH-CNT), cited in Guillamón, *La Revolución de los comités*, 150, 353, and 393, respectively.

125   Guillamón, *La Revolución de los comités*, 85: Guillamón points out once the army revolt had been put down in Barcelona, "within days upwards of one hundred and fifty thousand volunteers had signed on to fight the army mutiny wherever required."

126   Fraser, *Recuérdalo tú y recuérdalo a otros*, I, 182.

127   Per Juan García Oliver: "an army with reserves but with plentiful munitions is more effective than one with huge units in reserve but running short of munitions." García Oliver, *El eco de los pasos*, 272.

128   Abad de Santillán, *Por qué perdimos la Guerra*, 139.

129   Jacques de Gaule (pseudonym of Juan Gómez Casas), *El frente de Aragón 1937–1938* (Madrid: Círculo de Amigos de Historia, 1973), 100.

130 For a detailed study, see Francisco Javier Madariaga Fernández, *Las industrias de guerra de Cataluña durante la Guerra civil*, Thesis, Universitat Rovira i Virgili, 2003, http://www.tdx.cat.

131 Abad de Santillán, *Por qué perdimos la Guerra*, 150. See also Mompó, *El Comité Central de Milicias Antifascistas*, Section 3.9: "The response from the Madrid government was categorical and revealed the state republican authorities' stance. 'Catalonia will never make cartridges.'" Ultimately, with regard not only to the case of the Toledo munitions plant but also to the overall boycotting of the libertarian movement by the central government, there is also the highly revealing report from Eugenio Vallejo Isla—a member of Catalonia's War Industries Commission—to the Regional Plenum of Anarchist Groups of Catalonia on February 14, 1937. *Actos de los Plenos Regionales de Grupos Anarquistas de Cataluña, celebrados los días 6 de diciembre de 1936 y febrero de 1937* (pamphlet) (Barcelona, June 1937), cited in Agustín Guillamón, *Los Amigos de Durruti. Historia y antología de textos* (Barcelona: Aldarull-Dskntrl-ed!, 2013), 259–60.

132 Márquez Rodríguez and Gallardo Romero, *Ortiz*, 115–17: "Do you think that I am about to hand you this money so that you can arm the FAI and mount a coup d'état against me?" That was what Largo Caballero flung into Ortiz's face when the latter approached him in late September with a proposition to purchase arms from a central European consortium with which the general secretary of the IWA, Pierre Besnard had put him in touch. The arms would be destined for the whole of Spain, but Largo Caballero had his doubts because the arms would be transiting across the Catalan border: "If the arms go in via Catalonia, in Catalonia they will stay," Pierre Besnard, cited by Paz, *Durruti en la revolución española*, 598–603, 608. After that initial fruitless overture and within a few days of it, Durruti and Besnard showed up in the company of the agents of the aforementioned consortium for a meeting with Largo Caballero. Things went better this time and the cabinet agreed to place an order to the tune of 1,600 million, with one third of the gear to remain in Catalonia and Aragon. However, with things at that stage, in stepped the Russians and "Largo Caballero—who in actual fact was none too keen on our proposition—must have let himself be persuaded, or else Rosemberg [the Soviet ambassador] *managed to persuade him* that it was more important to wait for disinterested aid from Russia" [italics in the original], and "The Russians . . . even went so far as to depict the vendors as agents of Franco." The likelihood is that this was a set-up or a fraud (something that was commonplace, by the way): the *Informe y resoluciones de la delegación de la CNT al congreso extraordinario de la AIT, Barcelona, Diciembre 1937* (IISH-CNT-61C1), 14, described the consortium involved as a "ghostly entity," which does nothing to diminish the—quite reasonable—mistrust felt by the central government towards the regions of Aragon and Catalonia and its grounds for boycotting them.

133 See note 105 above.

134 Abad de Santillán, *Por qué perdimos la Guerra*, 143–44: "After several months of fighting and of dead-end incidents with the central government . . . when we were told repeatedly that we would receive no help from it as long as the Militias

Notes to pages 58–59

Committee's power was so blatant ... we were obliged to give in. ... Anything just to secure the arms and financial help to prosecute our war successfully." Abad de Santillán, cited in Paz, *Durruti en la revolución española*, 588–89: "In response to our asking for hard currency, we were constantly being told by the central government (Giral or Largo Caballero) that we would get no help for as long as the Central Militias Committee's power was so visible. The Russian consul in Barcelona was bringing pressures to bear along the same lines. In order to secure arms for the front and raw materials for our industries, we acquiesced in the dissolution, which is to say, the abandonment of a significant revolutionary position."

135 Agustín Guillamón (2013), 109: second sitting of the Union Anarchiste congress on October 30 to November 1,1937, statement by Louis Mercier Vega (*aka* Charles Ridel), who served in the Durruti Column as a militian up until mid-October 1936: "Durruti's threat to 'seize the money from the Bank of Spain' should have been carried out." Paz, *Durruti en la revolución española*, 599–601, offers a few additional details furnished by Abad de Santillán in a letter to the author. See also the meeting between Santillán and Lieutenant-Colonel Felipe Díaz Sandino, Generalitat Councillor for Defense, as reported in Azaña, *Memorias políticas y de guerra*, 180–81.

136 Paz, *Durruti en la revolución española*, 600; and Márquez Rodríguez and Gallardo Romero, *Ortiz*. See in the documents section "Ortiz's letter to Juan García Oliver, sent from Marin (Venezuela) regarding the book *El eco de los pasos*."

137 Abad de Santillán, *Por qué perdimos la Guerra*, 140–41.

138 It is commonly believed that the Bank of Spain's gold was sent in its entirety to the USSR. In fact, seventy-odd per cent of those reserves and a remaining twenty-odd per cent remained in France. For more details see Ángel Viñas Martín, *El oro español en la Guerra Civil* (Madrid: Instituto de Estudios Fiscales, Ministerio de Hacienda, 1976).

139 As Mompó states in Section 5.2.7 of *El Comité Central de Milicias Antifascistas*: "Contrary to what one might suppose from the comments and accusations emanating from some newspaper media linked to the PSUC and the rest of the organizations making up the Front d'Esquerres, the need to endow the militias with a unified command was felt by all factions." There is very telling testimony to this lack of coordination, if not outright sabotage, between columns of differing political persuasions: "Fernando Aragón, a middle-aged peasant and CNT member, sourly watched the rivalries in the village of Angüés. ... The anarchist 'Roja y Negra' column was on one side of the village and the POUM militia on the other. 'When the former went into action, members of the other militia sat around with their hands in their pockets and burst out laughing. Whenever it was POUM guys who were going into combat, the anarchists did the same.'" Fraser, *Recuérdalo tú y recuérdalo a otros*, I, 183.

140 Paz, *Durruti en la revolución Española*, 614–17, reprints a tiny fragment from the original document, held at the Hoover Institution, albeit in a rather mangled form, skipping over a couple of comments from Durruti that might offer a rather harsher picture of the protagonist of Paz's book. A complete copy can be found in José Del Barrio's *Memorias políticas y militares* (Barcelona: Pasado y

Presente, 2013), 169–89, and, under the title *Informe textual del encuentro de Jefes Políticos y Militares en el Frente de Aragón en septiembre de 1936*, in Julián Casanova (*Anarquismo y revolución*), though many of the sentences in the latter are very blurred or outright unreadable. Note that that meeting cannot possibly have taken place in September because there are references to the taking of Leciñena by the rebels, which happened during the second week of October. Likewise, *La Vanguardia* of October 14, in "Towards a Unified Command Right Across the Aragon Front," 13, reports the aforementioned meeting as having occurred the previous day. As for Durruti, his stance at this meeting is at odds with the account that García Oliver offers us regarding the meeting held in mid-August to launch the Aragon Front War Committee, García Oliver, *El eco de los pasos*, 271. There, on learning of the creation of that Committee, Durruti seemed about to quibble before asking: "I . . . would like to know if discussion is possible." In answer to which García Oliver, guillotining the discussion, stated: "No, Durruti, the time for discussion is over now. But any column commander unwilling to toe the line could be replaced on the spot and he, and he alone, could turn to his organization or his party and spell out his disagreement." Nevertheless, one must handle García Oliver's opinions of Durruti as set out in his book with care, since he was engaged in a definite settling of scores with his former fellow group member.

141   García Oliver, *El eco de los pasos*, 266.
142   García Oliver, *El eco de los pasos*, 270–72.
143   As is plain from the report cited in note 140 above.
144   For further detail, see Maldonado Moya, *El Frente de Aragón*; and Guarner, *Cataluña en la Guerra de España*, 201–02.
145   Guarner, *Cataluña en la Guerra de España*, 255.
146   For more details see Mira, *Los guerrilleros confederales*, 120–24; Guarner, *Cataluña en la Guerra de España*, 170–72; and Maldonado Moya, *El Frente de Aragón*, 118. Also, newspaper reports in *Solidaridad Obrera* of September 11, 12, and 13; *El Frente* of September 19; and *Solidaridad Obrera* on October 1.
147   The expression was coined by Luis Miguel Limia Ponte y Manso de Zúñiga, the general who was in command of the Aragon front from August 21, 1936. See "When Aragon was an Anvil" in *Revista Ejército*, March 2, 1940.
148   Maldonado Moya, *El Frente de Aragón*, 90, 109.
149   Martínez Bande, *La invasión de Aragón*, 96.
150   Martínez Bande, *La invasión de Aragón*, 94–95; and Maldonado Moya, *El Frente de Aragón*, 91.
151   Maldonado Moya, *El Frente de Aragón*: much of his book is given over to studying the organization on both sides. On the other hand, Vicente Guarner represents an exemplary summation: "collating intelligence about the enemy, which was arriving from throughout the front, it came to light that General Ponte, who was in command inside Zaragoza, had practically quintupled the normal strength of the Fifth Division, totalling almost 30,000 troops, plus a hundred artillery pieces. The names we were being sent of the local commanders suggested compartmentalization into well-armed precincts complete with artillery, with a motorized mobile reserve force that could strike anywhere, and which

Notes to page 62

posed serious problems for our mediocre militians." Guarner, *Cataluña en la Guerra de España*, 178–79.

152   Quotation taken from Guarner, *Cataluña en la Guerra de España*, 163. See also Martínez Bande, *La invasión de Aragón*, 135–36; Mira, *Los guerrilleros confederales*, 125–30; Ramos, *Una vida azarosa*, 51–52; Gimenez, *Del amor, la Guerra y la revolución*, 81–82; and Mira/Anónimo, *La 26 División*, 17–19. Martínez Bande points out that the clash occurred on the 8th, whereas José Mira mentions the 6th: I credit the former with greater likelihood because he is using sources drawn from the Military Archives in Ávila rather than personal reminiscences. I should highlight Mira/Anónimo where he explains that such was the dearth of ammunition that in order to outfit the reserve column "munitions were gathered up from the rest of the column's units, leaving quiet sectors of the front to militians issued with ten bullets." Mira/Anónimo, *La 26 División*, 38. Likewise, as an indication of the straitened circumstances in which the Column was living, there is the following fragment from a contribution by Durruti to the conference of Political and Military leaders on the Aragon front, which would take place a few days later (see note 140 above): "If you were to ask me how we held Farlete and Monegrillo the other day, my answer to you would be that we defended as best we were able and in our mind' eye the time when we set off racing in the direction of Fraga and lost those two positions." Paz, *Durruti en la revolución española*, 615; and del Barrio, *Memorias políticas y militares*, 177. Finally, let me point out that a short documentary film was made of the clashes that occurred around Farlete and it is accessible as part of the *Archivo cinematográfico de la Revolución española. CNT 1936–1939*, Vol.1, DVD1.

153   Martínez Bande, *La invasión de Aragón*, 136; and Maldonado Moya, *El Frente de Aragón*, 122. A more detailed account appears on Grossi Mier, *Cartas de Grossi*, 77–78. With regards to arms and munitions, Manuel Grossi, throughout his book, on many occasions exposes the consistent boycotting of POUM forces by the PSUC and the CNT alike (see for instance Grossi Mier, *Cartas de Grossi*, 73). Likewise, as already mentioned, at the conference of Political and Military Leaders on the Aragon front due to be held a few days later (see note 140 above), reference was made to the recent loss of that village: it is worth highlighting the following exception taken by Rovira to what he took to be a criticism from García Oliver: "They abandoned the place [Leciñena] for want of munitions. We were cut off." Paz, *Durruti en la revolución Española*, 615; and del Barrio, *Memorias políticas y militares*, 186.

154   Mira/Anónimo describes the take-over of Monte Oscuro in the wake of the abortive attack on Perdiguera and says that the enemy "offered scant resistance," but his testimony does not seem believable with respect either to its having come after the Perdiguera incident or of the resistance from the enemy. Mira/Anónimo, *La 26 División*, 21. Manuel Ramos took part in the occupation of Monte Oscuro, and places the operation in October, providing no specific date but speaking of it after an account of the clashes in Farlete. Ramos, *Una vida azarosa*, 53–54. Similarly, Vicente Guarner points out that "Durruti's reaction [to the enemy push against Farlete] consisted of capturing Monte Oscuro a few days

later." Guarner, *Cataluña en la Guerra de España*, 163. Gimenez was also a participant in the capture of Monte Oscuro, and he places it toward late September and indicates that Berthomieu took part in it: once the position had been seized, they stayed there for several days, after which they handed over to the Spaniards to finish off fortifying it and they, the internationals, fell back to Farlete to take part in the attack on Perdiguera. Gimenez, *Del amor, la Guerra y la revolución*, 90. Antoine Gimenez's book is riddled with chronological mistakes such as one might expect in a memoir written after such a long time, but it is hard to see Berthomieu's taking part in the takeover of Monte Oscuro if he actually did not, especially as he was the International Group's delegate-general and not just another number. On all these grounds the operation must have taken place after the attack on Farlete and a few days ahead of the attack on Perdiguera, in which Berthomieu was to lose his life: sometime between October 9 and 12, being our conclusion. Besides Manuel Ramos and Antoine Gimenez are agreed in pointing out that they ran into no resistance, although, as the climb began they had no idea what or whom they were likely to meet at the top, which supports the argument that this must have been prior to the attack on Perdiguera, as it is very doubtful whether Durruti and his high command would have been so outrageously imprudent as to attack Perdiguer without first knowing if the enemy was or was not digging in on Monte Oscuro, a position from which any attack on Perdiguera might be easily spotted and the element of surprise thus destroyed.

155   Abel Paz, himself a member of the CNT, the FAI, and the Defense Committees back then, attests that by late September the activist grassroots "were obsessed with nothing beyond finishing off Huesca and Zaragoza so that they might turn to the [higher] committees and tell them "that that was an end of the concessions and that the time had now come to face down the counter-revolution, proclaiming libertarian communism." Paz, *Durruti en la revolución Española*, 597.

156   For more details of the muddled Perdiguera episode see Mira/Anónimo, *La 26 División*, 20; Paz, *Durruti en la revolución española*, 619–20; Gimenez, *Del amor, la Guerra y la revolución*, 97–117; and Los Gimenólogues, *En busca de los Hijos de la Noche*, 314–31.

157   As can be verifying by consulting the official dispatches from the front published in the Catalan press at the time.

158   Maldonado Moya, *El Frente de Aragón*, 119–20.

159   For the actual figures on both sides but a month apart, see Maldonado Moya, *El Frente de Aragón*, 96–100; on the rebel side, a document from October 1936 states that the Fifth Division had a total strength of 32,247 men; on the other side, according to a document from the Aragon Front Delegation dated November 29, there were 33,087 men fighting who were answerable to the Generalitat, plus 10,500 answerable to Valencia, making a total of 43,587.

160   Abad de Santillán, cited in Paz, *Durruti en la revolución española*, 645.

161   Lorenzo, *Los anarquistas españoles*, 119. The scene outlined by Horacio Martínez Prieto himself in *Utopistas*, an unpublished manuscript held at the IISH, 121–22, https://search.socialhistory.org/Record/ARCH03264 (visited June 19, 2016).

162   See note 132 above.

Notes to pages 64–66

163 "Companñera" was the word normally used in anarchist circles to designate partner. "*Reunión de Comités, celebrada el día 16 de octubre de 1936* (IISH-CNT-94D11). Although the minutes are not specific on this, it looks as if the money was meant to keep the Column supplied.
164 Published in *Gaceta de la República*, September 29.
165 Published in *Gaceta de la República*, September 30.
166 Published in the *Butlletí Oficial de la Generalitat de Catalunya*, October 28.
167 "*Reunion de Comités celebrada el día 31 de octubre de 1936*" (IISH-CNT-94D11). As to the opposition to the decree militarizing the militias, see also "No to the Resurrection of the Old Army," in *Solidaridad Obrera*, October 31, 1936.
168 The text in question can be found in the appendices to Guillamón, *Barricadas en Barcelona*. Likewise, for Durruti's opinion of the militarization decree and how the column reacted to it, see *L'Espagne Nouvelle*, November 1936, cited in Abel Paz, *Durruti en la revolución española*, 623–24. Also available in French in André Prudhommeaux and Dori Prudhommeaux, *Catalogne libertaire 1936–1937. L'Armement du people. Que sont la CNT et la FAI?* (Paris: Cahiers Spartacus, 1940), 18–19.
169 Joan Peiró took over at Industry, Juan López at Trade, Federica Montseny at Health and Social Assistance and Juan García Oliver at Justice. Whilst it could be said that these were actually two and a half ministries because, as José Peirats remarks in "Sense and Nonsense in Libertarian Participation in the Republic's Government" in *Polémica*, nos 22–25 (Summer 1986). Industry and Trade had always been just one ministry and Health just a General Directorate.
170 Agustín Guillamón reconstructs the speech on the basis of the transcription carried in *Solidaridad Obrera* plus fragments that José Peirats captured for *Acracia*, both published on November 6 (Guillamón, *La Revolución de los comités*, 371). The reason for this is that the *Solidaridad Obrera* version was sweetened and bowdlerized; see for instance Marcos Alcón in a letter to the author, cited in Paz, *Durruti en la revolución española*, 633. Similarly, to get some idea of what that speech must have been like, it is worth looking at the transcript published in the November 7 edition of *Cultura y Acción: Órgano de la Regional de Aragón, Rioja y Navarra*, which is somewhat more abrasive and explicit than the *Solidaridad Obrera* one and therefore potentially closer to the actual one.
171 Guillamón, *La Revolución de los comités*, 372.
172 "Acta de la reunió celebrada sota la presidencia de S.E. El president de la Generalitat pels consellers i representants dels partits I sindicats que tenen representació en el Consell, els dies 5 i 6 de noviembre de 1936," cited in Agustín Guillamón, *La Revolución de los comités*, 373–74.
173 Felipe Díaz Sandino.
174 Mary R. Habeck, Ronald Radosh, and Grigory Sevostianov, *España traicionada. Stalin y la Guerra civil* (Barcelona: Planeta, 2002), 122.
175 Habeck et al., *España traicionada*, 122.
176 Diego Abad de Santillán "Buenaventura Durruti (1896–1936)" in *Timón*, November 1938. See also José Borrás: "The CNT's Regional Committee for Catalonia wanted to raise its profile a little by dispatching a column of its own to that front,

Notes to pages 66–68

under the most prestigious and courageous militant it had available. It summoned Durruti to spell out the decision it had reached and sound him out about accepting it. He replied: 'I disagree. The most effective contribution to Madrid's defense is an attack on Zaragoza. Give me the weapons and reinforcements planned for the trip to Madrid and I will attack the city on the Ebro. In which case, we either capture it, which would be a success, or at the very least we will force the enemy to leave the Madrid front depleted.'" José Borrás *Del radical-socialismo al socialismo radical y libertario. Memorias de un libertario* (Madrid: Fundación Salvador Seguí, 1998), 59.

177 Habeck et al., *España traicionada*, 128.
178 Or at any rate according to Abad de Santillán, cited in Paz, *Durruti en la revolución Española*, 649: "Durruti told Santillán: 'If you could see the trams down in Zaragoza, the way I can can see them, you would not go to Madrid' To which I replied that given the situation we were in, it was pointless considering an attack on Zaragoza. Whereupon he told me to send somebody else: send Miguel Yoldi, who was more up to it than he was." Joan Llarch also recounts this episode: Joan Llarch *La Muerte de Durruti* (Esplugas de Llobregat, Spain: Plaza & Janés S.A. Editores, 1976)], 24–25. In English as *The Death of Durruti*, trans. Raymond Batkin [Hastings, England: Christie Books, 2013]).
179 Habeck et al., *España traicionada*, 122–23.
180 Habeck et al., *España traicionada*, 123. José del Barrio offers his own version of that meeting which overlaps on some points and differs on others (del Barrio, *Memorias políticas y militares*, 205–11). Nevertheless, I believe the secret report from the soviet consul is more reliable than a set of memoirs written fifty years after the event.
181 David Antona, "When Durruti arrived in Madrid!" in *Nosotros*, November 22, 1937. The plenum's motion, the petition forwarded to Durruti asking him to move swiftly to Madrid, can be found at (IISH-CNT-39C-2).
182 David Antona, "When Durruti Arrived in Madrid!"
183 Enzensberger, *El corto verano de la anarquía*, 220–21: author's interview with Federica Montseny on April 21, 1971.
184 García Oliver, *El eco de los pasos*, 328–38; "Letter from Ortiz to Juan García Oliver, from Marín (Venezuela) regarding the book *El eco de los pasos*" in the "Documents" section of Márquez Rodríguez and Gallardo Romero, *Ortiz*.
185 *Utopistas*, unpublished manuscript held at the IISH, 123.
186 Diego Abad de Santillán, cited in Paz's *Durruti en la revolución Española*, 649, mentions this meeting and places it on the night of November 11–12, but that cannot be true because at the morning meeting on the Committees on the 11th, it was mentioned that that part of the Durruti Column that was staying in Aragon had been left under the command of Ruano and Cantón [recte Campón], from which we may deduce that Durruti must have already agreed to leave for Madrid (See "Reunión de Comités celebrada el día 11 de Noviembre de 1936" (IISH-CNT-94-D11). This fits in with the article "The Death of Freedom's Guerrilla in Madrid" in *Mi revista*, October 15, 1937, which recounts how, on the night of November 9, 1936, Durruti told two reporters he had come across that he had

157

Notes to pages 68–70

to be off swiftly to Madrid. Moreover, Ricardo Sanz appears to be referring to the same meeting as Abad de Santillán and places Federica Montseny at it (Sanz, *Los que fuimos a Madrid*, 111).

187   This is mentioned by Diego Abad de Santillán, in a letter cited by Paz, *Durruti en la revolución española*, 651: because Antonov-Ovseenko mentions the Winchesters only. Likewise, Abad de Santillán offers details as to the quality of the gear: the Winchesters had "five-bullet magazines like the Mauser rifles but were not the Spanish caliber, which entailed all sorts of problems in the procurement of ammunition, added to which there was the fragility of the rifle butts, which could be snapped by a single blow, all of which were major drawbacks with the weapon. The Swiss rifles were even worse since they were of a model dating from 1886 with ammunition of the same vintage that used to jam the barrel after a few shots fired." That the shipment comprised mostly of Winchesters is clear in Ricardo Sanz's *Buenaventura Durruti*, cited in Enzensberger, *El corto verano de la anarquía*, 225–26; the Durruti Column in Madrid "showed up with spanking new, recently arrived war materials, especially Winchester rifles of great fire-power but non-repeaters and very dangerous to handle."

188   See note 124 above.

189   I have summarized and cobbled together this section of the report which I consider reliable, because it can be a bit muddled in places. For the original text, see Habeck et al., *España traicionada*, 123.

190   Diego Abad de Santillán "Buenaventura Durruti (1896–1936)" in *Timón*, November 1938, 20.

191   A similar process had occurred at national level with the Socialist Youth and the Communist Youth, the upshot of which was that the brand-new Unified Socialist Youth fell under communist control as well.

192   Paz, *Durruti en la revolución española*, 641–48. See also the depiction offered by Juan García Oliver, *El eco de los pasos*, 330.

193   Mira, *Los guerrilleros confederales*, 161: the column was still being described as the Del Barrio Column. Was this the Stalin Regiment of which Antonov-Ovseenko spoke? Habeck et al., *España traicionada*, 123.

194   Jesús Arnal argues that from his column Durruti took with him from Aragon "a sizable escort of maybe a thousand men and the remainder of the troops that left for Madrid were militias recruited in Barcelona by the anarchist organizations; I do not know how many of them there were, but they can be estimated to account for another thousand or one thousand two hundred." Arnal, *Por qué fuí secretario de Durruti*, 130. So, all in all, some two thousand-odd men: even though Arnal's testimony may be somewhat open to question, especially regarding those thousand to twelve hundred-odd militias recruited in Barcelona, looks as if he was going on hearsay or sheer intuition. Koltsov, *Diario de la guerra de España*, 285, Enrique Líster, *Nuestra Guerra. Aportaciones para una Historia de la Guerra Nacional Revolucionaria del Pueblo Español 1936–1939* (Paris: Editions de la Librairie du Globe, 1966), 88, and Louis Fischer, the American correspondent (cited in Enzensberger, *El corto verano de la anarquía*, 225) all mention the figure of three thousand. Salas Larrazábal, *Historia del Ejército Popular de la República*, I, 754,

says 3,200. Ricardo Sanz, *Los que fuimos a Madrid*, 112, and Eduardo de Gúzman, *Madrid rojo y negro* (Madrid: Oberon, 2004), 183, speak of about four thousand. Finally, Cipriano Mera, *Guerra, exilio y cárcel de un anarcosindicalista*, 129–30, reproduces the following dialogue: "Looks like you've brought sixteen thousand men . . . No [replied Durruti]: only four to five thousand." I am inclined to think that the true figure must have been somewhere between 3,000 and 4,000 and that the missing one or two thousand men referred to in the conversation reproduced by Mera must have been due to Durruti. In his response, having included the Libertad-López Tienda Column and/or the regiment from the K. Marx Division that were to have been placed under his orders—something that never came to pass. Abel Paz counted as Durruti's troops in Madrid only the fighters drawn from his own column (*Durruti en la revolución española*, 65), yet it appears to be established fact that those fighters were joined by others drawn from different sectors along the front or in the rearguard. Nevertheless, it is still striking that Vicente Guarner also alludes solely to those 1,500 fighters (Guarner, *Cataluña en la Guerra de España*, 176); Mira, *Los guerrilleros confederales*, 141–42, 181; Mira/Anónimo, *La 26 División*, 25; Los Gimenólogues, *En busca de los Hijos de la Noche*, 395–96. As to those who joined the Column off their own bat whilst it was marching off to Madrid, see Mira, *Los guerrilleros confederales*, 142, 143. Jesús Arnal reduces the numbers of militians that Durruti took away from the Aragon front to "maybe around a thousand," Arnal, *Por qué fuí secretario de Durruti*, 130: however, the evidence from Mira, an eyewitness offering hard figures regarding the make-up of that force seems much more believable. Likewise, "The Column Reaches Madrid" (Dispatch from Headquarters), *El Frente*, November 13, 1936, says: "Durruti and a few hundred more brothers have left to fight outside of the Column's territory." It ought to be made clear here that the press, and especially the press circulating along the front, was subject to censorship and was manipulative, for the purpose of avoiding the leak of information useful to the enemy. It is logical for it to have minimized the numbers of veteran fighters who had set off.

195   Paz, *Durruti en la revolución española*, 650.
196   "The Column Reaches Madrid" (Dispatch from Headquarters), *El Frente*, November 13, 1936. Los Gimenologos make it clear that the reference was to *Pablo* (Paolo) Vagliasindi rather than Pablo Ruiz. Los Gimenólogues, *En busca de los Hijos de la Noche*, 564.
197   Habeck et al., *España traicionada*, 123. The inference appears to be that Durruti manged to extract about two thousand five hundred Mauser rifles from the Civil Guards and Assault Guards in order to arm his column. However, no other source supports that possibility. In the light of the testimonies in note 187 above, it is clear that Durruti's troops in Madrid were armed with those elderly Winchesters and Swiss rifles that had recently arrived in Barcelona. As for the Mausers there are three possibilities: either they were not extracted, or that they finished up with different forces (such as the Libertad-López Tienda Column) or ended up back in the hands of the Civil and Assault Guards.
198   Paz, *Durruti en la revolución española*, 651; "The Column Reaches Madrid" (Dispatch from Headquarters), *El Frente*, November 13, 1936.

Notes to pages 71–74

199 Enrique Líster, *Nuestra guerra. Aportaciones para una Historia de la Guerra Nacional Revolucionaria del Pueblo Español 1936–1939* (París: Libr. du Globe, 1966), 88.
200 See note 178 above.
201 Regarding the death of Durruti there is a multitude of contradictory testimony that can be broken down into several theories. Anyone wanting to delve deeper into this mystery will find the following anthologies and analyses of interest: Enzensberger, *El corto verano de la anarquía*, 238–56; Paz, *Durruti en la revolución española*, 667–78; and Los Gimenólogues, *En busca de los Hijos de la Noche*, 397–413.

III. Durruti and his Column Between the Ideal and the Reality of War

1 Durruti from a balcony is the testimony of Ricardo Rionda, cited in Hans Magnus Enzensberger, *El corto Verano de la anarquía* [*Anarchy's Brief Summer*]. "Findings: The Army and the People" in *Solidaridad Obrera*, August 2, 1936: "July 19, 1936. Two tactics, two fighting strategies at loggerheads, each ready to win a duel to the death; graduation from the Military Academy, with all the experiences of the wars for territorial expansion and governmental economic greed with all its criminal refinements, and the spontaneous, intuitive one of the anarchist-influenced people. The anarchist approach … has demonstrated … the superiority of its tactics, free of subjugation, *caudillismo*, no minds stemming revolutionary action, no single commands to curtail the personal freedom of action of each fighter." Another fragment from this article appears in the chapter "Armed Agencies and Debates Around Defense of the Revolution during the Second Republic"; by way of an exception, since it does not appear at all to have been the usual tone, Alejandro Soteras Marín points out: "The head of my *centuria* was a Catalan by the name of Silvio. He was put in command of my *centuria* by Durruti himself," Alejandro Soteras Marín, *Mis memorias* (Zaragoza: Asociación Casa Libertad de Gurrea de Gállego, 2003), 50–51.
2 Mercedes de los Santos Ortega and Javier Ortega Pérez, *El devenir revolucionario de Buenaventura Durruti. Durruti y las tradiciones del antimilitarismo* (Estella, Spain: Hiru, 1997), 132, 137.
3 Ramón Salas Larrazábal, *Historia del Ejército Popular de la República* (La Esfera de los Libros, Madrid, 2006), I, 590–91: "the militias … that the libertarian movements raised for themselves [sic] had already introduced the precept of order, subordination, hierarchy, and discipline, which implies a remarkable deviation from Spanish anarchism's traditional theses."
4 There is no recorded instance of rape within the Durruti Column. Antonio Ortiz does mention an attempted rape in his own column and how the two culprits were punished by him by being shot. See the documentary *Ortiz, Général sans dieu ni maître*, Ariel Camacho, Phil Casoar, and Laurent Guyot, 1996, Pt.1, minutes 28–30, available at https://www.youtube.com/watch?v=OnF1PO WI6CA; and indicated by, say, Simone Weil: "I know that within the anarchist

Notes to page 74

columns, thievery and rape were considered deserving of the death penalty" Simone Weil, *Escritos históricos y políticos* (Madrid: Editorial Trotta, 2007), 525.

5 "Francoist sources [the Causa General] themselves cite many instances in which Durruti ordered the brakes applied to the repression (Gelsa, La Almolda) or set supposed right-wingers loose (two from Alfajarin and one from Tauste) only for them to be shot later by their neighbors. This bears out the oral sources from places that endure the so-called 'scourge' of the man (e.g. in Pina). It also happens that the repression was no greater in the comarca in which he was active than in any other that it was indeed minimal or nonexistent in places such as Monegrillo and Bujaraloz where his headquarters were established," José Luis Ledesma, *Los días de llamas de la revolución. Violencia y política en la retaguardia republicana de Zaragoza durante la Guerra civil* (Zaragoza: Institución Fernando e Católico, 2002), 242–43. For a concrete example, see AHN FC—Causa General, Pina de Ebro, 10: "on the outbreak of the Glorious Uprising, my son Angel Caro Andrés, sixteen years old, marched off as a volunteer to defend his imperiled Homeland, being posted to Falange 29 on the Quinto front. On August 22, 1936, in a night-time battle, he was taken prisoner by the international reds who hauled him in front of the column commander, Durruti. This latter commander spared his life because of his tender years and ordered him taken to the town hall in Pina preparatory to his imprisonment. The following day, the reds fleeing from Tauste asked Durruti to hand the prisoner over to them for shooting and Durruti turned them down because of his youth. Then, carried away by their criminal instincts, they arranged to raid the prison at daybreak to seize him and having taken him off to the outskirts of the town out by the Ebro, they murdered him." For more information regarding this incident and its possible connection with an incident recounted by Simone Weil, *Escritos históricos y politicos*, 524, and Mathieu Corman, *Salud camarada! Cinq mois sur les fronts d'Espagne* (Paris: Editions Tribord, 1937), 14–19, see Les Gimenólogos "Retour sur la lettre de Simone Weil à Bernanos," June 8, 2009, text digitalized at http://Gimenólogos.org (consulted online on June 11, 2014). Those documents, plus the testimony of Jesús Arnal (*Por qué fui secretario de Durruti*), who could scarcely be charged with being soft on anarchism, utterly dismantle the image of a bloodthirsty Durruti depicted in several writings.

6 Quotation from Los Gimenólogos, "Retour sur la lettre de Simone Weil à Bernanos," 85.

7 See for instance the description of her male comrades offered by the militian Georgette Kokoczinski, aka Mimosa, in her diary; Los Gimenólogues, *En busca de los Hijos de la Noche. Notas sobre los Recuerdos de la Guerra de España de Antoine Gimenez* (Logroño, Spain: Pepitas de calabaza, 2009), 546–48. Likewise in *Ortiz. Général sans dieu ni maître*, Ariel Camacho, Phil Casoar, and Laurent Guyot (1996) Pt. 1, minute 28–29. Antonio Ortiz recounts how, among the volunteers setting off for Aragon, there were out and out adventurers, people with nothing better to do in Barcelona.

8 A copy of the text is included in the appendices of Agustín Guillamón's *Barricadas*: "its individual members [referring to the Column] defer to whatever tends

to further their aim of beating fascism… the work done on the front by our militians and the ongoing advancement of our positions are our finest testimonials to that self-discipline," Agustín Guillamón, *Barricadas en Barcelona: La CNT de la Victoria de Julio de 1936 a la necesaria derrota de Mayo de 1937* (Ediciones Espartaco Internacional, 2007).

9   Emma Goldman, *20 de noviembre*, a pamphlet published by the CNT in 1937. See Abel Paz, *Durruti en la revolución española* (Madrid: La Esfera de los Libros, 2004), 571.
10   *El Frente*, August 27, 1936.
11   "THIS IS THE TIME FOR SACRIFICE," *El Frente*, August 29, 1936.
12   "When the war-like action ends, we must win over the consciences of the people," *El Frente*, August 29, 1936.
13   *El Frente*, September 2, 1936.
14   José Mira, *Los guerrilleros confederales* (Barcelona: Comité Regional de la CNT, Sección de Propaganda y Prensa, 1937), 73–74; "Durruti in Madrid," *Solidaridad Obrera*, October 8, 1936.
15   Testimony of various members of the Column. Ilya Ehrenburg also refers to this in *La Nuit Tombe* (Paris: Ed. Gallimard, 1968). See Paz, *Durruti en la revolución española*, 549.
16   Ilya Ehrenburg mentions this in *Ljudi, gody, Zisn'*, published in German as, *Menschen, Jahre Leben. Autobiografía, primera parte*. See also Hans Magnus Enzensberger, *El corto verano de la anarquía: Vida y muerte de Durruti* (Barcelona: Anagrama, 2002), 139. The words in quotation marks are lifted from there.
17   José Mira, *Los guerrilleros confederales*, 73.
18   "Durruti in Madrid," *Solidaridad Obrera*, October 8, 1936.
19   *España Libre* (Toulouse), September 11, 1949; cited in Enzensberger, *El corto verano de la anarquía*.
20   Though he did come close: See Victoria Priego "Heroic Discipline" in *La Noche*, August 18, 1936; she recounts how Durruti came within an ace of shooting five militians who had stolen from the house in which they were billeted, but in the end he forgave them: "On this occasion and on this occasion only, you are forgiven. But let us have no repetition because militians cannot thieve." Jesús Arnal Peña, oral evidence to the journalist Ángel Montoto Ferrer in the autumn of 1970; see also Enzensberger, *El corto verano de la anarquía*, 184–85: he also tells of a similar episode, perhaps the very same one: "After the capture on Monegrillo some militians made their way to an abandoned house and made off with clothing belonging to the absent residents. When the fugitives returned home, they reported the looting to the committee.… Those guilty were identified. Durruti ordered that they be shot. At the last moment he spared their lives. He said: 'You are my men and I am sparing your lives this time. But any further looting and I will have you shot. I have no need for thieves nor bandits.'"
21   I have uncovered references to just five shootings. The first are cited in *Salud camarada!*: "One had been caught in possession of twenty thousand pesetas, for the origins of which he was unable to account. The other had indulged in defeatist talk. An initial council of war sentenced them both to death, but as

they were two trade union militants with impeccable past records, their files were looked at again. A second council of war, following further interrogation, reckoned that their offences had been clearly established and that an example had to be set" Corman, *Salud camarada*, 104–05. The third appears in *Del amor, la Guerra y la revolución*: a certain Carrillo, who headed a centuria and was a member of the FAI, was tried and convicted by the rest of the centuria delegates for having pocketed some jewelry, Gimenez, *Del amor, la Guerra y la revolución*. In a footnote, the Gimenólogos remark: "This may well be the episode to which Ridel alludes in the columns of *L'Espagne Nouvelle* in the summer of 1939: "The unfortunate militian got himself shot for having pocketed a ring discovered in one village." Our fourth instance comes from Hans Magnus Enzensberger's interview with the liberal physician Martínez Fraile on May 7, 1971: "I was called one day to the Durruti Column's headquarters in Madrid. A dead militian lay sprawled on the ground.... I had to make out a death certificate so that they could bury him. I asked what had killed him. Their chilling response was that *they* had put two bullets into him [note the use of the plural pronoun here] because, in the course of a house search, he had stolen a watch and two bracelets," Enzensberger, *El corto verano de la anarquía*. And the fifth instance comes from Soteras Marín's *Mis memorias*: it refers to a certain Silvio, centuria commander. But the reference mentions no details and offers no clues as to how the trial had been conducted or who had determined the sentence, mentioning only that he was punished for "immorality," specifically for extortion directed at the former warden of Pina prison and his family, Soteras Marín, *Mis memorias*, 51.

22 A telling piece of evidence here comes from Gaston Leval, interviewed on May 27, 1971, in *El corto verano de la anarquía*: "As a military leader he demonstrated courage and caution, as well as a stunning sense of proportion. He was not one of those who blindly ordered the shooting of fascists or alleged fascists. Because he was only too aware that in such muddled circumstances the direst slanders proliferate. I remember, for instance, that he rescued from execution a foreign comrade who had spoken out about certain abuses," Enzensberger, *El corto verano de la anarquía*, 133.

23 Jesús Arnal, *Por qué fui secretario de Durruti* (Andorra la Vieja, Andorra: Edicions Mirador del Pirineu, 1972), 141.

24 "The Notion of Discipline" *El Frente*, October 9, 1936. The capital letters and italics appear in the original.

25 Some examples: Augustin Souchy's interview on June 3, 1971, in Enzensberger, *El corto verano de la anarquía*, 199: Jacinto Toryho, *No éramos tan malos* (Madrid: G. del Toro, 1975), 76; Ariel *¿Como murió Duruti?* (no date, no place cited) in Enzensberger, *El corto verano de la anarquía*, 216: Ilya Ehrenburg *Ljudi, gody, zisn'*, cited in Enzensberger, *El corto verano de la anarquía*, 138: Mira, *Los guerrilleros confederales*, 124.

26 Carl Einstein, "Die Kolonne Durruti" in *Buenaventura Durruti* (Barcelona: Helmut Rüdiger and the CNT-FAI's German-language News Service, 1936), 13–17, originally it was a speech in commemoration from a "Durruti Column

Notes to page 79

militian," broadcast over the CNT-FAI radio station in Barcelona. See Carl Einstein, *La Columna Durruti y otros articulos y entrevistas de la Guerra Civil Española* (Barcelona: Uwe Fleckner, 2006), 17; Manuel Ramos, *Una vida azarosa. 44 años de exilio en Francia* (Sant Feliu de Guixols: self-published, 1993), 52; Mira, *Los guerrilleros confederales*, 93, 124, and 127; Marín, *Mis memorias*, 49; José Fortea Gracia, *Mi paso por la Columna Durruti/26 Division* (Badalona: Centre d'Estudis Llibertaris Federica Montseny, 2005), 35; Juan García Oliver, *El eco de los pasos. El anarcosindicalismo en la calle, en el Comité de Milicias, en el gobierno, en el exilio* (Barcelona: Fundació d'Estudis Llibertaris i Anarcosindicalistas, Llibrería La Rosa de Foc y CNT Catalunya, 2008), 335; the latter's testimony stands out because of his disapproval of Durruti's approach, as when he encountered him fighting in the front lines in Madrid and taunted him: "This is not a command post, Durruti. This is not your place. For as long as you are in Madrid, remember to steer clear of the rabble-rousing. In the same vein, he offered similar advice to Mera; since there had ... to be an end to the slaughtering of anarcho-syndicalist militants! Because, if things carry on this way, we're going to find that we don't even have enough concierges for our trade union locals," García Oliver, *El eco de los pasos*, 339.

27 José Mira/Anónimo, *La 26 División* (Barcelona: Sindicato de la Metalurgía CNT, 1938), 10.

28 AGCC, Salamanca, E.M. (2) 54.5.8.5 (6.4) See also Maldonado Moya, *El Frente de Aragón*, 84.

29 Interview with Antonio Ortiz dated June 5, 1995, kindly made available to the author by Juan José Gallardo Romero. In addition, this can be inferred from the following remark by Ortiz, who was critical of it: "Letter from Ortiz to Antonio Téllez, 9-10-1978, included in the "Documents" section of Márquez Rodríguez and Gallardo Romero, *Ortiz*: "I stayed in Bujaraloz for a few hours, trading impressions with Durruti and emphasizing to him for the nth time that we should agree to operate our forces jointly and try to mop up Quinto and press on to Mediar ... [sic] [Perhaps he meant Mediana de Aragón?] but there was no budging Durruti and ... there were too many war committees within his Column." The September 2, 1936, edition of *El Frente* reported the establishment on the new Pina war committee. In *Solidaridad Obrera* of August 29, 1936, there was a decree from the "War Committee—Osera," signed by José Espluga[s], the delegate from the *centurias*. The decree applied to every part of Durruti Column territory, so it cannot have come from the committee overseeing sub-sector but from the Central War Committee which must have been based or met often in that locality; the text forwarded to the Generalitat on November 1, 1936, on behalf of the War Committee and signed by Durruti was also sent from the "Osera Front" (the document is included in the appendices to Agustín Guillamón, *Barricadas en Barcelona*). See also how the article "We are Freedom's army and should obey those watching over our lives." The September 2, 1936, edition of *El Frente* speaks of "war committees" in the plural. By contrast, Abel Paz mentions no war committee other than the central one made up of Durruti and his confidants, but divides the Column up into three sectors,

each comprised of three *agrupaciones* (Paz, *Durruti en la revolución española*, 544–45).
30   Mary R. Habeck, Ronald Radosh, and Grigory Sevostianov, *España traicionada. Stalin y la Guerra civil* (Barcelona: Planeta, 2002), 122.
31   Fraser, *Recuérdalo tú y recuérdalo a otros*, I, 203.
32   Julián Casanova, *De la calle al frente*, 174: "The civil war ... the 'artificial' splitting of Spain into two zones and the beginning of a phase when social frictions were going to be resolved through armed means was no guarantee that broad swathes of the population would commit to ideas that had hitherto been clearly backed by an activist minority. To put that another way, the overthrow of bourgeois socioeconomic structures was not as straightforward as had been imagined and, in any event, was being delivered, not through the labor movement's revolutionary maturity but by military means."
33   Casanova, *De la calle al frente*, 175: "it is sloppy thinking to think of this process as 'spontaneous,' but it is equally so to argue that the Aragonese peasantry rejected collectivism out of hand. Within that segment of society there were groups with very different interests and in some of these the revolutionary situation ushered in in July 1936 raised tremendous expectations ... those with more wretched living conditions displayed a greater readiness to avail of the benefits of collectivization. The landless laborers and poorest owners who did just that bettered their standard of living and above all gained in terms of power and dignity. The very same power and dignity lost by the well-off owners and family heads from the leading village families who found themselves bereft of authority, autonomy, and control over the process of production that they had previously enjoyed as the chief beneficiaries of the pre-war social order."
34   Julián Casanova, *Anarquismo y revolucion en la Sociedad rural aragonesa, 1936–1938* (Madrid: Siglo Veintiuno Editores, 1985), 128. For a more optimistic alternative view of the collectivization process, see Alejadro R Díez Torre, *Trabajan para la eternidad: colectividades de trabajo y ayuda mutua durante la Guerra Civil en Aragón* (Madrid: LaMalatesta – Prensas Universitarias de Zaragoza, 2009).
35   Ronald Fraser, *Recuérdalo tú y recuérdalo a otros. Historia oral de la Guerra civil española* (Barcelona: Crítica, 1979), II, 65; and Bolloten, *La Revolución Española*, 234. One example directly relating to the Durruti Column is cited in Simone Weil, *Escritos históricos y políticos* (Madrid: Editorial Trotta, 2007), 510–11. "Conversing with the peasants of Pina. Are you all agreed upon farming together? First response (over several occasions); Whatever the committee says will be done. Old man: Yes—provided that we are given everything that we need—and that I am not all the time straining to pay off the carpenter, the doctor, the way I am now.... Another said: We will have to see how everything works out ... Would you rather farm together than divide things up? Yes (but none too categorically). The sense of inferiority was quite vivid, Weil, *Escritos históricos y políticos*, 525: "to the militians these impoverished and magnificent Aragonese peasants, bearing their degradation with such dignity, were not even items of curiosity. Without any insolence, insult or brutality—or at any rate I saw none— ... there was a gulf between the armed men and the unarmed populace, a gulf like the one between

the poor and the rich. There was always something humble, submissive, and fearful in the attitude of some and the swagger, lack of care and condescension coming from the others."

36   Fraser, *Recuérdalo tú y recuérdalo a otros*, II, 65.
37   Fraser, *Recuérdalo tú y recuérdalo a otros*, II, 65. As *El Frente* had pointed out in its edition of August 27, 1937, "IT IS ONE OF LIFE'S RULES THAT ARMIES LIVE OFF THE LAND THEY CONQUER".
38   "Minutes of the Regional Plenum of the Anarchist Groups of Aragon, Rioja and Navarra," September 1936, published in Barcelona: see also Miguel Amorós, *Francisco Carreño y los arduos caminos de la anarquía* (Vitoria, Spain: Asociación Isaac Puente, 2013), 39.
39   The full decree appeared in *Solidaridad Obrera*, August 14, 1936.
40   This road was known as the "gypsies' road": Ledesma, *Los días de llamas de la revolución*, 151; José Peirats, *De mi paso por la vida* (Barcelona: Flor del Viento Ediciones, 2009), 382–83; Ricardo Sanz, *Buenaventura Durruti* (pamphlet) (Toulouse: 1945). See also Enzensberger, *El corto verano de la anarquía*, 186; Gaston Leval, interviewed on May 17, 1971, in Enzensberger, *El corto verano de la anarquía*, 186–87.
41   "A Few Words from Comrade Durruti" in *El Frente*, September 2, 1936. Apropos of the need to set aside "ideological disquisition" and apply methods theoretically at odds with anarchist principles, the following testimony from then *Solidaridad Obrera* staffer, Vicente Galindo Fontaura is telling: "One day when two or three of us were doing editorial work at the paper, we were informed that a phone call had come in from Bujaraloz. Durruti was at the other end. He asked to speak to the editor-in-chief, that is, Callejas. He was told that Callejas was not there just at that moment. He replied that it made no matter. After I had identified myself, he pointed out that we should be careful about publishing certain items. He said: 'I am as much an anarchist as any one of you. But bear in mind that I am living in a war setting and in wartime there are factors that depart from current views of libertarian ethics. This needs to be borne in mind when reference is made to our struggle.' He explained that sometimes moral and material coercion were needed to salvage a situation in combat that was overwhelmingly necessary to achieve an essential purpose, in the absence of which defeat was a certainty and its implications injurious," Vicente Galindo Fontaura, *La estela de los recuerdos (ideas y figuras)* (Vitoria: Asociación Isaac Puente, 1986), 10.
42   *Verbatim Report on the Meeting of Political and Military Leaders on the Aragon Front in September 1936*, included in the appendices to Casanova, *Anarquismo y revolución*, 14–15, and José del Barrio, *Memorias políticas y militares* (Barcelona: Pasado y Presente, 2013), 180–81. These two contributions are the ones I cited in note 140, and in the Abel Paz biography, he skips over them.
43   These anecdotes were passed on to the author by militians from the Column such as Teresa Margalef or Francisco Subirats; see also Paz, *Durruti en la revolución española*, 548–49: "There was a brutality about the war and Durruti was more aware of that anyone else, because the way of life imposed by the war wound up

degrading even the most revolutionary. 'It is not man's purpose to be stalking and killing but rather to live, to live!' Durruti would interject from time to time as he strode around the room in which the War Committee had established itself. 'If this situation carries on, it will put paid to the revolution because the man that emerges from it will be more beast than human. . . . We need to step on it really hurry up and finish it as soon as possible.' Such considerations triggered a gnawing impatience in Durruti. On many a night, unable to sleep, he would leave his bunk and take off for the forward positions, spending hours on end in the company of the sentries just gazing at the lights of Zaragoza. Daybreak would often find him there." See also the scene recounted in Paz, *Durruti en la revolución española*, 662.

44 *L'Espagne Nouvelle*, November 1936; see also Paz, *Durruti en la revolución Española*, 624. Available in French in André Prudhommeaux and Dori Prudhommeaux, *Catalogne libertaire 1936–1937. L'Armement du people. Que sont la CNT et la FAI?* (Paris: Cahiers Spartacus, 1940), 19.

45 So described by Francisco Carrasquer: "Durruti, child-like as he was," Francisco Carrasquer, *Ascaso y Zaragoza. Dos pérdidas: la pérdida* (Zaragoza: Alcaraván, 2003), 65. A similar description is offered by García Oliver in *El eco de los pasos*. In "Letter from Ortiz to Juan García Oliver from Marin (Venezuela), regarding the book *El eco de los pasos*"—see the 'Letters' section of Márquez Rodríguez and Gallardo Romero's *Ortiz*, which states: "It pains me, Juan that you have been so harsh in your remarks about Durruti . . . and I cannot argue that you are not right, but you might have shown somewhat more generosity." Likewise, "Antonio Ortiz Archive. Juan Campá's interview with Antonio Ortiz, Márquez Rodríguez and Gallardo Romero, *Ortiz*, 77: "Durruti was much given to stereotypical phrases, being a bit of a yokel, a child's mind in a huge body he was a bit of a loose cannon and enjoyed playing fast and loose with the group's decisions, because he was what he was . . . and liked attention and I sometimes had the impression that he was somewhat prisoner to his aura and reputation."

46 Eduardo Pons Prades, "Verano de 1936. ¿Por que no se tomó Zaragoza?," in *Nueva Historia* 26 (March 1979).

IV. Militarization of the Column and the Eclipse of the Libertarian Movement: The End of the Dream

1 Carl Einstein, "The Aragon Front" in *Die Soziale Revolution. Frontzeitung*, published by the German Anarcho-Syndicalists and the Spanish National Committee of the CNT-FAI, No. 12, May 1, 1937, 1–2. *Internacional*, June 1938, cited in Burnett Bolloten, *La Revolución Española. Sus origenes, la izquierda y la lucha por el poder durante la Guerra civil 1936–1939* (Barcelona: Grijalbo, 1980), 289. Miguel González Inestal, *Cipriano Mera. Revolucionario* (Havana: Editorial Atalaya, 1943), 60.

2 "Hugely Important Accords of the CNT National Plenum in Madrid" in *Solidaridad Obrera*, September 19, 1936.

Notes to pages 86–88

3 For the minutes of the Plenum, see *Fragua Social*, November 17, 1936. Similarly, for instance, at the Meeting of Committees from Catalonia held on October 31, 1936, Federica Montseny had stated that: "we must see to it that within the *centurias* of these brand-new militias, all that belongs to the people must be preserved—the people being consubstantial with us, as are their Delegates, the Committees, etc. (IISH-CNT- 94D-11). And in a speech published by *Fragua Social* on October 18, 1936, Juan López declared: "We do not want uniformed, disciplined, mobilized, marshalled, or pip-wearing militias."

4 Bolloten, *La Revolución Española*, 433–35.

5 Bolloten, *La Revolución Española*, 441–45.

6 This a National Committee representative told the Plenum of Confederal and Anarchist Columns held in Valencia on February 5, 1937, that Largo Caballero, asked by him how come he was not delivering arms to the confederal columns, had supposedly replied: "The State's arms are for the State's forces and if you refuse to join them, you can get your weapons from your own organizations," CNT-FAI Acta del Pleno de Columnas Confederales y Anarquistas celebrado en Valencia el día 5 de febrero de 1937, http://www.fondation-besnard.org/2024/03/13/cnt-fai-acta-del-pleno-de-columnas-confederales-y-anarquistas-celebrado-en-valencia-el-dia-5-de-febrero-de-1937, 10.

7 Julián Casanova, *De la calle al frente: el anarcosindicalismo en España (1931–1939)* (Barcelona: Crítica, 1997), 189.

8 See for instance the Acta del Pleno de Columnas Confederales y Anarquistas celerado en Valencia el día 5 de febrero de 1937. To borrow the words of the article "No to Resurrection of the Old Army," in *Solidaridad Obrera*, October 31, 1936.

9 José Mira/Anónimo, *La 26 División* (Barcelona: Sindicato de la Metalurgía CNT, 1938), 23.

10 Mira/Anónimo, *La 26 División*, 44.

11 It was 7,054 of them in fact according to one document from the Operations branch of the Aragon Front Delegation dated November 29, 1936, as reproduced in José María Maldonado Moya, *El Frente de Aragón. La Guerra Civil en Aragón (1936–1938)* (Zaragoza: Mira Editores, 2007), 98–99. Vicente Guarner, on the other hand, indicates that "by late 1936, the column had managed to assemble 59 centurias," Vicente Guarner, *Cataluña en la Guerra de España* (Madrid: G. del Toro, 1975), 161. It needs to be understood, however, that this book is based mainly on the personal reminiscences of its author, meaning that there is a high likelihood that it may contain mistakes when it comes to the concrete figures or the facts it cites. *La 26 División* mentions that by September 1936 they had successfully "organized the 62nd Centuria," Mira/Anónimo, *La 26 División*, 14. Moreover, we need to appreciate that to the fighting militians marshalled in their centurias must be added others working in the Column's administrative, medical and other services.

12 As Manzana, for one, indicated in the report he forwarded to the CNT Regional Committee for Catalonia, "*Al Comité Regional de la 'CNT' de Cataluña en Barcelona*" (IISH-CNT-94E1), 2.

13 See for instance the evidence of the journalist José Gabriel *La vida y muerte en*

Notes to pages 88-90

Aragón (Buenos Aires: Edicions Imán, 1938), 166–78, and of the militiamen Manuel Ramos, *Una vida azarosa*. *44 años de exilio en Francia* (Sant Feliu de Guixols: self-published, 1993), 55; Antoine Gimenez, *Del amor, la Guerra y la revolución. Recuerdos de la Guerra de España del 19 de julio de 1936 al 9 de febrero de 1939* (Logroño, Spain: Pepitas de calabaza, 2009), 155; and Edi Gmür in his diary entry for January 18, 1937, Edi Gmür, *Spanish diary. A Swiss 'miliciano's' war diary of the Aragon front and Barcelona's 'May Days'* (Hastings, England: Christiebooks, 2015). Likewise, Léo Voline's very telling statement published in the *Bulletin du CIRA*, Marseilles, No 26–27, 1986.

14 Ricardo Sanz, *Los que fuimos a Madrid* (Barcelona: Petronio, 1977), 113–14. See also Cipriano Mera, *Guerra, exilio y cárcel de un anarcosindicalista* (Madrid: La Maltesta-Solidaridad Obrera, 2011), 131. For a complete account of how things went for the Durruti Column in Madrid prior to the death of its leader, see Abel Paz, *Durruti en la revolución española* (Madrid: La Esfera de los Libros, 2004), 649–67; Sanz points out that the casualty rate was 60%, *Los que fuimos a Madrid*, 120. Mira/Anónimo, *La 26 División*, p. 27 speaks of "upwards of 50% of all its personnel on the ground, not counting the many wounded who were evacuated."

15 Ricardo Sanz, *El sindicalismo y la política. Los 'Solidarios' y 'Nosotros'* (Toulouse: 1966), cited in Hans Magnus Enzensberger, *El corto verano de la anarquía: Vida y muerte de Durruti* (Barcelona: Anagrama, 2002), 233.

16 Ricardo Sanz, *Buenaventura Durruti* (Toulouse: 1945), cited in Enzensberger, *El corto verano de la anarquía*, 241–42. Regarding those militians that left Madrid see the minutes of the meetings of the higher committees on November 26 (IISH-CNT-94-D11) and December 2 (IISH-CNT-85-C1).

17 "*Reunión de Comités celebrada el día 11 de noviembre de 1936*" (IISH-CNT-94-D11).

18 Los Gimenólogues, *En busca de los Hijos de la Noche. Notas sobre los Recuerdos de la Guerra de España de Antoine Gimenez* (Logroño, Spain: Pepitas de calabaza, 2009), 569.

19 Joan Llarch *La Muerte de Durruti* (Esplugas de Llobregat, Spain: Plaza & Janés S.A. Editores, 1976), in English as *The Death of Durruti*, trans. Raymond Batkin (Hastings, England: Christie Books, 2013), 23–24.

20 Which fits in with the role that García Oliver thought that an intelligent revolutionary should perform once the revolution was under way: See *Colección de Historia Ora* (Vol 2): "One day I happened to hear that some comrades were bemoaning the fact that the bourgeois newspapers were—according to them—defaming the revolutionaries of Asturias because they said (the bourgeois newspapers) that a bunch of revolutionaries had raped a girl and they took a dim view of this. I seized upon the comrades' expressing this view in order to spell out in a talk what I understood social revolution to mean, and I ventured to state that the social revolution was an explosion that burst free of all restraints: legal restraints, political restraints, economic restraints, military restraints, family restraints—all of it! Of course—I added—an explosion that bursts free of all restraints strides recklessly into the infinite and the infinite proves to be something akin to madness. So—I instructed them—the intelligent revolutionary should have brand-new restraints standing by, some new conception of family, a new idea of

Notes to pages 90–92

economics and a brand-new conception of justice. All the restraints. Therefore, instead of allowing everyone to stride towards infinity, the revolutionary has to become a reactionary but not a counter-revolutionary. Meaning that he needs to backslide in order to impose restraints upon everything, and if you think that libertarian communism has ideas of its own, this is when it needs to be called upon," *Colección de Historia Oral: El movimiento libertario en España*, 2 (Madrid: Fundación Salvador Seguí, 1990), 16.

21 Llarch *La Muerte de Durruti*, 24.
22 Los Gimenólogues, *En busca de los Hijos de la Noche*, 565.
23 Los Gimenólogues, *En busca de los Hijos de la Noche*, 566.
24 Antonio Campos claims that he was political commissar, but I would rather refer to him as a delegate because commissars as such did not then exist within the unit: they would be appointed once the Column had been comprehensively militarized.
25 Antonio Campos Crespo, *Guerra y cárcel en España 1936–1975. Memorias del comandante Antonio Campos Crespo* (Barcelona: Virus, 1999), 39–43.
26 See Manzana's report *"To the Regional Committee of the 'CNT' in Catalonia in Barcelona,"* (IISH-CNT-94E1), 2: "The inactivity into which our Column had sunk over several months due to shortage of arms and munitions conjured up a climate of festering grumbling, even about things that were right."
27 Mira/Anónimo, *La 26 División*, 21.
28 Mira/Anónimo, *La 26 División*, 21–22.
29 "Al Comité Regional de la 'CNT' de Cataluña en Barcelona," IISH-CNT-94E1, 1.
30 Notice included in IISH-CNT-94E1.
31 Miguel Amorós, *La revolución traicionada. La verdadera historia de Balius y Los Amigos de Durruti* (Barcelona: Virus, 2003), 150. Thus, in his report Manzana accused Ruano of being "lacking in tact, being unduly opinionated in his judgment of actions which, just because they had been carried out by comrades of ours whose previous conduct had made the success of the revolution possible, ought to have merited greater indulgence on the part of those who, without an exemplary moral record of their own, set themselves up as the executioners of their own comrades-in-arms," "Al Comité Regional de la 'CNT' de Cataluña en Barcelona" (IISH-CNT-94E1), 1.
32 Published in *La Noche*, December 15, 1936.
33 "Shelling Enemy Concentrations in the Perdiguera-Leciñena Sector. FIGHTING IN THE VICINITY OF QUINTO"
34 Proclamation in IISH-CNT-94E1. It was also printed in *La Noche* on December 15, 1936.
35 Set up under the decree of November 21 that was carried in the *Butlletí Oficial de la Generalitat de Catalunya* on December 6: it was amended in the later, December 10 edition of the *Butlletí Oficial de la Generalitat de Catalunya*.
36 For more on this "Army of Catalonia," see Michael Alpert, *El ejército republican en la guerra civil* (Paris: Ruedo Iberico, 1977), 87–88.
37 Vicente Guarner, Cataluña en la Guerra de España (Madrid: G. del Toro, 1975), 270. Also of interest here is the "*Acta de la reunió del Consell Executiu de la*

Generalitat del dia 22 d'abril del 1937" cited in Agustín Guillamón, *La Guerra del pan. Hambre y violencia en la Barcelona revolucionaria. De diciembre de 1936 a mayo de 1937* (Barcelona: Aldarull-Dskntrl-ed!, 2014), 483: at which Isgleas, the Generalitat's Defense Councillor representing the CNT, reported that "his demand for arms for organizing the divisions in Aragon had been subjected to further postponement even though 'our divisions on the Aragon front are already organized in accordance with the orders from the central government.'"

38   Juan Giménez Arenas, *De la Unión a Banat. Itinerario de una rebeldía* (Madrid: Fundación Ansemo Lorenzo, 1996), 55–56.

39   Giménez Arenas, *De la Unión a Banat*, 56.

40   "The Army is of the People and For the People," in *Via Libre*.

41   For a list of the demands translated into Castilian, see Miguel Amorós, *La revolución traicionada. La verdadera historia de Balius y Los Amigos de Durruti* (Barcelona: Virus, 2003), 154. The complete resolution (in French) can be found in André and Dori Prudhommeaux, *Catalogne libertaire 1936–1937. L'Armement du people. Que sont la CNT et la FAI?* (Paris: Cahiers Spartacus, 1940), 25–26.

42   "Reunión de Comités celebrada el día 18 de Diciembre de 1936" (IISH-CNT-85-C1): "RC [Regional Committee]: Opens by saying that, in addition to the Delegation that turned up complaining about Ruano." It should be added that the general secretary of the Regional Committee, Valerio Mas himself, was there when Ruano threatened to shoot the delegation that had come to object to militarization (See Juan Giménez Arenas (1996), 56).

43   "Reunión de Comités, Consejeros, Concejales y Jefes de Columna, celebrada el día 18 de diciembre, a las 10 de la noche" (IISH-CNT-85-C1). Capitals reproduced from the original.

44   It should be made clear that there were Spaniards in the International Group.

45   Edi Gmür, *Spanish diary. A Swiss 'miliciano's' war diary of the Aragon front and Barcelona's 'May Days'* (Hastings, England: Christiebooks, 2015): "This afternoon there was a get-together of all the Internationals. Topic: Militarization. The proceedings were quite shrill. Mostly it was the French and the Spaniards who were against militarization of the militias. The Germans and the other Internationals are for it, but with certain stipulations. The meeting ended in chaos."

46   In his report, Manzana mentions that the Committees from several villages "had handed over . . . cash sums to the tune of around ninety thousand pesos. Moreover, CAMSA, presented an invoice for one hundred thousand pesos, which, by its reckoning, was the cost of the gasoline ordered by the preceding Committee [Ruano's committee] and sold to a variety of villages." "Al Comité Regional de la 'CNT' de Cataluña en Barcelona" (IISH-CNT-94E1, 5) Similarly, in "Reunión del Comité Regional de Cataluña celebrada el día 27 de 1937, a las diez de la noche," Ascaso had pointed out that the commission that showed up to look into the Column's finances agreed with Manzana that the latter "would require of Ruano that he return the hundreds of thousands of pesetas that he had improperly seized" (IISH-CNT-85-C1).

47   As suggested by the fact that, just prior to his being executed by some of his CNT comrades, Ruano had been planning to flee the country in a yacht laden

Notes to pages 95–97

with the money that he had been embezzling. For the fate of Ruano and his "treasure," see Los Gimenólogues, *En busca de los Hijos de la Noche*, 567–69.

48 Los Gimenólogues, *En busca de los Hijos de la Noche*, 396. *Solidaridad Obrera* reported his arrival in an article on January 17, 1937, headlined "With the Durruti Division... This Is the Man..."

49 "Al Comité Regional de la 'CNT' de Cataluña" (IISH-CNT-94E1), 2: "My first move was to relieve all of the personnel who had aided and abetted the poisonous handiwork of the previous Committee so that comrades coming to me to tell me what they needed might not run into those who, just days before, had been threatening them at rifle-point. That move went down well with the Column but, because previously there had been a personal type of politicking going on, some personnel who identified with the outgoing Committee asked to leave."

50 "Al Comité Regional de la 'CNT' de Cataluña en Barcelona" (IISH-CNT94E1), 2–3: "In order to make it more palatable, Manzana preferred to talk about 'organizing ourselves militarily; rather than mention militarization." See also "With the Durruti Division... This Is the Man..." in *Solidaridad Obrera*.

51 One eloquent example might be Camillo Berneri's article "The Slandered Aragon Front" in the May 1, 1937, edition of *Guerra di Classe*, the Italian-language anarchist weekly paper published in Barcelona as his response to a caricature that had appeared in *Las Noticias* depicting the front as a portly militiaman sitting without a care in the world in the shade of a tree with a flagon by his side and fishing in a river.

52 As is stated in the article "The War and the Revolution" *in El Amigo del pueblo*, no 1: "The petit bourgeois parties and the official marxists are the ones putting the greatest effort into dissevering the revolution from the war. They tell us that we anarchists should wait until we have won the war before making the revolution. They tell us not to be impatient, that there will be time enough for everything. But in the meantime, those who champion the revolution's postponement until after the war, are out to secure a monopoly on positions of command and on the levers of power, with the aim of strangling the revolution."

53 Juan Giménez Arenas, *De la Unión a Banat. Itinerario de una rebeldía* (Madrid: Fundación Ansemo Lorenzo, 1996), 56.

54 Los Gimenólogues, *En busca de los Hijos de la Noche*, 364; "To the comrades from the confederal columns., The opinion of a majority of the Durruti Column's comrades" (IISH-CNT-94E-1).

55 "Informe para el Comité Regional de la CNT," January 13, 1937, (IISH-CNT-94E-1), 1: "But on the 20th, our delegates were informed that they would not be recognized at headquarters.... Comrade Manzana informed us that, for one thing, the manifesto issued by the outgoing headquarters no longer held any validity and that, secondly, a military reorganization along lines acknowledged by himself, Manzana, would now begin."

56 "Informe para el Comité Regional de la CNT," 2.

57 We know the actual date thanks to Edi Gmür, *Spanish diary*.

58 "The Militarization Question. To the comrades, to the confederal comrades" in *El Amigo del Pueblo*, July 20, 1937.

59 "Acta del Pleno de Columnas Confederales y Anarquistas celebrado en Valencia el día 5 de febrero de 1937," 22. Accessible at http://www.fonation-besnard.org.
60 "Acta del Pleno de Columnas Confederales y Anarquistas celebrado en Valencia el día 5 de febrero de 1937," 31, 59.
61 Guarner, *Cataluña en la Guerra de España*, 253 explains how, on February 20, he signed off on the order covering the definitive organization of the front, by forming four Divisions, flanked by two *Agrupaciones* covering the Pyrenean and Southern sectors: one such Division was the 'Durruti' Division."
62 "Al Comité Regional de la 'CNT' de Cataluña en Barcelona," (IISH-CNT-94E1), 3–4. This fact appears also to be borne out by Collado from the Durruti Column's "official" delegation, as the Gelsa sector also sent its own delegation which was not allowed to participate. See "Acta del Pleno de Columnas Confederales y Anarquistas celebrado en Valencia el día 5 de febrero de 1937," 29, http://www.fondation-besnard.org/wp-content/uploads/2025/01/CNT-FAI-Acta-del-Pleno-de-Columnas-Confederales-y-Anarquistas-v-3-1.pdf.
63 The lines in quotation marks are taken from "Al Comité Regional de la 'CNT' de Cataluña en Barcelona," 4.
64 "Informe que este Comité de Relaciones de Grupos Anarquistas de Cataluña presenta a los camaradas de la región" (undated/no place of publication given (April 1937?), cited in Agustín Guillamón, *Los Amigos de Durruti. Historia y antología de textos* (Barcelona: Aldarull-Dskntrl-ed!, 2013), 220.
65 "Reunión celebrada el día 12 de febrero de 1937. [a] las diez de la noche, estando presente el compañero Manzana de la columna Durruti, C.R. de la FAI, Federación Local, JJ.LL y Comité Local de Cataluña," (IISH-CNT-85C1).
66 "Informe que este Comité de Relaciones de Grupos Anarquistas," in Guillamón *Los Amigos de Durruti*, 220.
67 Guillamón, *Los Amigos de Durruti*, 220, note 229; "Pablo Ruiz talks about the civic action carried out by the Durruti Column on Aragonese soil," in *La Noche*, March 24, 1937; "FAI: *Informe que este Comité de Relaciones de Grupos Anarquistas de Cataluña presenta a los camaradas de la región*" (undated/no place of publication given) [April 1937?], cited in Guillamón, *Los Amigos de Durruti*, 219–20: "Not only did they refuse to be militarized, but they also ignored the stipulation from both Committees that they lay down their arms and quit the front."
68 For further detail regarding the origins of the *Agrupación*, see Guillamón, *Los Amigos de Durruti*.
69 Los Gimenologos write: "It looks like Sergeant Manzana may have drawn his gun during a tussle with one of Durruti's comrades, José Mira." Nevertheless, in light of "Acta de la reunión celebrada (3), it seems that Manzana was not the only one to draw his weapon: "Comrade Mamet offers a justification [clarification?] of what passed between comrade Mira and Manzana, mentioning the business with the pistols and some other minor details," Los Gimenólogues, *En busca de los Hijos de la Noche*, 424.
70 As the Gimenologos put it: "Might possible suspicions as to his part in Durruti's death have generated these tensions?," Los Gimenólogues, *En busca de los Hijos de la Noche*, 424. For more about Durruti's death and the theories as to whether

that gunshot may have been premeditated, intentional or accidental mentioned in the books cited, see note 201 in the chapter "Zaragoza Bound: The Revolution Awaits" above.

71 Letter dated March 28, 1937 (IISH-CNT-63D-II-2): "Some signs indicated that it was Manzana had a mental breakdown: he was desmoralized, according to his own statements, he was full of 'inferiority complexes according to others.'"

72 Letter dated March 28, 1937 (IISH-CNT-63D-II-2): The Estado Mayor of the Aragon Front and the Central Government [saw] the sergeant in Manzana. The difficulties experienced by our division because of these two bodies is nuanced. This may have been one of the reasons for Manzana's resignation

73 I Letter dated March 28, 1937 (IISH-CNT-63D-II-2): So, if all goes well, Manzana will go to Sariñena, where some taciturn Russians are currently plotting shady things with a republican militarist.

74 Letter dated March 28, 1937 (IISH-CNT-63D-II-2): "Manzana returned, involuntarily, but at the insistence of the organization. A four-man commission, in which I was included, received Manzana on behalf of the division. The meeting took place in the presence of two delegates from the regional committee and a delegate from the Consejeria de Defensa. The result is to be treated confidentially. Manzana officially returns to our division as chief and, with the support of three comrades, and forms the headquarters as before. Also confidential, Manzana will remain with us until the Confedracion manages to replace the current chief of the Estado Mayor of the Aragon Front with Manzana"; "Acta de la reunión celebrada en el Cuartel General el día 26 de Marzo de 1937" (IISH-CNT-94E-1): Gaston Leval opined "Manzana's return is crucial as far as general business is concerned . . . one such item is that there is no one to replace him in this Division a promptly as would be required." This was not the meeting with Manzana that I mentioned by Rudolf Michaelis in his letter, but an earlier one that took place a day or two before.

75 For more details see José Manuel Márquez Rodríguez and Juan José Gallardo Romero, *Ortiz: general sin dios ni amo* (Barcelona: Editorial Hacer, 1999), 164–74: Ricardo Sanz, *La política y el sindicalismo* (Barcelona: Petronio, 1978), 286–87; Eduardo Pons Prades, "Verano de 1936: ¿Por qué no se tomó Zaragoza?," *Nueva Historia* 26 (March 1979). The latter article, based mainly on the evidence of Saturnino Carod Lerín, explains that the planning behind and proposal for the operation took place prior to Durruti's departure for Madrid. Nevertheless, by my reckoning, Carod, naturally enough after such a long time, must have mixed up, and in his testimony, conflated scenes and dates from different points in the war: so Antonio Ortiz in Márquez Rodríguez and Gallardo Romero's *Ortiz* states that it occurred during the first few weeks of 1937, and Sanz, in *La política y el sindicalismo*, though mentioning no date, points out that it began to come under consideration because "Zaragoza, given the enemy pressure on Madrid, was completely undermanned." Which inclines me to think that its planning and proposal, as Ortiz mentioned, must have come during the first few months of 1937.

76 Maldonado Moya, *El Frente de Aragón*, 146; Valentín Solano Sanmiguel, *Guerra Civil Aragón Tomo III, Teruel* (Zaragoza: Delsan Libros, 2006), 83–84; José Manuel Martínez Bande, *La invasión de Aragón y el desembarco en Mallorca*

Notes to pages 101–03

(Madrid: Editorial San Martín, 1989), 239–40; Vicente Guarner, *Cataluña en la Guerra de España* (Madrid: G. del Toro, 1975), 259–60; and Mira/Anónimo, *La 26 División*, 52.

77   Guarner, *Cataluña en la Guerra de España*, 263.

78   Guarner, *Cataluña en la Guerra de España*, 263–64; Maldonado Moya, *El Frente de Aragón*, 148, and Mira/Anónimo, *La 26 División*, 52–53.

79   Mira/Anónimo, *La 26 División*, 52–53; and Maldonado Moya, *El Frente de Aragón*, 151. Likewise, there is a wide range of testimonies in greater detail concerning this incident in Los Gimenólogues, *En busca de los Hijos de la Noche*, 430–34, 480–82, and 487.

80   Juan García Oliver acknowledged: "Ever the ingenues, ever the hot-heads.... We made bad politicians," García Oliver, *El eco de los pasos*, 414.

81   For more detail, see Agustín Guillamón, *La Guerra del pan. Hambre y violencia en la Barcelona revolucionaria. De diciembre de 1936 a mayo de 1937* (Barcelona: Aldarull-Dskntrl-ed!, 2014), passim.

82   For the full battery of these decrees, see the *Butlletí Oficial de la Generalitat de Catalunya*, March 4, 1937.

83   For more details regarding their origins, functions, and make-up, see García Oliver, *El eco de los pasos*, 210–11.

84   Josep Antoni Pozo González explains that following the frustration of the army's would-be coup, a lot of members of the police forces made overtures to the workers' organizations, working hand in glove with them, especially during the first few weeks. "Nevertheless, despite such inroads made by the revolution into the policing bodies, most of their personnel maintained a degree of aloofness.... The very same mind-set that had traditionally shaped the cadre structure lived on, and so, of course did the same conservative mentality with little liking for revolutionary processes. Besides, it needs pointing out that a goodly proportion of the positions available within the Security and Assault Guard Corps and the Investigation and Watch Corps, were overhauled and filled with fresh personnel in 1934.... During that period, a lot of militants from the Esquerra Republicana-Estat Català Youth had joined ... leading to a significant 'Catalanization' of them," Josep Antoni Pozo González, *Poder legal y poder real en la Cataluña revolucionaria de 1936. El Gobierno de la Generalidad ante el Comité Central de Milicias Antifascistas y los diversos poderes revolucionarios locales* (Seville: Ediciones Espuela de Plata, 2012), 130–31.

85   "*Acta de la sessió del Consell Executiu de la Generalitat pels dies 12/13 de març del 1937*," cited in Guillamón, *La Guerra del pan*, 358; Regarding the reasons behind this resignation, see Guillamón, *La Guerra del pan*, 359: "Acta de la reunión del Comité Regional celebrada el día 20-3-37," (IISH-CNT-85-C1); and "Reunión de comités responsables, consejeros, delegados de comarcas y Toryho. Que se celebró el día 23 de marzo de 1937. A las 12 del mediodía," (IISH-CNT-85-C1).

86   Examples of this alarm might be the contributions of the Barcelona Manufacturing Union or the Barcelona Woodworkers' Union to the thirteenth sitting of the congress of the CNT of Catalonia: *Memoria del Congreso Extraordinario de la Confederación Regional del Trabajo de Cataluña. Celebrado en Barcelona los*

Notes to pages 103–04

días 25 de febrero al 3 de marzo de 1937, Talleres gráficos (Juan, Barcelona, 1937) (CDHMS-DIGITAL-A-02501); the *"Acuerdos tomados por el Pleno de Locales, Comarcales e Intercomarcales de GGAA de la región, celebrado el día 8 del corriente [marzo],"* (IISH-FAI-CP-17-B1): the *"Pleno del Comité regional. Reunión con los Delegados de zona de la Región, celebrada el día 14 de Marzo de 1937,* (IISH-CNT-85-C1); and the Argentinean Jacobo Prince's letter to his FACA comrades back in Buenos Aires, see *"Correspondencia de la FACA. Carta 40 del 22 marzo 1937"* (BAEL) cited in Guillamón, *La Guerra del pan,* 375–76; *"Reunión de comités responsables, consejeros, delegados de comarcas y Toryho. Que se celebró el día 23 de marzo de 1937. A las 12 del mediodia,"* (IISH-CNT-85-C1).

87   Notably the resolution passed at the "Second sitting of the local plenum of Barcelona anarchist groups . . . summoned in the meeting-hall of the Casa CNT-FAI and attended by the confederal Defense groups and the Libertarian Youth, Barcelona, April 24, 1937," (SA-PS-Barcelona 1307-7), cited in Guillamón, *La Guerra del pan,* 427–41. At it, it was agreed "1—That all personnel currently holding posts in antifascist governing circles should withdraw. 2—That an antifascist revolutionary Committee should be formed to coordinate the armed struggle against fascism, and 3—That industry, trade and agriculture be taken into social ownership immediately."

88   Guillamón, *La Guerra del pan,* 444, note 441, or also in Guillamón, *Los Amigos de Durruti,* 226, note 222. Francisco Pellicer was to give clear expression to this belief in "The Present Moment," published in *La Noche,* April 14, 1937, as Jaime Balius also did in "Grave Times. Let's Make the Revolution" in *Ideas,* the weekly mouthpiece of the Libertarian Movement in the Lower Llobregat Comarca, April 8, 1937, cited in Guillamón, *Los Amigos de Durruti,* 215.

89   For a detailed listing of their activities at the time, see Guillamón, *Los Amigos de Durruti,* 22–23.

90   See the full program, Guillamón, *Los Amigos de Durruti,* 220–21.

91   This list has been based in part on theone set out by José Costa Font in "Background to and Chronology of the Events of May 1937 in Barcelona," in *Polémica,* available in digitalized form at https://revistapolemica.wordpress.com/2014/01/22/antecedentes-y-cronologia-de-los-sucesos-de-mayo-de-1937-en-barcelona.

92   For further details, see "To What End? Twelve tanks removed from a Depot holding War Materials," *Solidaridad Obrera,* March 7, 1937.

93   For a translation in Castilian, see *Germinal. Revista de Estudios Libertarios* 3 (April 2007).

94   Juan Gómez Casas, *Historia del anarcosindicalismo Español. Epílogo hasta nuestros días: La España del éxodo y del llanto* (Bilbao: Zero, 1978), 292; and Tomás Caballé y Clos, *Barcelona roja. Dietario de la revolución (julio 1936–enero 1939)* (Librería Barcelona: Argentina, 1939), 93–94.

95   Burnett Bolloten, *La Revolución Española,* 556. See the recent study by Antonio Gascón and Agustín Guillamón into the death of Antonio Martín in *Catalunya.Organ d'exppressió de la CGT de Catalunya,* nos 166 and 167, November and December of 2014, respectively.

Notes to pages 105–10

96   Carl Einstein, "The Aragon Front," in *Die Soziale Revolution. Frontzeitung*, published by the German Anarcho-syndicalists and the Spanish National Committee of the CNT-FAI, no 12, May 1, 1937, 1–2, cited in Einstein, *La Columna Durruti*, 22–27. The German-language original can found at https://www.anarchismus.at/zeitungen-bis-1945/die-soziale-revolution/file/237-die-soziale-revolution-nr-12.
97   Carl Einstein, "The Aragon Front."
98   Gómez Casas, *Historia del anarcosindicalismo Españo*, 292, and Bolloten, *La Revolución Española*, 558. This is reflected, albeit more ambiguously, in Caballé y Clos, *Barcelona roja*, 96.
99   Caballé y Clos, *Barcelona roja*, 95.
100 *Solidaridad Obrera*, 12.
101 Agustin Guillamón, *Los Amigos de Durruti*, 48.
102 For a detailed account of events, see Bolloten, *La Revolución Española*, 559–96; and Agustín Guillamón, *Insurrección. Las sangrientas jornadas del 3 al 7 de mayo del 1937* (Barcelona: Descontrol Editorial, 2017).
103 Guillamón, *Insurrección*.
104 Notably Felix Morrow, *Guerra Civil en España. Revolución y Contrarrevolución* (Publicaciones Trece Rosas, n.d.), 126; and as indicated by "Senex" in *Vanguard* of February 1939 and cited in Bolloten, *La Revolución Española*, 578–79: "It may be readily taken for granted that the workers, backed by the CNT units, might have stood a very good chance of victory had this new civil war erupted. But that victory would have been a Pyrrhic victory at best, because it must be plain that a civil war in the rearguard, with a resultant demoralization in the front lines and troops being withdrawn in order for them to participate in the new civil war would have thrown the gates wide open to a triumphant advance by the fascists. . . . No one with the slightest knowledge of the situation is going to say that . . . the masses of the French people and British people were ready to go to war for Spain."
105 Here we have the interesting testimony of Juan Manuel Molina aka *Juanel*, the then under-secretary at the Defense Department, as articulated in "From the Defense Department, May 1937 in Catalonia," *Historia Libertaria*, 4, (March–April 1979).
106 This episode is explored in detail in Bolloten, *La Revolución Española*, 597–618.
107 See the *Butlletí Oficial de la Generalitat de Catalunya* for June 5, 1937.
108 For more detail regarding the make-up of the government and the debates and circumstances leading up its formation, see Agustín Guillamón, *La represión contra la CNT y los revolucionarios. Hambre y violencia en la Barcelona revolucionaria de mayo a septiembre de 1937* (Barcelona: Descontrol Editorial, 2015), 186–93.
109 The last to be raised was the premises of the Centre Defense Committee on September 20. For more details, see Guillamón, *La represión contra la CNT y los revolucionarios*, 402–07.
110 Guillamón, *La represión contra la CNT y los revolucionarios*, passim.
111 It is worth highlighting here: "How could the CNT have failed to come up with a determined collective political action in opposition to state repression? How

come the RC [Regional Committee] or the CAP [Policy Advisory Commission] failed to mount a defense and stoically put up with blow after blow? As far as the higher committees were concerned, there were two priorities to which they subordinated everything: thwarting the emergence of an internal revolutionary opposition within the CNT's own ranks, and, at all costs, preserving antifascist unity in," Guillamón, *La represión contra la CNT y los revolucionarios*, 220. "Revolutionary prisoners and minorities distanced themselves from the collaborationist approach of the higher committees in such a way as to make a split look inevitable. That split was averted thanks to the SELECTIVE policy of the Stalinists, consisting of cracking down on and weakening the revolutionary opposition and absorbing the higher committees into the machinery of the state," Guillamón, *La represión contra la CNT y los revolucionarios*, 447.

112 Carlos Engel specifies April 28, Carlos Engel, *Historia de las Brigadas Mixtas del Ejército Popular de la República* (Madrid: Almena, 1999), 210.

113 Mira/Anónimo, *La 26 División*, 42; Sanz, *Los que fuimos a Madrid*, 127; and Sanz, *La política y el sindicalismo*, 275; "Ricardo Sanz at the head of the Durruti Division" in *Solidaridad Obrera* May 16, 1937, reported: "Our comrade Ricardo Sanz arrived in Bujaraloz yesterday and has assumed command of the Durruti Division." For more details regarding the rest of the Division's ranking officers see "OUR MEN," *El Frente*, July 19, 1937.

114 Maldonado Moya, *El Frente de Aragón*, 168.

115 Gimenez, *Del amor, la Guerra y la revolución*, 169.

116 "*Informe que presenta la sección de defensa al comité regional de la CNT*," 5, (IISH-CNT-39C-2).

117 Maldonado Moya, *El Frente de Aragón*, 191.

118 Maldonado Moya, *El Frente de Aragón*, 193.

119 Decree published in the *Gaceta de la República*, August 11.

120 José Borrás, *Aragón en la revolución española* (Barcelona: César Viguera, 1983), 208; Maldonado Moya, *El Frente de Aragón*, 210; and Márquez Rodríguez and Gallardo Romero, *Ortiz*, 214.

121 Sanz, *Los que fuimos a Madrid*, 154.

122 For an account of the battle, see Maldonado Moya, *El Frente de Aragón*, 200–23.

Epilogue: A Hard Lesson to Swallow

1 For further details regarding the outlooks of each current, see Ángel Herrerín López, *La CNT durante el franquismo*: "Each faction's approach may be summed up briefly as follows: in the view of the orthodoxes, the experience of what had passed during the civil war, with the odd honorable exception such as the collectives, had been a nightmare to be banished from their memories as soon as possible. To which end they sought to take a step back from all of the 'ideological deviations' that they saw as having been behind the loss of the war and the position in which the libertarian movement found itself … as if nothing had happened. For their part, the possibilists suffered from the same delusion as the other faction,

but, far from wanting to forget the bad experience, they were not prepared to write the civil war off as lost and they stuck to the organization's civil war-time policy line, which is to say, collaboration with the other antifascist organizations, entry into the republican governments, championing republican legality, etc., which, essentially, entailed a jettisoning of anarcho-syndicalist ideals, which should have necessitated an ideological re-think. The basic problem for that faction was that they had a purely circumstancialist policy, which is to say one based on the circumstances of the moment, without making the changes necessary to guide them in the future." Ángel Herrerín López, *La CNT durante el franquismo. Clandestinidad y exilio (1939–1975)* (Madrid: Siglo Veintiuno, 2004), 76–77.

2 Another notable exception, albeit of a shall we say reformist bent, which is not to say uninteresting, would be Horacio M. Prieto: for information regarding his thinking and the Libertarian Party he suggested should be launched, see "Regarding the Present and Future of the Libertarian Movement" in *Timón*, July 1938 and "Controversial Study" in *Timón*, September 1938: Also Horacio Martínez Prieto, *El anarquismo español en la lucha política* (Paris, 1946); and Horacio Martínez Prieto, *Posibilismo libertario* (Val-de-Marne, France: Ivry-sur-Seine, 1966).

3 Agustín Guillamón, *Los Amigos de Durruti. Historia y antología de textos* (Barcelona: Aldarull-Dskntrl-ed!, 2013), 95.

4 Jaime Balius, *Towards a Fresh Revolution*, cited in Guillamón, *Los Amigos de Durruti*, 331.

5 As is evident from the following commentary: "At the present time an understanding between the CNT and the revolutionary wing of the UGT is feasible," Guillamón, *Los Amigos de Durruti*, 329.Nevertheless, the fact is that there was still some ambiguity surrounding the make-up of the Revolutionary Junta which was never well-defined at all.

6 Regarding the Revolutionary Junta, see Guillamón, *Los Amigos de Durruti*, 331.

7 Guillamón, *Los Amigos de Durruti*, 332.

8 Guillamón, *Los Amigos de Durruti*, 328. "The workers will enforce revolutionary order. We insist upon the disbandment of the uniformed bodies that offer no guarantee of revolution. The trade unions must vouch for those put in charge of watching over the new order we want to establish," Guillamón, *Los Amigos de Durruti*, 330.

9 Guillamón, *Los Amigos de Durruti*, 320.

10 As is also explained by Miguel Gómez from the Aldarull publishing house, cited in Guillamón, *Los Amigos de Durruti*, 16.

11 Jaime Balius, *Towards a Fresh Revolution*, cited in Guillamón, *Los Amigos de Durruti*, 333.

12 For further exploration of this interesting point, see Guillamón, *Los Amigos de Durruti*, 122–34.

Index

Abad de Santillán, Diego: on arms, 55, 56, 151–52n134, 158n187; on Blanquism, 128n54; Column in Madrid, 63, 68; Column moving out, 42; Column trapped, 50; on disarming libertarians, 56; on Durruti's request for arms, 55; on high command anarchists, 142–43n55; on manpower, 44, 69; on seizure of gold, 58; on Zaragoza attack, 157n178
abstention, 17
"Acción y Alegría" Group, 95, 96–97, 172n55
action groups, 6
administration, 48
affinities, 42
age, 126n36
Agrupación Committee, 49
Los Aguiluchos, 64
aid, 56, 57
air force, 47
AIT/IWA. *See* Workers' International Association

Alberola, José, 80
Alcalde, Juan J., 135n15
ammunition, 57, 62, 66, 154n152, 158n187. *See also* arms
"Anarcosindicalismo: cómo afianzaremos la rev-ón" (Prieto), 8–9
Los anarquistas españoles y el poder 1868–1969 (Lorenzo), 135n15, 147n103
Andalusia, 130n78
antifascists: collaboration with, 34–36, 46, 59, 101, 135n7, 152n139 (*see also* Central Antifascist Militias Committee of Catalonia); Higher Council of War as overseers, 86; optimism of, 44
Antona, David, 67
Antonov-Ovseenko, Vladimir, 66
Aragon: as "anvil," 60; and arms for Barcelona, 69; Column and Ruano, 89–90; as fallen to rebels, 39; and Generalitat, 57–58, 151n132; March/April

181

1937, 100–01; optimism on, 105; Regional Defense Council of Aragon, 53. *See also* Zaragoza; *various towns/cities*
Aragón, Fernando, 152n139
Aragon Front War Committee, 59
Arendt, Hannah, 1–2
arms: for Barcelona, 68–69, 158n187; for Column in Madrid, 159n197; and desertion, 98; and Gelsa comrades, 99; and integration into People's Army, 86, 110, 168n6; libertarians disarming, 56, 106, 150n124; for Madrid, 67; and militarization, 96–97; moving to the front, 63; for rearguard, 55–57; rearguard vs. front, 44, 143n55, 150n120, 150n122; as responsibility of defense committees, 8; shortages of, 44, 54–57, 100, 149n116, 149n118, 151n132, 151–52n134, 167n6; and socialists' stockpile of, 131n83; sources for, 57, 59, 151n131; training, 140n39. *See also* ammunition
army: CNT's libertarian communism, 26–30; as danger to revolution, 29; Faure on, 9–10; and guerrilla warfare, 53–54; molding of new, 85; mutiny, 18, 128n53; need for, 115; as rearguard, 44, 143n58; revolt of, 33–34, 134n4; and revolution, 2, 8, 16–17, 122n4, 124n14; standing, 13; and traditional anarchism, 5–7, 10–11, 22, 25, 28–29; unity of rebels, 136n16; and workers control, 12, 124n24. *See also* Assault Guard; Civil Guard; militarism/militarization; Proletarian Army proposition; rearguard; Republican National Guard
Army of Catalonia, 92
Arnal, Jesús, 47, 74, 77, 142n50
Arquer, Jordi, 46, 56–57
arrests, 106
Arshinov Platform, 121n1
Ascaso, Francisco: action and Los Solidarios/Nosotros group, 128n52; death of, 140n35; Los Indomables, 121n9; and Madrid, 67; and Makhno, 117; Regional Defense Committee of Catalonia, 13–14; on Ruano's theft, 171n46
Ascaso, Joaquín, 17, 127n49
Ascaso Column, 64
Assault Guard, 102, 104, 105–06, 108, 175n84
Asturian revolutionaries, 18–19, 24–25, 70, 131n83
authority, 77–78
AWOL, 74, 76–77, 91. *See also* desertion; mutiny
Azaña, Manuel, 52

Bakunin, Mikhail Aleksandrovitch, 1, 14, 122n4, 126n35
Balbé, Manuel, 126n36
Balius, Jaime, 113, 114–16
La Banda Negra, 49, 145n84
"La baraja sin fin" (Oliver), 14
Barcelona, 42, 68–69, 106–08, 134n4, 135n10, 158n187

Index

Barcelona Manufacturing and Textile Union, 26–27
Bargalló (comrade), 70
barrio defense committees, 20–21. *See also* Local Defense Committee
De Barrio-Trueba Column. *See* Karl Marx Division
Basque Nationalist Party (PNV), 52
Battle of Belchite, 112
The Bears of Berne and the Bear of St Petersburg (Bakunin), 1
Belchite, 112
Berneri, Camillo, 103–04
Berthomieu, Louis, 62, 155n154
Besnard, Pierre, 63–4, 151n132
Black Army, 117
Blanco, José, 48, 92
Blanquism, 128n54
Bloody Week in Seville, 7
Boguña, Jaime, 91–92, 94
Bolshevik-Leninist Section of Spain, 107–08
Bolsheviks, 11
Boncour, Paul, 25
Bonet, José, 15, 126n38
book overview, 2–3
Borrás, José, 156–7n176
Bueno Pérez, Justo, 49
Bujaraloz Decree, 80
bullets. *See* ammunition
Busquets, 70

CAMC. *See* Central Antifascist Militias Committee of Catalonia
Camón, Agustín, vii
Campón (comrade), 70

Campos, Antonio, 90
capitalism, 105
Carbó, Eusebio, 15
Carlists, 36, 135n16
Caro Andrés, Angel, 161n5
Carod, Saturnino, 56–57, 81–82
Carrasquer, Francisco, 146n90
Carreño, Francisco, 49
Casanova, Julián, 35, 126n36, 129n65, 130n77, 133n101, 134n1, 134n4
Caspe, 46–47
Catalonia, 34–35, 57, 64, 70. *See also* Central Antifascist Militias Committee of Catalonia; Generalitat of Catalonia
Causa General, 161n5
Central Antifascist Militias Committee of Catalonia (CAMC): birth of, 35–36, 135n11, 135–36nn13–15, 135n14; as contradictory, 137n18; Control Patrols, 102, 175n84; disarming rearguard, 55–56, 150n124; end of, 51; and Generalitat, 37, 58, 137n18; Majorca expedition, 51, 146–47n96; proclamation on arms, 150n120; and PSUC arms, 55; radio address 1936, 42
Central War Committee, 164n29
centurias (general), 21, 27–28, 36, 48–49, 145n80, 160n1, 168n3
Civil Guard, 46, 140–2n42
civil war (general), 11–12, 22
clandestinity, 6, 20
class, 44–5
CNT. *See* National Confederation of Labor
Code of Military Justice, 64

183

coercion, 74–75, 79, 166n41
collaboration: with antifascists, 34–36, 46, 59, 101, 135n7, 152n139 (*see also* Central Antifascist Militias Committee of Catalonia); at any cost, 101–02; as ending, 103, 176n87; justifications for, 113, 178–79n1
collectivization, 79–80, 140n38, 165nn32–33
Comerera, Joan, 65
Los Comités de Defensa de la CNT (Guillamón, Agustín), 132n92
Commissions and Councils (of Supplies, Economy, Culture, Defense), 51
Communist Party, 24
Communist Youth, 158n191
communists: 1937 actions in Zaragoza, 111–12; overview, 70; and CNT split, 178n111; Durruti as threat to, 66, 68, 88–89; and Friends of Durruti, 116; and libertarian victory, 108; March campaign in Catalonia, 101; murdering anarchists, 104; refusing Durruti's orders, 70; and removal of Largo Caballero, 109; revolution ideas, 95, 171n51; and Telephone Exchange, 107; theft from CNT, 103; Unified Socialist Youth, 158n191; and USSR supplying arms, 59. *See also* antifascists
Companys, Don Luis, 39, 40, 65. *See also* Generalitat of Catalonia
compartmentalization, 59–60

compliance, 65–66
concessions, 95, 101–02, 155n155. *See also* collaboration
Conejos Vicente, Antonio, 16–17
"Confederal Conception of Libertarian Communism" resolution, 29–30
confederal defense cadres, 7–8
Control Patrols, 102, 109, 175n84
corrective actions, 30
Cortada, Roldán, 104
Council of Aragon, 53
countryside: anarchist support, 23; and CNT, 15; collectivization, 79–80, 165n33, 165–66n35; guerrilla detachments, 23–24; revolution starting in, 130n74, 130nn77–78, 131n80; vs. towns, 45, 79–80, 131n80, 146n95, 165n32
coup d'états, 13, 22, 26, 36, 57
crime, 29–30
Crónicas del 36 (Camón), vii
Cuba (comrade), 70
currency, 57–8, 152nn134–5

decrees for desertion, 34
decurias, 49, 73
defense committees (overview), 8, 21, 106–07, 109, 129n64. *See also* discipline; *individual committees*
Defense Department, 63, 92, 101, 102
"In Defense of the Revolution" (El Pájaro Rojo), 132–33n92
defense vs. offense, 40
desertion, 34, 45, 90, 97–98. *See also* AWOL; mutiny

Index

dictatorship, 29, 38, 138n24
Los Dinamiteros, 49
discipline: overview, 73–77; vs. authority, 44–45, 77–78, 143n60, 143n63; vs. courage, 56; and Durruti as leader, 78–79, 164n26; early introduction of, 160n3; and militarization resistance, 87; Pérez Farrás on, 142n50; the Platform, 12; and rearguard, 44, 79, 164n26; and *Solidaridad Obrera*, 133n99; workers in arms plants, 9. *See also* punishment
District Defense Committee, 21. *See also* Local Defense Committee
dual powers, 37, 137n18
duplication of powers, 37, 137n18
Durruti, José Buenaventura: arms for Barcelona, 68–69, 158n187; on arms shortages, 149n116; Camón meeting, vii; and Caro Andrés's son, 161n5; and collaboration, 46, 59; and collectivization of harvest work, 80; Column set up, 39; and Companys, 40; criticized, 51; criticizing privilege, 65–66; death of, 71, 88–89, 99; and defeat, 128n52; and discipline, 78–79, 164n26 (*see also* punishment); on ending war quickly, 81, 167n43; as figure manipulated, 131n89; and Friends of Durruti, 99; and García Oliver, 26, 152n139; Generalitat Nov. 1936 meeting on, 65; January 1933 rising, 41, 139n34; Largo Caballero meeting for arms, 151n132; as leader, 78, 167n45; and Makhno, 117; on militarization decree, 65; as murdered, 88–89, 99; optimism, 46, 143–4n65; and Ortiz, 164n29, 167n45; Perdiguera attack, 155n154; and police reinforcements, 42; and POUM unity, 46; and punishment, 74–75, 76–77, 162–63nn20–22; radio address 1936, 42, 65; Regional Defense Committee of Catalonia, 13–14; respect for, 77; on retreat, 54; on a revolutionary win, 81–82; revolutionary gymnastics, 18, 128n52; on rifle numbers, 54–55; and the Ruanos, 89–90; Sanz on, 146n95; seizure of gold, 58, 152n135; and Los Solidarios/Nosotros group, 121n7; on the Spanish Republic, 5; and strategy, 146n95; Toryho on, 131–32n89; on war as serious, 81; War Committee, 49, 70, 75; on wartime factors, 166n41; and Zaragoza, 63, 81–82, 145n84, 157n176, 157n178, 167n43; Zaragoza revolutionary committee meeting, 17; on Zaragoza strike speed, 48; as Zaragoza's liberator, 81–82
Durruti Column/Division: overview, 2–4; as absorbed into People's Army, 110–11; administration, 48; air force attack,

47; arms in Madrid, 159n197; assets of, 42–43, 50, 54–55, 62, 110–11, 149n116, 149n118, 154n152; AWOL, 74; bulletin of, 75; campaigns against, 95, 171n51; captures in Aug. 1936, 49–50; in Caspe, 46–47; and Code of Military Justice, 64; coordinating failures, 91; and discipline, 73–77; discontent in, 97–98; and executions, 162–63n22 (*see also* punishment); fighting ability of, 79; and foreign support, 104–05; guerrilla detachments, 54–55; Huesca, 60; and integration into republican army, 88–89; internationals in, 104–05; and Karl Marx Division, 66; on left bank of Ebro, 47; and Madrid, 63, 66–68, 70–71, 157–58nn186–87, 158–59n194; Manzana as leader, 94; Manzana returning, 100; morale decline, 91; murdered comrades, 88–89; numbers of men, 43–44, 88, 141–42n48, 168n11; October 1936, 61–64, 153–54n151; organization of, 49, 145n79; and Pérez Farrás, 43, 142n50; POUM column meeting, 46; power of Durruti, 43; Ruano as leader, 89–90, 92, 94, 95, 172n49; Sanz as leader, 110; set up of, 39, 41–42; Siétamo, 60; split over mititarization, 88; as spontaneous, 73, 160n1; as trapped, 50, 146n93; as 26th Division, 110; wages of, 74; waiting for Oritz Column, 50; War Committee, 164–65n29; to Zaragoza, 42, 43–44, 100–01

Durruti en la revolución española (Paz), 135n10, 135n14

Ehrenburg, Ilya, 82, 149n116
Einstein, Carl, 85, 104–05
El Amigo del Pueblo (newspaper), 114
El Comité Central de Milicias Antifascistas (Mompó), 138nn25–26
El eco de los pasos (Oliver), 121n1
El Pájaro Rojo, 132–33n92
Enzensberger, Hans Magnus, 125n29, 128n52, 143n59, 160n1
ERC. *See* Republican Left of Catalonia
Esplugas (comrade), 70
executions, 77, 91–92, 94, 161n5, 162–63n21, 170n31
Exèrcit de Catalunya, 92
Extraordinary Plenum, 53

Fabbri, Luigi, 25
FAI. *See* Iberian Anarchist Federation
Falangists, 36, 135n16
Farlete, 62, 154n152, 154–55n154
fascism, 33–34, 56, 105, 113, 123n9, 134n1
Faure, Sébastien, 9–11
Fernández Sánchez, Aurelio, 3
"Findings: The Army and the People" (article), 133n102
First International Company,

95–97, 99, 101, 172n55. *See also* International Group
Fourth Agrupación, 95, 96–97
France, 24–25
Franco, Francisco, 24, 113
FRE. *See* Spanish Regional Federation
Friends of Durruti Agrupación, 99, 102–03, 107–08, 114–16

Galindo Fontaura, Vicente, 165n33
gangs, 120n5
García Oliver, Juan: on Aragon falling, 39; Aragon Front War Committee, 59; and attacking Zaragoza, 145n84; on CNT and FAI roles in revolution, 138n24; on defense committees, 45; and Durruti, 26, 152n139; and habit of revolutionary action, 13–14; Higher Council of War, 86; at Justice ministry, 156n169; as leader of Regional Defense Committee of Catalonia, 13; Majorca expedition, 146–47n96; and Makhno, 117; Mera criticizing, 29; paramilitary ideas, 8, 17–18, 26, 123n12; positions of, 3; on preparedness, 123n9; radio address 1936, 33; on Republic, 125n29; revolution envisioned, 37–38, 40–41, 132n92, 137–38nn19–20, 139–40n34, 169–70n20; on revolutionary being, 126n35; self-aggrandizement, 125n29; and Los Trienta, 121n1; Zaragoza revolutionary committee meeting, 17–18. *See also* Los Solidarios/Nosotros group
Gaule, Jacques De, 57
Gelsa comrades, 98–99
general strikes, 13, 48, 119n2, 146n93
Generalidad Council, 58, 147–48n105
Generalitat Defense Department, 63
Generalitat of Catalonia: anarchist ministers joining government, 156n169; and CAMC, 37, 51, 58, 137n18; and CNT, 37, 102–03, 109, 137n18; defense vs. offense, 40; Exércit de Catalunya, 92; Liaison Committee, 35; Majorca expedition, 51; and Manzana returning, 99–100; and militarization resistance, 65; November 5 1936 meeting, 65; and war materials, 57. *See also* Companys, Don Luis; Largo Caballero, Francisco
Germen, 21–22
Gilabert, Alejandro, 18
Gimenez, Antoine, 55, 110, 149n119
Giménez Arenas, Juan, 92, 94, 95
Gmür, Edi, 94
gold seizure, 152n135, 152n138
Goldman, Emma, 74–75
Gómez Casas, Juan, 57
grenades, 140n39
Grossi Mier, Manuel, 46, 142n50
Group of Russian Anarchists, 124n24
Guarner, Vicente, 134n4, 143n58, 153n151, 154–55n154

guerrilla detachments/warfare: overview, 23–24, 53–55, 130n74; Column fighting as, 149n118; El Pájaro Rojo on, 132n95; leaflets about, 131n79; as necessary, 6; as useless, 148–49n115; and victory, 148n112
Los guerrilleros confederales (Mira), 145n84
Guillamón, Agustín, 21, 51, 129n56, 137n18, 140n38
Guillén, Abraham, 148n112

hard currency, 57–58, 152nn134–35
hierarchy, 44–45, 143n60
High Command, 59–60, 99–100
Higher Council of War, 86
Hilario-Zamora, 120n6
Historia del Ejército Popular de la República (Salas Larrazábal), 136n16
Hobsbawm, Eric, 120n5, 130n78
Home Security, 102
Huesca, 60, 63, 101, 111, 155n155

Iberian Anarchist Federation (FAI): abstention, 17; and CAMC, 35, 135n14; civil war and structure, 22–23; and CNT, 19–20, 23; denied guerrilla campaigns, 23; Durruti criticizing, 65–66; and Gelsa comrades, 99; limit of, 129n56; and new military code demands, 93–94; strategies in 1933, 24
Ignacio Taibo, Paco II, 131n83
ignorance, 45

incontrolados, 74
individualism, 11
Los Indomables, 21–22, 121n9
Inestal, Miguel, 67
insurrection of January 1933, 14, 126n35
Internal Security Corps, 102
International Group, 49, 62–63, 93. *See also under* Durruti Column/Division; First International Company
internationals in Durruti Division, 104–05
Investigation Group, 49
Iron Column, 97, 145n80
Isgleas, Francisco, 99, 102
IWA. *See* Workers' International Association

journalists, 126n33
Jover Column, 64
Juanel (Juan Manuel Molina), 16

Karl Marx Division, 66, 67, 79
Koltsov, Mikhal, 82, 149n116

Languedoc Anarchist Federation, 9–10
Largo Caballero, Francisco, 52–53, 57, 86, 109, 151n132, 167n6. *See also* Generalitat of Catalonia
leaders (overview), 3–4, 9, 12
Leciñena, 62
Lenin Column, 62
Libertad-López Tienda Column, 70
Libertarian Youth, 90, 98
Líster, Enrique, 71
Llarch, Joan, 89–90

Index

Local Defense Committee, 8, 20–22, 123
Local Federation of Anarchist Groups, 21–22
Local Plenum of Barcelona Anarchist Groups, 132n92
Local Revolutionary Preparedness Committee, 21–22
López, Juan, 156n169, 168n3
Lorenzo, César M., 31, 63, 121n1, 135n15, 139n34, 147n103
Luis Jubert Division, 100. *See also* Ortiz Column

Madrid: and Barcelona, 135n10; and Durruti Column, 66–68, 70–71, 88–89, 143n59, 158n187, 158–59n194; as nearing capture by rebels, 63–64; vs. Zaragoza, 157n176
Majorca, 50–51, 146–47n96
Makhno, Nestor Ivanovitch, 117
Malato, Charles, 25
Maldonado Moya, José María, 40
Manuel Molina, Juan (Juanel), 16
Manzana, José: as Column leader, 94, 95, 172n49, 173n74; on discontent, 98; and Durruti, 43, 70; and militarization, 171n50; and Mira, 99, 173n69; resigning, 99, 173nn71–72; on Ruano, 91, 94, 170n31, 171n46
Marestan, Jean, 9–10
Marianet, 65
Marine Transport Union, 51, 146n96
Marqués de Marchelina, 148n114
Martín, Antonio, 104
Martínez Bande, José, 154n152

Martínez Prieto, Horacio, 8–9, 53, 63, 124nn14–15
Marxism, 116
Mas, Valerio, 91, 171n42
maverick (*incontrolados*) groups, 74
May Days, 106–08
Mera, Cipriano, 17, 29, 133n96
Mercier Vega, Louis, 152n135
Merino Martínez, Julián, 15, 126n38
Michaelis, Rudolf, 99
militarism, 133n96
militant columns. *See* Central Antifascist Militias Committee of Catalonia; defense committees; Durruti Column/Division; *individual columns*
militarism/militarization: and arms, 96–97; CNT's militias, 85–86; and discipline, 87; Durruti Column, 95, 171n50; and Germans, 94; and integration into republican army, 86; and international volunteers, 95; and Mera; opposition with resistance, 88, 92–93; resistance and Generalitat, 65; and traditional anarchism (*see* traditional anarchism). *See also* discipline
military discipline. *See* discipline
military production, 57–59, 151n131
"militiaman X," 90
Mira, José: on ammunition, 154n152; on centurias, 48; on guerrilla warfare, 149n118; homeward journeys, 76; and

189

Manzana, 99, 173n69; on Monte Oscuro, 154n154; on Siétamo capture, 70
Miravitlles, Jaume, 79, 140–42n42
moderates, 7
Moix (PSUC leader), 55
Mola, Emilio, 148n114
Mompó, Enric, 137n18, 138nn25–26
Monegrillo, 154n152
Monte Oscuro, 62, 154–55n154
Montseny, Federica: on centurias, 168n3; Durruti and Republic, 125n29; Durruti as active, 128n52; Durruti as leader, 67–68; on García Oliver and Durruti, 146n90; on guerrilla warfare, 130n74; positions of, 156n169; revolution in countryside, 131n80
Montserrat, Juan, 26
Mora, 70
Morin, Emilienne, 64
Moya, Maldonado, 111
murder, 88–89, 99, 104. See also executions
mutiny, 18, 46, 128n53. See also AWOL; desertion

Napoleon I (French Emperor), 130n74
National Committee, 13, 15, 68, 97, 127n42, 129n65
National Confederation of Labor (CNT): abstention, 17; and anarchist thought, 14–15, 126n37; Bloody Week in Seville, 7; boycotting POUM, 154n153; and CAMC, 35, 51, 135n14; communists stealing from, 103; confederal defense cadres, 7–8; and countryside, 15, 130n77; Durruti criticizing, 65–66; and Durruti in Madrid, 67; and FAI, 19–20, 23; Farlete and Perdiguera and revolution, 62, 155n154; and Generalitat of Catalonia, 37, 102–03, 109, 137n18; Higher Council of War, 86; and Largo Caballero's new cabinet, 52–53, 147n103, 147–48n105; Local Revolutionary Preparedness Committee, 21–22; and long records of struggle, 128n54; Marine Transport Union, 51, 146–47n96; membership revoked, 77; motion in 1934, 20–22, 23; National Committee meeting July 29, 1936, 41; National Defense Council, 52; and powers at top, 37–38, 138nn24–5; priorities of, 178n111; and Regional Defense Committee of Catalonia, 13, 15; and repression following May Days, 109–10, 177–78n111; and revolutionary theory, 113, 114, 178–79n1; and Ruano, 89; social revolution as magic, 31; strategies in 1933, 24; and Telephone Exchange, 106–07, 108; and UGT, 135n10, 179n5; unity with POUM, 46; and uprising outbreaks, 18, 128n54; voluntarism and credibility, 18, 127–28n51; Workers' And Soldiers' Councils, 102; and

Zaragoza's foothold, 40. *See also* National Committee; National Defense Committee

National Defense Committee: overview, 8; and antifascist militias, 86; beginnings of, 13; as bi-partisan, 123; as correspondence bureau, 129n65; on preparedness, 19; and Regional Defense Committee of Catalonia, 15; and revolt solidarity, 127nn41–43; seizure of gold, 58, 152n135

National Defense Council, 52, 85, 114–15

National Railway Industry Federation, 13

Negrete (Civil Guard), 46

Negrín, Juan, 104

Nosotros group. *See* Los Solidarios/Nosotros group

"The Notion of Discipline" article, 77–78

October 1934 Revolution, 18–19, 24–25, 129n56

offense vs. defense, 40

optimism, 14, 44, 46, 105, 142–43n55, 143–44n65

"Organizational Platform of the General Union of Anarchists" (pamphlet), 11–12, 124n24

Ortega Pérez, Javier, 48

Ortiz, Antonio, 41, 100, 151n132, 164n29, 167n45

Ortiz Column: overview, 43; Durruti Column waiting for, 50; and Madrid, 67; objections to militarization, 64; operation in 1937, 100; and Quinto attack, 91; and rape, 160n4; on right bank of Ebro, 47

Orwell, George, 143n60

"Our Anarchism" (Ascaso), 128n52

pay. *See* wages

Paz, Abel: on CAMC, 135n14; centurias, 48; on CNT and FAI roles in revolution, 138n24; on CNT and UGT alliance, 135n10; on concessions, 155n155; on Durruti and defeat, 128n52; on Durruti Column men, 142n52; on revolutionary army, 132n92; Los Solidarios/Nosotros group formation, 7; on training, 140n39; on Zaragoza as important, 127–28n51

peasants, 131n80, 165n33, 165–66n35. *See also* countryside

Peirats, José, 24, 120–21n7, 129n55, 148–49n115, 156n169

Peiró, Joan, 123n8, 156n169

people in arms, 5–6, 121–22n3

People's Army, 86–87, 110–12. *See also* militarism/militarization

People's Militias, 21

Perdiguera, 62–63, 155n154

Pérez Farrás, Enrique, 39, 42, 43, 139n29, 142n50

Pestaña, Ángel, 119n1

Plenum of Catalonia's Local and Comarcal FAI Group, 36–37, 140n34

Plenum of Confederal and Anarchist Columns, 97

191

Plenum of Local and Comarcal Federations of the Libertarian Movement of Catalonia, 51, 139n34
Plenum of the Barcelona Federation of Anarchist Groups, 21
police: Control Patrols, 102, 175n84; and Durruti Column, 42; Faure on, 9–10; as rearguard, 44, 143n58; signifying stop to revolution, 17; and Telephone Exchange, 107; traditional anarchism and, 5–6, 10–11. *See also various towns/cities*
Popular Front, 52, 65
Por qué perdimos la Guerra (Abad de Santillán), 142–43n55
POUM. *See* Workers' Party of Marxist Unification
poverty, 10
power, 37, 137n18
Pozo González, Josep Antoni, 175n84
press, 95, 171n51
Proletarian Army proposition, 27–29, 127n19, 132n92, 132–33n95
propaganda, 103, 108, 115
propaganda by deed, 125n31
PSUC. *See* Unified Socialist Party of Catalonia
Public Order forces, 143n58
Puente, Isaac, 17, 25
punishment: and "Confederal Conception of Libertarian Communism," 29–30; and Durruti, 74–75, 76–77, 161n5, 162–63nn20–22; for rape, 74, 160–61n4; for retreat/desertion, 90, 91, 170n31; for theft, 91–92, 94 (*see also* executions)

Quinto, 90

rape, 74, 160n4
Ratner, Iosif, 66
rearguard: overview, 43–44, 55–57; AWOL in, 74; columns becoming, 87; and discipline, 79, 164n26; Durruti's ideas on, 69; vs. front, 43–44, 142–43n55, 150n120, 150n122; and Internal Security Corps, 102; "legitimate" violence, 102; retreat to, 74, 76, 97
Red Cross, 43
Regional Committee for Catalonia, 135n7, 156–57n176
Regional Defense Committee, 8
Regional Defense Committee of Catalonia, 13–15, 99–100, 123, 127nn41–43
Regional Defense Council of Aragon, 53
Regional Plenum of Local and Comarcal Trade Union, 34, 135n7
Regional Plenum of the Anarchist Groups of Aragon, Rioja, and Navarra, 80
Regional Plenum of the Anarchist Groups of Catalonia, 150n120
repression, 54, 109–10, 148n114, 161n5, 177–78n111
Republican Left of Catalonia (ERC), 43, 106

Index

Republican National Guard, 102, 104, 105–06, 175n84
responsibility, 11, 30
revolution: vs. army, 16–17, 122n4; and backlash, 115; CNT motion in 1934, 22; communists' ideas of, 95, 171n51; and defense committees' goals, 48; García Oliver's vision, 137–38nn19–20; intervals of, 18, 129n55; and intervening stage, 30–31; postponing, 34, 95, 135n7, 171n51; and single party, 138n24; as starting in countryside, 130n74, 130nn77–131, 131n80; success Oct. 1934, 18–19; as totalitarian, 115; and underworld, 120n5; vs. uprisings, 18; as war, 1–2, 6–8, 105; without bloodshed, 16–17, 119n2
revolutionary being, 126n35
"Revolutionary Defense: Capitalism throws…" (article), 133n99
revolutionary government, 115, 116, 179n8
revolutionary gymnastics, 13, 18, 125n31, 128n52
Revolutionary Junta, 103, 108, 114–15
Revolutionary Ward Committees, 42, 140n38
Reyes, Alfonso, 59–60, 100
Rionda Castro, Ricardo, 49, 70, 82–83
Rivas, Manuel, 15
Rodríguez Vázquez, Mariano, 65
Roja y Negra column, 152n139

romanticism, 133n101
Rovira, José, 154n153
Ruano, Lucio: overview, 89–90; and Column in Madrid, 70, 89–90; fleeing, 171–2n47; and Internationals, 62–63; leaving Column, 94–95; and militarization, 92, 95, 171n42; punishment, 91, 94, 170n31; theft of village money, 95; in War Committee, 49
Rüdiger, Helmut, 133n101
Ruiz Trillo, Leopoldo, 122–23n7
rural areas. *See* countryside
Russian Revolution, 11–12. *See also* USSR

Sabadell expedition, 63–64
sabotage, 115
Sáez, Ángel, 90
Salas, Rodríguez, 106
Salas Larrazábal, Ramón, 136n16
Salillas Artigas, Jesús, 70
Sanjurjo, José, 5
Sanz, Ricardo: on 1937 actions in Zaragoza, 112; Column set up, 39; Durruti's death and Column, 88; importance of Zaragoza, 100; leading Column, 110; Oliver's revolution envisioned, 41, 139n34; positions of, 3; on Proletarian Army proposition, 28; Los Solidarious groups, 120n7, 140n35; on streetfighting, 146n95
secret societies, 122n4
seizure of gold, 58–59, 152n135, 152n138
self-criticism, 113

self-discipline, 74
selfishness, 74
Shapiro, Alexander, 8, 13, 15, 123, 125n30, 131n80
"Sheer Fascism" article, 17
Siétamo, 60
social revolution. *See* revolution
Socialist Youth, 158n191
socialists/socialism, 18–19, 25, 70, 129n56, 131n83
Solidaridad Obrera (newspaper), 166n41
Los Solidarios/Nosotros group: and action, 128n52; and J. Ascaso, 127n49; and F. Ascaso death, 140n35; and FAI, 121n7; and formation of defense committees, 21–22; history of name, 120–21n7; last gathering of, 41; on Republic, 125n29; union membership, 26; urbanity of, 23. *See also* García Oliver, Juan
"Sons of Night," 49, 55, 98, 145n84, 149n119
Soteras Marín, Alejandro, 49, 149n116, 160n1
Spanish Regional Federation (FRE), 6
Spanish Republic: Assault Guard, 102, 104, 105–06, 108, 175n84; Civil Guard, 46, 140–42n42; and democracy, 126n36; Durruti on, 5; Largo Caballero's new cabinet, 52; libertarian integration into army, 86; People's Army, 86–87, 110–12; searches for libertarians, 105–06; Second Republic vs. revolution, 125n29; workers and, 34. *See also* army; rearguard
spontaneity, 31, 133n102
stand-down, 106–07, 109
street vs. war fighting, 45, 146n95
strikes, 146n93. *See also* general strikes
success/victory, 56–57

Tardienta sector, 101
Telephone Exchange, 106–08
Terrer, Martín, 43
Teruel area, 100
theft, 74, 76, 92, 94, 103, 161n4, 162–63nn20–21, 171n46
theory vs. action, 128n52
Tierra Libre, 21–22
Tierra y Libertad Column, 58
Tierra y Libertad (newspaper) survey, 12–13, 16
Tolstoyans, 119n2
Torres-Benedito column, 79
Toryho, Jacinto, 131–32n89
totalitarianism, 115
Towards a Fresh Revolution (Balius), 113, 114–16
"Towards a New Dawn for Society" (Montseny), 130n74
traditional anarchism: and army, 5–7, 10–11, 22, 25, 28–9; and discipline, 77–78 (*see also* discipline); as failed, 113; and militarism, 5–7; and police, 5–6, 10–11; reality in wartime, 166n41
training, 42
Los Treinta, 121n1
Trotsky, Leon, 128n53

26th Division. *See* Durruti Column/Division

UGT. *See* Workers' General Union
underworld, 120n5
Unified Socialist Party of Catalonia (PSUC), 51, 55, 70, 154n153, 158n191
unions: CNT as dictatorship, 38, 138n24; and concessions of libertarians, 102; confederal defense cadres, 7; and defense committees, 21; and Friends of Durruti proposal, 103; and July revolution workers, 138nn25–26; and Oliver's revolution, 38, 138n25; Peiró's ideas, 123n8; as rearguard, 44; and revolutionary government, 115, 179n8; and Revolutionary Junta, 114. *See also* general strikes
unity, 36, 46, 59, 70, 136n16, 152n139. *See also* collaboration
Urales family, 131n80
urban vs. rural, 45, 79–80, 131n80, 146n95, 165n32
Urrutia (Lieutenant-Colonel), 61
USSR, 59, 108, 151n132, 152n134

Vagliasindi, Pablo [Paolo], 70
Valdés, Blanco, 69–70
Van Paassen, Pierre, 143–44n65
vanguardism, 14, 20–21
victory/success, 56–57, 108–9, 148n112, 177n104
Villalba Rubio, José, 59

Vilna Terytoriya (Free Territory), 117
violence, 2, 119n1
volunteering, 12, 18, 22, 127–28n51

wages, 74, 87, 93
War Committees, 70, 75, 80, 109, 164–65n29
War Delegation, 95
"We are Freedom's Army and Should Obey…" (article), 76
weapons. *See* ammunition; arms
Weil, Simone, 143n63
women, 44
workers: and army, 12, 124n24; and committee democracy, 138nn25–26; and economic issues, 15; faith in mobilization, 29, 123n8; focus on, 103; and military discipline, 9. *See also* revolution
Workers' And Soldiers' Councils, 102
Workers' General Union (UGT): and CNT, 135n10, 179n5; and communists, 70; in Durruti Column, 43; and Largo Caballero's new cabinet, 52; and National Defense Council, 52; and October 1934 Revolution, 24; and Telephone Exchange, 106–07; Workers' And Soldiers' Councils, 102
Workers' International Association (AIT/IWA), 15, 137n18, 138n34
Workers' Party of Marxist Unification (POUM): boycotting, 154n153; Column meeting, 46;

Leciñena, 62; outlawed, 109; and Roja y Negra, 152n139; and Telephone Exchange, 107–08

Yoldi, Miguel, 49, 67, 70, 157n178

Zaragoza: overview, 40; bridges blown, 50, 146n93; and CNT, 40; and Durruti, 63, 81–82, 145n84, 157n176, 157n178, 167n43; Durruti and Jan. 1933 rising, 41, 139n34; Durruti Column halting before, 50, 146n90; Durruti Column leaving for, 42, 43–44; and ending concessions, 155n155; general strikes, 48; importance of, 81, 100; vs. Madrid, 66, 157n176; 1937 action, 100, 111–12; and People's Army, 111–12; as protected, 61, 153–54n151; shortage of combatants, 43–44; strategy of Ebro banks, 47; street fighting, 100. *See also* Aragon

Zaragoza Congresses: CNT's libertarian communism, 25–30; FAI denied guerrilla campaigns, 23; Proletarian Army proposition, 27–29, 132n92, 137n19; set up of revolutionary committee, 17–18